£7.95

PLI

WARWICK JOURNAL IN PHILOSOPHY

General editors:
Justin Barton & Joan Broadhurst

PLI is published from the Department of Philosophy at the University of Warwick. First published in 1989, *PLI* concentrates on contemporary work coming from the the European Neo-Kantian and phenomenological tradition. Post-structuralist thought has not been welcomed in the Anglo-American academy. *PLI* hopes to demonstrate to a somewhat hostile anglophonic audience that the 'continental' school is philosophically rigorous, using its precision, in part, to problematize and augment the other lines of philosophical debate.

DELEUZE & THE TRANSCENDENTAL UNCONSCIOUS

Guest Editor: JOAN BROADHURST

PLI
WARWICK JOURNAL OF PHILOSOPHY
UNIVERSITY OF WARWICK
1992

Published October 1992

ISBN 1 897646 00 3

British Library Cataloguing-in-Publication Data.
A catalogue record for this book is available from the British Library.

CONTENTS

ILLUSTRATIONS
Between pages 40 & 41 *La Vittoria* by Jean Tinguely from *A Magic Stronger Than Death,* Jean Tinguely and Pontus Huxley, Thames and Hudson 1987.

ACKNOWLEDGEMENTS

...in particular thanks to Greg Hunt, Chair of the Lord Rootes Memorial Fund at the University of Warwick. He has given much time and technical expertise to make the production of this journal much easier than it could have been. The Lord Rootes Memorial Fund generously gave me financial support to produce this journal and go to the Trent Conference in Canada as part of this project.

Constantin Boundas, organiser of the Trent University (Canada) Conference on Deleuze also in May 1992. He helped finance my visit there and acted as an excellent host for a premature guest. He also generously gave us permission to print the Lingis paper. A revised version of the paper will appear in *Deleuze and the Theatre of Philosophy* edited by Constantin V Boundas and Dorothea Olkowski, (New York, Routledge, forthcoming.)

Roger Broadhurst, for his intermittent support throughout the whole of this project, his advice and criticisms and for his help in the production, editing and compilation of this volume.

David Wood, Director of the Centre for Research in Philosophy and Literature at the University of Warwick. Throughout this project he has always given abundant advice, encouragement and support and, in very many ways, made this whole thing possible.

EDITORIAL NOTE

All the papers included in this volume were presented at a "conference" at the University of Warwick on 23rd & 24th May 1992 entitled

DELEUZE AND THE TRANSCENDENTAL UNCONSCIOUS.

As well as those published within this volume, there were also papers given by John Welchman from Monash University who did an audio-visual presentation entitled: NOTES ON FACIALITY and Martin Joughin, translator, who led an improvised session entitled PHILOSOPHY IN THE DEBATING CHAMBER. Unfortunately the format of their presentations means that they could not be adequately reproduced herein. We would like however to acknowledge their presence, thank them for their participation and regret the inflexibility of this presentational format.

There was no attendance list made for the conference but we would like also to thank everyone (over one hundred and fifty bodies) who came and joined in throughout the weekend. This volume is much weaker for the omission of their discussions.

Joan Broadhurst
Coventry, September 1992

ALPHONSO LINGIS

The Society of Dismembered Body Parts

The notion of societies formed by contract posits law as the transcendent, universally valid and transtemporal, horizon of the contents of contracts. The notion of contract posits individuals as autonomous agents, individuals individuated as seats of understanding and will.

Our culture also maintains the image of a social body, the multiplicity of individuals integrated as so many functions of an organism. The body writ small that serves as the analogon for societies consists of a set of parts and organs defined by their functions, which are fixed and complementary with one another.

Recent structuralism identified the social fabric with the system regulating the exchange of words, women, goods, and services. Ferdinand de Saussure's linguistics had separated the value of terms from their meaning: to consider the meaning of a term is to consider the way it designates its referent; to consider the value of a term is to consider the other terms which can substitute for it. It was this view of language as an economic system, a field of circulation of terms bearing messages, that made it possible to view the kinship structure which determines the division of tasks and of power in tribal societies as rules made by men for the distribution and exchange of women. The icons and practices of power, ritual, ceremonial, and religious practices, myths and ideologies will also be envisioned as structured fields for the circulation of different kinds of values.

In the exchangist model, the terms of the social field are not individuals, the personae presupposed by the social contract theory. It is fundamental to the exchangist model that the terms be susceptible of several uses, be interchangeable. It is this feature that makes it incompatible with the old organic image of society, which depicted society as an integrated hierarchy of terms defined by their functions.

Gilles Deleuze and Felix Guattari's *The Anti-Oedipus* offers a new mapping of the libidinal body--the libidinal body of the primary process--which will serve to guide what they have to say about societies. If when we envision our bodies as organisms we envision them as integrated sets of functions, the libidinal body being depicted in Deleuze and Guattari is not an organism; it is the anorganic body, the orgasmic body. What we call the body as organism is rather the body of secondary process libido, the Oedipalized body.

An anorganic body is not defined by its constitutive organization, but by its states. *The Anti-Oedipus* distinguished different states of the body. On the one hand, the orifices couple on to organs they find contiguous with them, and draw in nutritive flows. With the forces of its own strong jowls the infantile mouth draws into the milk, along with gulps of air and warmth. These forces produce plenitude, satisfaction, and contentment, which is not simply an affect shimmering over the inner content. For contentment is itself a force; the infantile body closes its orifices, curls up upon itself, closes its eyes and ears to outside fluxes, makes itself an anorganic plenum, a "body without organs," in Artaud's expression. This undifferentiated and closed plenum produces and reproduces itself; Deleuze and Guattari identify the Id, and the primary repression that produces the Id, with this state of the body. Its contentment is a primary mode of death drive, which is not a compulsion to disintegrate into the quiescence of the inert, but the primary catatonia.

Freud discerned libidinous pleasure already in the slavering and drooling with which the infant, over and beyond contentment, spreads a surface of pleasure. Every organ-coupling can, by an anaclitic deviation, be turned to the excess production of erotogenous surfaces; the mouth can draw in the nutriment but also slaver and drool, google and babble, the

2

anus can release the excrement but also spread it in a surface of warm pleasure. The pleasure surfaces that are thus extended are surfaces of contact, undiscernibly infantile face and maternal breast, infant cheeks and blanket. Here the organs figure not as orifices leading into the inner functional body, but as productive apparatuses attached to the surfaces of the closed plenum of the body, functioning polymorphously perversely to extend pleasure surfaces. The surfaces are surfaces of sensuality, surfaces not of contentment but of what Freud called excitations, freely-mobile excitations. Flows of energy that irradiate, condense, intersect, build, ripple. Excitations are not properly "sensations," that is, sense-data, givens of meaning and orientation, information-bits that would be fed into the inner functional body. They are contact phenomena, and reveal the other as the convex reveals the concave face of a surface. The infant extends its surplus energies in extending surfaces, discovers the pleasures of surfaces, discovers the pleasures of having surfaces, of being outside, being born. This extension of pleasure-surfaces to which life attaches itself blocks the compulsion to return to the womb, the primary death drive.

These freely-mobile excitations converge, affect themselves with their own intensities, discharge in eddies of egoism. Nomadic, multiple, ephemeral surface egos, where surplus energies are consumed in pleasure, eddies of egoism that consume themselves.

The infant contented, mouth, eyes, ears, fists closed, gives us the very image of the anorganic plenum to which the organs are attached, the "body without organs". Freud even reduced a great deal of the charm of babies to our fascination with the image of narcissism, of closed individuality. Yet the infantile body is anything but a separate substance. From the first it is in symbiosis with mother, earth-mother, earth. In symbiosis with mother harassed, preoccupied, weighed down with the weight of the world, the social, imperial world. The closed plenum upon which organs are attached, producing surface effects, pleasure-surfaces and eddies of egoism, reduces to the individual mass of the body only in the discourse

3

and practices of our epoch. The closed plenum upon which our organs are attached identified with the mass of our own individual bodies is the residue of a historical process of deterritorialization, abstraction, formalization.

The Deleuze-Guattari analysis distinguishes productive apparatuses, "machines" or engines where energy is produced, reproduced, distributed, consumed. Genetics places, at the point of origin of living systems in the non-living, the maintenance of codes--the DNA and RNA molecules. If vital systems can be called "machines," it is because their operations are not simply random; they are coded, or rather are loci where coding forms and maintains itself.

For Deleuze and Guattari the question of the nature of the social system or structure or fabric is formulated as a question of code. "Society is not first of all a milieu for exchange where the essential would be to circulate or to cause to circulate, but rather a "socius of inscription where the essential thing is to mark and to be marked." (CSI 142) The social machinery operates essentially to record, channel, regulate the coded flows of libidinal energies. Three different kinds of codings determine the socius as the body of the earth in nomadic societies, as the body of the despot in imperial societies, and as the body of capital in capitalist societies.

Savage societies, nomadic, hunter-gatherer society, subdivide the people but not the territory. The earth is the body without organs, the undivided plenum upon which the productive machinery, the organs of men are attached; the societies are territorial or terrestrial. Men are not viewed or treated as disconnected, separated, from the earth, sovereign lords of the earth. Savages therefore do not experience human bodies as integral whole units. The organs and limbs, experienced as productive of substances, flows, and energies, are so experienced not as integrated into one another but as separately attached to the earth.

4

An individual does not enter the society by assuming civic rights and responsibilities, as a juridic person. An individual does not enter the society by taking up a post in the distribution of tasks which the society organizes, by fulfilling a productive or defensive role. In nomadic societies pretty much every individual performs the whole gamut of tasks. An individual enters the society by initiation. In the initiation ceremonies he will be marked; more exactly, energy-productive organs and limbs will be separately marked. He will be tattooed, scarified, perforated, circumcised, subincised, clitoridectomized. Among the Lani of Irian Jaya, the eagle people perforate the ears of the initiate, and insert into them the plumes of eagles, marking his belonging to the high crags where the eagles dwell; among the Kapuaku the initiated will have the septum of their nostrils perforated and the tusks of wild boars inserted, marking their belonging to the dense forest; among the Azmat the initiated will have the ridges of their ears perforated and the teeth of crocodiles inserted, marking their belonging to the swamps and rivers. Among the Australian aborigines men at initiation will have the opening of their penis cut back, in monthly operations, until it is open to the root, so that they will urinate stooping like women, marking their belonging to the fertile body of maternal earth. The myths tell of these couplings, these marked and separate productive organs and limbs, and their attachment to the earth: Parvati is dismembered, and her body parts fall to the earth; at Varanasi her vulva falls and, attached to the Ganga, form a whirlpool; at Rishikesh her eyes fall and form lakes in the Himalayan clefts; at Brindabar her breasts fall and form mountains on the plains. The marked penis of Shiva falls to the earth, forming linga, stalactites and outcroppings in rivers, in caves, in high mountains.

It is by attaching the impulsive organs of the bodies of the clan to the earth that the social body constitutes itself. Primitive societies are not constituted by a pact among its members but by an attachment to the earth; the tribe is a group that inhabits, and that hunts and gathers together on, the productive surface of the earth that is not divided and parcelled out among them. It is in being marked--in being tattooed, scari-

5

fied, circumcised, subincised--that these men constitute a society, a social body or socius.

This conception Deleuze and Guattari direct against the exchangist conception of society, such as that presupposed by Claude Levi-Strauss. Society is not a network that gets elaborated in the measure that individuals exchange women, goods, services, messages with one another, and, in the delay between giving and receiving, contract obligations which are represented by claims. In primitive society I do not have relationships only with those individuals with which I have exchanged women or goods. I may owe no one anything, but when the clan goes on a hunt, is attacked by wild beasts or human enemies, or pulls up its camp and moves elsewhere, I who live in this area, who have been marked with the tattoo of the leopard people or wear in my perforated septum the tusks of wild boars, have obligations to all those who are so marked. It may well be that I will suffer loss without getting the equivalent in return from the others, or even that I will risk or lose my life. The original obligation, the original debt, is not something contracted personally, when I received something in a transaction where I agreed to give the equivalent in return. The original subject of obligation is not the persona, the subject as autonomous and independent agent of initiatives; it is my body, more exactly, my productive body parts which have been incorporated into the social code by being marked, inscribed, incised, circumcised, subincised, scarified, tattooed. When danger threatens the group, all those who by initiation have been marked with the sign of the boar are obliged to lend their arms to the task. When the group needs to reproduce, and approaches the moiety during the annual betrothal feast, all women who have been clitoridectomized are obliged to bring their reproductive bodies to the feast and accept a man of the other moiety.

Savages do not belong to society as persons, individuals, juridic subjects, but as organs attached to the full body of earth. The society is the marking of this attachment. The multiplicity of the attached organs extends a productive surface. Deleuze and Guattari do not conceive of the social bond between individuals to be formed by each legislating for the others, nor do they take it to be formed by contracts among individuals who exchange words, women, goods, and services. They conceive it not as a contract nor as an exchange, but as couplings. Couplings not of individuals, but of organs.

Savage society is constituted by the coupling up of voice with hearing: primitive cultures are epic, narrative, oral cultures. In New Guinea, the hunter-gatherer societies, divided into 700 mutually incomprehensible languages (fully a third of the languages of humanity), have never engaged in any empire-building. They have no hereditary or elected chiefs. Most of these societies are headhunting societies. Headhunting is not war; neither territory, nor booty, nor women are captured in their battles. Rather each young man seeks out the most brave and the most spectacular warrior on the field to kill, and to cannibalize his body so as to interiorize his spirit. Men who have killed more than one are not respected and do not gain power over the group; they are regarded as twisted killers. Big men are big by virtue of two things: the power of language, and the capacity to organize feasts in which the people assemble, reaffirm their bonds, and communicate with distant peoples. They have astonishing memories and linguistic capabilities; they are capable of telling their ancestries back dozens of generations, capable of recalling and retelling in captivating ways the history of the people, its luck and its feasts, its heroisms and its ordeals. It is especially this power to hold an audience spellbound long nights that constitutes their prestige. The languages themselves are extraordinarily difficult to learn; not only is their grammar extremely complex but they develop great elaborations of ceremonious, poetic, and epic styles.

A second coupling is that of hand with surfaces of inscription. Primitive societies are not manufacturing, but graphic societies. They inscribe the earth, with their paths, their dances, they inscribe the walls of their caves or huts, they inscribe their bodies. Savages do not so much build things, shelters and monuments, as do handcraft; they develop not architectural

7

powers but manual dexterity. They cut twigs to mark their paths, carve tools, weave baskets and clothing. The markings made do not express ideas, but reveal the dexterity of hands. The inscription is not related to the voice; they develop no alphabet or ideograms. Hands learn skills not by being explained the meaning and the methods of handling and manipulating, not by being shown the diagram or the model, but instead by immediate induction: the hands of the child imitate the movement of hands of the men and women. One learns to throw the boomerang by throwing it oneself in the company of the skilled. Like in Zen archery; there are no manuals, no discussions with the master; the master holds and tightens and releases his bow; one does the same, again and again.

The third coupling is that of eye with pain. The pain inflicted, in the initiation rites, is public, theatrical: one watches, the eye does not circumscribe, survey, comprehend, it winces, it senses the pain. As the young Maasai maiden is being scarified, the thorn inserted again and again to raise scars in regular patterns across her back, down her thighs, all afternoon, the others watch, eyes like flies feasting on the pain.

Savage inscription cuts into living flesh; the markings, perforations, inscriptions, incisions, circumcisions, subincisions, clitoridectomies are painful. Savage societies are machines of cruelty. The pain is by no means minimized; initiation rites redouble the pain, include gratuitous fastings, long incarcerations in dark men's houses, beatings, bleedings. Infections, deaths occur. The markings are done in long public feasts. It is clear that there is a collective pleasure in this savagery, this cruelty that so revolts us. And that also excites us, childhood readers of *National Geographic*, colonialists, missionaries, who are evidently excited by these societies of pain, who soon indulge our own cruelties, unleashing upon the savages insults, beatings, hard labor, enslavement. Those who live long among savages soon acquire cruel habits. I remember spending a week with a missionary, a member of the order of Saint Francis, who had been in Irian Jaya for 27 years, and helping him each morning in the clinic he had set up and personally staffed. I was surprised, then intrigued, then revolted by the roughness with which he tore off bandages, by the extra touch of cruelty with which he manhandled and jabbed children while vaccinating them. Those he baptized, initiated into his parish, were also perforated, scarred, marked.

Nietzsche, in the Second Essay of *The Genealogy of Morals* spoke of the excitant that pain is for the spectator. When one lies with the sick one, the suffering and the moanings invade the space, invade one's own body, depress and devitalize in the contagion of suffering. But when one actively inflicts pain, on oneself or on others, there is excitement and jubilation in the spectacle of the pain. The eye is this crystal ball where the pain suffered is transfigured into pleasure received.

Nietzsche observed that the one who is cheated by another who owed him some commodity or service is satisfied not when justice intervenes and forces the debtor to bring what he owed, but when justice punishes the debtor. What is this? Nietzsche asked. How is it that the creditor could accept the transaction contracted for to be fulfilled when the goods were not delivered but the debtor suffered? How can pain be some kind of payment? It is that the original social contract was not for goods and services, but for the pleasure of those goods and services. It is that the spectacle of the pain of another can be a pleasure equivalent to the pleasure in those goods and services.

But the original marking is not the result of transactions between individuals freely entered into by which one becomes creditor and the other debtor, a marking that will be effaced when the goods contracted for is delivered. The prime marking, the prime coding, is the socialization itself, which isolates the productive organs of the body and codes their coupling with the body of the earth: the tattooing, scarifying, circumcising, subincising, clitoridectomizing. These markings sear with pain. Nietzsche does not go far enough, when he says that these brandings serve to mark the memory--or to create a memory--with a few "Thou shalt nots." The rites in which they are inflicted are public rites, festive occasions in which the

9

clan affirms its unity. They are destined for the eyes that watch, and that derive from them from the start the surplus value of pleasure. It was not originally a pleasure owed them, contracted for; it was the original surplus value that the socialization itself generates. It is only afterward that one so marked will enter into limited transactions with other members of the group, will deliberately and on his own contract debts that he will pay or not pay, and if he does not pay, he will have to give his creditors the pleasure of seeing him suffer.

The markings with which savage societies record, channel, regulate the coded flows of the energies produced in the couplings are not *read*. Savage inscriptions are not signs that refer to concepts; they are diagrams and paths for the hand. The leopard footprint one sees on the path does not refer to the name and notion of leopard, but links up directly with the leopard itself. The leopard claw-print that one sees inscribed by human hand on the path or on the body of the initiate does not refer to the voice that utters the name "leopard" and conceives the meaning of that name; it directly designates the leopard itself. The eye does not read this sign; it sees the mark of the beast, it winces, it senses the pain. But now it is the leopard itself that functions as a sign. One takes those marked with the mark of the leopard to be a tribe, a society. (I remember visiting a mine on the Arctic Ocean at the border between Finland and the Soviet Union; the young miner who showed me the mine put out every cigarette he smoked on his hand, which was covered with scar tissue. Then I saw that the other young miners all had the backs of their hands covered with scar tissue. When I saw them, I did not read them as marks of words that could be pronounced, like tattoos where one can read things "47th battalion, Nam"; rather when my eye fell on them it flinched, seeing the burning cigarette being crushed and sensing the pain. And it is this burning cigarette I took to be a sign of the fiery and defiant young men who had come from the south and gone there, to the mines on the brink of the Arctic Ocean, and whose branding of their own hands functioned as a seal of their fraternity. The eye does not read the meaning in a sign; it *jumps* from the mark to the pain and the burning cigarette, and then jumps to the fraternity signalled by the burning cigarettes.)

Savage societies are transformed or incorporated into barbarian societies, sedentary and imperial, in a change in the nature of the codings. By an overcoding, all the lines of filiation and alliance are made to converge upon the body of the despot. As the productive organs are attached to the closed plenum of the body of the despot, they are detached from the earth, deterritorialized.

Barbarian societies are also characterized by a change in the couplings of the organs that extend the productive surface of the social order. The hand is coupled onto a graphics that is aligned to the voice. The coupling of voice with hearing through the intermediary of writing produces wholly new effects. The eye is uncoupled from pain, anaesthetized.

Writing begins with empires.[1] It is contrived for use in imperial legislation, in a bureaucracy, for accounting, the collection of taxes, for the constitution of the state monopoly, for imperial justice, for historiography. But also it contains within itself a transcendent and despotic law.

Savages possess extraordinary manual virtuosity, and do not lack writing for lack of manual dexterity. Writing is produced when graphics are coupled with the voice to become signs of words spoken.

The graphics now do not, like in a claw mark incised on the back of the Yoruba initiate which invites the hand to gingerly feel it, serve as grooves for the movement of hand and body. The graphics are destined for tablets, stones, books, destined to be indefinitely reproduced on more tablets (the textbook explained in the classroom copied by students on notebooks, recopied by students on bluebooks at the end of the term, recopied later by graduates for articles to be published on more paper). When the savage eye saw the claw-mark cut into the white bark of the birch tree, it winced, it felt the wound of the tissue and sap of the tree and jumped to the wound on the flesh and the blood of the Yoruba initiate. Now the eye no longer winces when it sees the mark; it does not see the

11

incision with which the pen or the printer has cut into the white surface of the paper. The eye has lost the ability to see the cut, the incision, the wound, it passes lightly over the page, not seeing, not sensing the tissue of the paper at all, seeing the words as though they were flat patterns suspended in a neutral emptiness. The eye is no longer active, palpating the pain, jumping to the leopard; it is now passive before the flow of abstract patterns passing across it.

Writing is graphics now coupled an the spoken word; but in the coupling the voice is transformed. The voice in its savage relation with hearing exists in a reciprocal relation: the voice speaks, the other hears, and answers. The movement is zigzag from one to the other, and it is broken by pauses, by silences. The voice that is now written is linearized. The words no longer exist here, in this place, between these two savages stationed on the earth in front of one another; they now exist in a linear progression that has been deterritorialized. When I read, on paper, the lines: "The citizens of New Spain are hereby taxed five gold pesos each per year," all sense of a spot on the earth where these words were uttered is lost; I am not referred to this place but rather to the meanings of these signs, which exist transtemporally and transspatially. The meanings are there wherever the text is read or recalled; the voice of the speaker does not echo in them. Writing is a form of graphics, Deleuze and Guattari say, that is lined up with the voice, but also supplants the voice. When I come upon the lines: "When noble metals are roasted, phlogiston is released," it would be pointless for me to strain to hear the voice that uttered them. It is in reading on down the lines that I will discover that phlogiston was a concept of ancient chemistry, and will determine the meaning of "noble metals" from the lines of the writing that contrast the expression "noble metals" with "base metals."

Now the voice no longer resonates, chants, invokes, calls forth; one hears only the voice of a law that orders one to move on down the line. Writing remains aligned by the voice, a now mute, impersonal, remote voice. A transcendent voice detaches itself from the whole of discourse, and detaches the resonances from words. The voice is there only as that which once decreed that this inscription means this concept, that decrees that one no longer settle on the resonance of any sensuous sound but take it as but a sign that refers to other signs. To hear the message, the meaning, one must subject oneself to the law: the phonetic, taxonomical, syntactical, semantical laws of significant language, which are conventional, laid down by decree, by a law that regulates the meaning of language because it regulates the whole of society. To subject oneself to the law of written language is to subject oneself to the one law of the one language of the empire.

Siegfried, in the Enchanted Forest, hears the murmurs of the trees, what he hears is the substance of the trees, their individual substance and tensions and flexions that are being plucked by the wind and resound. Through the sound and in them he encounters the inner substances of the trees themselves. Then he drinks the magic potion brought to him by the bird descended from on high, from the throne of Wotan the Law-giver, and suddenly he hears what they *mean*. He no longer hears the trees resounding; he hears a message: he hears the warning that Alberich has bewitched him and is waiting to kill him.

You can wander the High Andes, and, by night, hear the murmurs of the people around the fire, hear their Qechoa tongue without understanding it, hearing the light, subtle, supple tripping of their sounds, hear their intonations and their murmurs, hear it as the very resonance of their substance, their gentle, unassertive, vibrant, sensitive way of vocalizing together like gentle animals, quail foraging a field or muttering in a thicket for the night, vocalizing their togetherness. You can look at their inscriptions, see the letters Saqsaywaman and intihuatana carved in stone or staining the weathered boards of their home, and see these marks as incisions and stainings in the substance of the stone or wood, forming patterns with the cracks and fissures in the stone, the grain and diverse colors of the wood. But if you were to drink some magic potion, some cocktail of coca tea and whisky, and

13

suddenly understand their language, and abruptly understand that they are speaking about "transporting cocaine into the hands of the Columbian agents", then abruptly you have subjected yourself to the codings of imperial society, you have suddenly related their sounds not to their own throats and substance but to the international code established by the reigning barbarian empire in Washington and Bonn and Tokyo, where cocaine means the same thing--crime-- whenever, wherever it is spelled out, and you cannot detach this meaning from their murmurings around the fire without subjecting yourself to the decrees that fix the international imperial code. And you at the same time insert yourself in the code, you find yourself designated as a tourist, an observer and reporter for the empire, another plunderer bringing back to the imperial metropolis handcrafts and idols, souvenirs and memories, and field reports on the activities of the outlaws. If you want to speak of them murmuring together, without subjecting them and yourself to the Law, if you want to speak a discourse of nomads and outlaws, if you want to tell of them speaking to you as outsiders, nomads and outlaws, you must never pronounce this word. But how then will others understand what you say--others who, like yourself, speak imperial English, which they have learned and continue to learn from the imperial media? At best you can speak of them in the imperial code, speak of them as cocaine traffickers and terrorists, in such a way the words begin to lose their consistency, become nonsensical, turn against the imperial order itself. You can try to make others conspirators who use the imperial formulas themselves as passwords by which the imperial discourse itself turns into babble and din.

Marx had spoken of the dismemberment of the human body in the social machinery of industrial capitalism. Labourers are coupled on to the productive process only as hands that assemble on assembly lines, or as legs and backs that bear burdens, or as arms that stoke furnaces. It is only the hands and eyes of clerks in offices that are paid for. Soldiers are limbs connected to weapons, disconnected from brain and imagination. Foremen are eyes disconnected from heart. The capitalist is the calculating brain disconnected from the capitalist's own taste and caprice. The industrial enterprise would be the whole body upon which these part-organs would be attached.

Marxism invokes the missing whole organism, that of the species individual, to which the diverse limbs and organs, attached to the body of industry, would in principle belong. The revolution Marx envisions would bring about the social ownership of the productive enterprise and the individual ownership of the bodyparts coupled on to that enterprise. But in fact capitalism itself invokes the private individual, owner of all his parts and members, motivated by self-interest, that is, interest in the consolidation and aggrandizement of the self as an integral whole. For the private ownership of productive enterprises to which large numbers of limbs and members of others are coupled invokes the subordination of the body of the productive enterprise to the integral body of the individual.

The private individual is constituted by a privatization of his organs, his productive engines. It is the social machine itself that privatizes the organs, decoding their couplings with their immediate objects, and making their flows of substance and energies abstract. The first organ to undergo privatization, removal from the social field, was the anus. We have long since ceased to use it to make contact with the earth, joining our excrement with the humus, wiping our asses with leaves, peeing in puddles and streams. We have long since ceased attaching an anus to the full body of the emperor. In the Middle Ages theologians long debated whether Jesus had an anus; his priestly role, mediator between God and man, God-man, seemed to require an integral human body, but an anus seemed fundamentally contradictory to his role as transcendont Word that inscribes the social coding on earth. Society decodes the flow of excrement, decrees that it cannot be spoken of, that meaning should not be sought in it. It becomes a pure residue, an abstract flow without significance, without coding. The first zone of privacy, of individuation that is constituted in the core of the symbiotic world of the infant is his anus. One has to cover up one's anus, stop playing with it, stop playing with excrement, stop leaving traces of it in the living room. It is about this private part that the privacy of a whole individual is constituted. The notion of a private individual is that of a source of flows, of substance and fluids and energies, what are of themselves abstract, without social determination, without coding. Freud understood that the phallic phase follows the anal phase, and builds on it: the pleasure that the boy feels in the hardening of his penis is felt as a prolongation outside of the pleasure he feels of a full bowel sliding outward. In the Oedipus complex, the boy will substitute for his real penis and this real pleasure the abstract pleasure of being a phallus, and make himself into an ego, an ego posited over against others, making demands on others. The individual is identified with the phallus, the core of his status as a private individual lies in the identity of the phallus which he can hide or reveal according to his own initiative. Deleuze and Guattari emphasize the decoded, deterritorialized nature of this phallic emanation. In primitive societies the boy's first ejaculation, the girl's menarche are highly significant, coded, public events. In our societies the flows of pubescent semen and blood are decoded, deterritorialized, privatized: it is supposed to take place behind locked doors, at night. No one is supposed to see the evidence of wet dreams on the sheets. The privacy of the individual is constituted about these privatized organs and flows.

Marx conceptualized as alienation the dismemberment of the body whose productive parts and organs are attached to the full body of industry, and invoked the idea of integral man, the man whose body parts would belong to himself. This notion of integral man, the species individual, has the status of a utopian concept. It would be necessary to show the constitution of this notion in the privatization of the individual about the privatization of his organs, beginning with the anus. But then the utopian notion of integral man can no longer maintain the function Marxism allots to it: that of figuring as the benchmark that enables Marxism to criticize the social coding of capitalism, as well as that of barbarism and of savagery. For the notion of the integral man, the privatized body, is a moment of the capitalist coding.

The schizophrenic apocalypse Deleuze and Guattari envision on the horizon of capitalism would not bring together the body parts dispersed across the social field It would rather free them for ever more diverse couplings with one another.

For the surface productive of the social is being extended, elaborated, transformed not simply by new laws being legislated, by new exchanges being contracted, by new enterprises being launched It is being extended, elaborated, transformed when hands clasp in greeting but also in parting, when arms embrace arms or shoulders or thighs or feet, when hands cleanse an oil-drenched cormorant, when eyes watch a sonar probe or a pregnancy, when hanggliding bodies circle one another, when lips kiss the pain of the AIDS victim, when fingers close the eyes of the one whose agony has at length come to an end.

NOTES

1   "What a strange thing writing is! It would seen that its apparition could not fail to determine profound changes in the conditions of existence of humanity, and that these transformations would have had to have been especially intellectual in nature. The possession of writing prodigiously multiplies the aptitude of men to preserve knowledge. We like to conceive of writing as an artificial memory, whose development should be accompanied with a better consciousness of the past, hence a greater capacity to organize the present and the future. After one eliminates all the criteria proposed to distinguish barbarism from civilization, one would like at least to retain this: the people with writing are capable of accumulating ancient acquisitions and progress more and more quickly toward the goal they have assigned themselves, while the peoples without writing, incapable of retaining the past beyond the fringe that individual memory suffices to fix, would remain prisoners of a fluctuating history which would always lack an origin and the durable consciousness of a project.
"And yet nothing of what we know of writing and its role in evolution justifies such a conception. One of the most creative

17

phases of the history of humanity took place during the approach of the neolithic age, responsible for agriculture, the domestication of animals and other arts. To reach it, it was necessary that during millennia little human collectivities observed, experimented and transmitted the fruit of their reflections. This immense enterprise was carried on with a rigor and a continuity attested to by success, while writing was still unknown. If writing appeared between the fourth and third millennia before Christ, we must see in it an already distant (and no doubt indirect) result of the neolithic revolution, but nowise its condition. To what great innovation is it bound? On the plane of technology, we can cite hardly anything but architecture at this period. But the architecture of the Egyptians or the Sumerians was not superior to the works of certain Americans who were ignorant of writing at the time of the arrival of Cortez. Conversely, from the invention of writing up to the birth of modern science, the western world lived some 5000 years during which its knowledge fluctuated more than it was increased. It has often been remarked that between the kind of life of a Greek or Roman citizen and that of a European bourgeois of the 18th century, there was hardly much difference. In the neolithic period, humanity took giant steps forward without the help of writing; with writing the historical civilizations of the West long stagnated. No doubt the scientific expansion of the 19th and 20th centuries would hardly be conceivable without writing. But this necessary condition is certainly not sufficient to explain it.

"If we want to correlate the apparition of writing with certain characteristic traits of civilization, we have to look in another direction. The sole phenomenon that faithfully accompanied writing is the formation of cities and empires, that is, the integration into a political system of a considerable number of individuals and their hierarchization into castes and classes. Such in, in any case, the typical evolution we see from Egypt to China, the moment that writing begins: it appears to favorize the exploitation of men before it favorizes their illumination. This exploitation, which make it possible to assemble thousands of workers to yoke them to extenuating tasks, better accounts for the birth of architecture than does the direct relation envisioned a moment ago. If my hypothesis is correct, *we have to admit that the primary function of written communication is to facilitate enslavement."* (Claude Levi-Strauss, **Tristes tropiques,** pp. 265-66)

KATH JONES

Response to Lingis

Alphonso Lingis submitted two papers for possible inclusion in this conference and I would like to begin my response by quoting from that paper which is today absent. In his paper entitled Segmented Organisms, Lingis tells us that once a paper is "finished", or at least "ended", that the "thinking is over", and that all one can do in presenting it to a conference such as this is to attempt to "read it with the right eloquence, performing it". For, he tells us, the thought has been expropriated; the enigma that may have held you spellbound in the many weeks, months of writing it, is simply "no longer thinkable". That:

"If someone asks you what you meant when you said this or that in your essay, you have to ask... where? what page? and then go back, and, just like him, try to figure out what the words themselves say." [1]

What we are presented with is a problem for and of writing. One could perhaps enunciate it in a quasi-Kantian fashion by saying that what writing delivers to readers, to their intellect, is a thought deprived of the faculty to bounce back, to start again, to ask again, to accept the question raw, to make room for a void of what is not yet thought, a materiality, a sensuous space of thought that can be moved through.

Or again, but this time following Lyotard [2], one could find a problem in the way that inscription, as a part of tradition (indeed, as tradition) betrays what it conserves. That is, that the time of transmission is dead. But is it the 'time of transmission' that Lingis is appealing to in his apparent mourning for the loss of a "reciprocal relation", of a "zigzag movement" from one speaker to another? [3] Surely the thought of reciprocity is itself merely a Kantian fiction that is ultimately nothing more than the vehicle for an ethics that can find no other way to insert itself into power relations. Reciprocity calls forth and creates an 'other' on the basis of which ethics can begin concocting its revolting fictions.

Perhaps, what this reciprocity marks for Lingis, is a fiction that he points to when he tells us that even the leopard, recalled by the inscription of the claw, is itself merely a sign. For what is at stake is not the mark of loss, of a lack, but the prime coding of socialization itself.

And yet what are we to understand when we are told that "The eye has lost the ability to see the cut" that it "No longer winces when it sees the mark" of ink etched on the paper?[4]

Is this then a call to an "ethic of the living word"[5], of the "dream in speech of a presence denied to writing, denied by writing"[6], an ethic of speech that is the delusion of a presence mastered?

In what sense are we to take this "loss" this "no longer"? Is this the "Illusion of full and present speech"[7] that Derrida warns us of? Of the "illusion of the presence within a speech believed to be transparent and innocent"[8]? Are we indeed being directed "toward the praise of silence that the myth of a full presence wrenched from difference and from the violence of the word is then deviated"[9]?

A persuasion ("suppleer") which we find being compensated for in "public force", in the "hands that cleanse an oil-drenched cormorant.... when lips kiss the pain of the AIDS victim"[10]?

Or perhaps we should follow Foucault [11] and say that the inability of writing to make the eye "wince" as it slices through the body of the page is no more than an indictment upon the status of writing - the fate of writing to be "infinitely reproduced" within the system of education, of discipline, the process of normalization - within our society?

An accusation that we stand under as readers, writers, philosophers. For insofar as we are the members of this community we too exist and act under accusation. We belong - are attached, bound - to the poverty we produce and reproduce within the closed system of a protection racket - of what it is to belong - to be properly classified, to be appropriate, to be in our suitable place.

The power to subvert, to cut, to incise, to turn the scalpel of the state, of theory, against itself lies, as Lingis suggests, within the very language, the power discourse, of the State.
"At best you can speak of them within the imperial code, speak of them as cocaine traffickers and terrorists, in such a way the words begin to lose their consistency, become non-sensical, turn against the imperial order itself. You can try to make other conspirators who use the imperial formulas them-selves as passwords by which the imperial discourse itself turns into babble and din."[11]

Yet for such a strategy to be effective we can acknowledge no "outsiders", indeed there can be no outsiders, for in order that danger, nomadic danger be effective, it must be seen to be bred and fed from within.

To summarize: Clearly we are not here dealing with either a mistaken attempt to privilege a form of inscription (verbal or bodily) over writing as a way of mastering or bringing to presence. Nor can the "anaesthetization" of the eye be understood and interpreted in terms of loss or lack. Rather, what is being advanced, I suggest, is an analysis of the devaluation of the mark occurring by way of the disciplinary model of writing in our society, that corresponds to the move-ment of Capitalism as Deleuze and Guattari diagnose it, in terms of the mark as the prime coding of socialization.

There remains in Lingis' reading however, within the couplings envisioned on the horizon of Capitalism, in the dispersion of body parts across the social field, a certain aura of (physi-ological) sympathy, a sensuality that seems to require a rela-tionship, perhaps even an ethical coding that, whilst it pre-cludes the public recognition, the coding, the celebration and suffering of the organs and flows of a unified body, formulates and projects upon an other, by way of a medium of sensuality, a coding that unites the body-parts in a relationship governed by what appears to be, in the end, something very close to a (Foucauldian) inscription of Care.

NOTES

1. A. Lingis. Segmented organisms page 16.
2. J-F. Lyotard. The Inhuman Polity Press. Cambridge. 1991.
3. A. Lingis. The Society of Dismembered Body Parts page 7.
4. A. Lingis. The Society of Dismembered Body Parts page 7.
5. J. Derrida Of Grammatology Trans GC Spivak John Hopkins University USA page 139
6. ditto
7. J. Derrida. ibid page 140.
8. ditto
9. ditto
10. A. Lingis. The Society of Dismembered Body Parts page 20
11. M. Foucault. Discipline and Punish Trans A Sheridan. Penguin Books. London. 1977.
12. A. Lingis. The Society of Dismembered Body Parts page 17

IAIN HAMILTON GRANT

Energumen Critique

I would like to begin with an anti-oedipal intervertion of Kant's *Critique of Pure Reason*: "Our age is, in especial degree, the age of universal schizophrenia, to which everything must submit". O Copernican Revolution! O critical sobriety! O submission and humiliation! A despot is being beaten. The great geopolitical sweep through nomadic, anarchistic and despotic regimes that heralds the call-to-arms of critical philosophy is not so much of historical as it is of geographical and strategic import: critical philosophy must secure the battlefield, the *Kampfplatz* of metaphysics; the latter's successive governments are of only incidental importance, since above all what impels the establishment of the Tribunal, "none other than the critique of pure reason" *(CPR Axii)*,[1] is the completely anarchic space these "endless controversies" have left behind; a flat and featureless extension over which to draw its boundaries, erect its fences and maintain its "perpetually armed state". Critique invests defensive stations at the extreme borders of this space, as well as at each of its internal limits: not only, that is, on the other side of the "continuous coastline of experience itself - a coast we cannot leave without venturing upon a shoreless ocean" *(CPR A 395)*, but also on this side, as the lines dissociating the courtroom from the battlefield - "the realm of this critique extends to all the claims that these powers make, in order to place them within the boundaries of their rightful use" *(CPJ Ak.176)*. Communicating spontaneously with each line of the defensive positions it occupies, critique has flattened out and striated the battlefield, which remains marked by the deep scars of its military ascendancy, continuously remarking the ground plan or architectonic of pure reason.

The critical revolution also spills over into other spaces. Notably the theatre. The theatre is above all an apparatus of energetic capture, a means of retaining the ennervation of the spectacle of "intestine wars" that racked the earth in its

Hobbesian "natural state", so as to continue to draw on its production of an indifferent earth on which Critique might build its enlightened edifice. Thus, encasted in the courtroom, observed from "the safe seat of the critic, these conflicts, now bloodless, continue:

Instead... of rushing into the fight, sword in hand, we should rather play the part of the peaceable onlooker, from the safe seat of the critic. The struggle is indeed toilsome to the combatants, but for us can be quite entertaining; and its outcome, certain to be quite bloodless, must be of advantage as contributing to our theoretical insight. Besides, (the conflict of dogmatic and sceptical) reason is already of itself so confined and held within limits by reason, that we have no need to call out the guard."(CPR A747/B775)

Towards the outer reaches of the critical plains, the same thing is repeated as Kant looks onto the "scene, over a hundred miles removed", of the French Revolution, which
finds in the hearts of all spectators (who are not engaged in the game themselves) a wishful participation that borders closely on enthusiasm ('An Old Question...', KH p.144)

Kant takes such enthusiasm to be an index of humanity's progress. In the *Critique of the Power of Judgement*, however, it is an affect bordering not only on participation, but on *Wahnsinn*, delirium, wherein the "unbridled imagination" is given free rein *(CPJ Ak.275)*. These assaults on the distinguishability of border states (which Deleuze and Guattari, in *Mille Plateaux*, call "zones of indiscernability") reach fever pitch with the case of the sublime. In consequence enthusiasm strikes us not so much as an index of humanity's progress, as it does an index of *deterritorialisation*. This is why, following *The Anti-Oedipus*,[2] critique must be regarded as a machinic assemblage of desire, such as function in "dreams, delirium, and phantasma" *(p.316)*, whose strata and substrata, these extensive spaces, revolve around the intensive space of the Body without Organs. We will return to intensive space later.

The Anti-Oedipus makes no secret of its critical affiliations:
In what he termed the critical revolution, Kant intended to

discover criteria immanent to the understanding so as to distinguish the legitimate and the illegitimate uses of the syntheses of consciousness. In the name of transcendental philosophy..., he therefore denounced the transcendent use of syntheses such as appeared in metaphysics. In like fashion we are compelled to say that psychoanalysis has its metaphysics - its name is Oedipus. And that a revolution - this time materialist - can proceed only by way of a critique of Oedipus, by denouncing the illegitimate use of the syntheses of the unconscious as found in Oedipal psychoanalysis, so as to rediscover a transcendental unconscious defined by the immanence of its criteria, and a corresponding practise that we shall call schizoanalysis. (A-Oe p.75)

A desirerevolution with which Deleuze and Guattari quite rightly credit Kant *(A-Oe p.25)*. Schizoanalysis in turn flattens the institutional, bureaucratic overcoded spaces of the Critical Tribunal, but follows Kant in deterritorialising the despots' territory, rendering it artificial, "more perverse". They, however, do not theatricise the bloodless conflicts in the core of the courtroom, they take despots as agents of de- and reterritorialisation, deterritorialising the "primitive territorial machine" and reterritorialising it as "the despotic machine". "Leave the tedious lingring method", bellows Hume, interrupting his schizo-stroll or getting up from the dinner table to hurl Molotovs into the citadel of human reason: "one can never go far enough in the direction of deterritorialisation" *(A-Oe p.321)*. It is in this direction that we will now briefly turn.

Deterritorialisation and Geology

Deleuze and Guattari are careful to insist that deterritorialisation and reterritorialisation form a circuit of intensities that circulate over the Body without Organs, "the ultimate residuum of a deterritorialised socius" *(A-Oe p.33)*.
Whether physical, psychological or social, D is relative insofar as it concerns the historical relations of the earth with the territories sketched on it or effaced from it, its geological relation with eras and catastrophes, its astronomical relation with the cosmos and the solar system of which it is a part. But

27

deterritorialisation is absolute when the earth passes into the pure plane of immanence of a thought-Being, a thought-Nature, towards infinite diagrammatical movements. (...) The deterritorialisation of such a plane does not rule out its reterritorialisation, but sets it up as the coming creation of a new earth. Further, absolute deterritorialisation can only be thought according to certain relations to be determined with relative reterritorialisations, not only cosmic, but geographical, historical and psychosocial. There is always a sense in which absolute deterritorialisation on the plane of immanence carries on from a relative deterritorialisation in a given field.(QP p.85)

The geological motif in this passage retains a geo-historical trajectory, based on eras, catastrophes and the new earth; Arnaud Villanni finds the "precise geographical sense of the plateau" in linear transformations of the erosion-sedimentation type,[3] but both remain within a very narrow band of the intensities that remain on the full body of the earth, constituting "relative deterritorialisations". It is in this sense that Kant's deterritorialisations must be understood. The sequence barbarian-despot-nomad-judge, i.e., the critical revolution, demonstrates relative deterritorialisations that are immediately followed by judicial "perversions" *(detournements)* or reterritorialisations. So it is with most revolutions, whether fascist, bourgeois or revolutionary: it makes little difference to the libidinal investments *(A-Oe p. 364)*. As Deleuze and Guattari put it concerning the discovery of the unconscious and its ensuing recoding on the analyst's couch and the machinery of neurosis, "psychoanalysis is like the Russian revolution: we don't know when it started going bad" *(A-Oe p.55)*. But critique has many unexploited intensive thresholds that are not at all stable. For example, the enthusiasm Kant finds in "the hearts of the disinterested spectators" of the French revolution is simultaneously an index of the progress of humanity and encroaching delirium. We must accordingly follow Dominique Noguez on the matter of revolutions when she insists that the Russian revolution constitutes a vast "dadaist prank on history".

The Anti-Oedipus proposes an intensive geology, an absolute deterritorialisation wherein the earth is stripped of the layers or "planes of resistance" that envelop the BwO, proceeding "with great patience, great care, by successively undoing the representative territorialities and reterritorialisations" *(A-Oe p.318)*.

One never deterritorialises alone; there are always at least two terms..., and each of these two terms reterritorialises on the other. reterritorialisation must not be confused with a return to a primitive or older territoriality; it necessarily implies a set of artifices by which one element, itself deterritorialised, serves as a new territory for the other, which has lost its own territoriality as well. (MP p.174)

Thus the cycles of deterritorialisation and reterritorialisation, endlessly revolving at different speeds and intensities, overlapping, feedbacking and breaking into multiplicities of other cycles, "there is no such thing as relatively independent circuits" *(A-Oe p.4)*. Asking Kant, with Deleuze and Guattari, "what drives your own desiring-machines?" *(A-Oe p. 290)*, we impatiently await the opportunity to seize on the delirium which heralds the breakdown and total collapse of the critical machinery, as it simultaneously approaches its highest and lowest intensities.

Incipient Delirium

We have seen that deterritorialisation moves from geology to cycles and circuits, from maps to diagrams and intensity. Critique, by the same token, moves from history to geography to geology to intensity. It is this "last" passage (geology - intensity) that we will examine here. Schizoanalysis replaces the maps of the old earth with circuit-diagrams of the new.

"There are no statues in the unconscious" *(A-Oe p.338).*[4] What then of Kant's battlefields, courts, theatres and architectonics? They are filled up with desiring-machines, "indices of deterritorialisation" *(A-Oe p.316)* which testify to immense perverse reterritorialisations: the Kant assemblage, as we shall see, constitutes a particular deleuzo-guattarian megamachine that operates prodigious deterritorialisations and reterritorialisations. The scorched earth left by Hume's imperialist expedient ("Here then is the only expedient, from which we can hope for success in our philosophical researches, to leave the tedious lingring method, which we have hitherto followed, and instead of taking now and then a castle or village on the frontier, to march up directly to the capital or center of these sciences, to human nature itself (...). From this station we may extend our conquests over all those sciences...[5]), is a vector of deterritorialisation on which critique seizes and reterritorialises, only to be caught up in a more intense deterritorialisation that digs up the subsoil of critical space. The *Critique of the Power of Judgement* institutes a "critique of the judging subject" *(CPJ Introduction VIII, Ak.194)* in order to explore "the terrain supporting this edifice to the depth at which lies the first foundation of our power of principles... so that no part of the edifice may give way, which would inevitably result in the collapse of the whole" *(CPJ Preface Ak.169)*. Here, the linear order of temporal succession is displaced: the *First Critique* provides the new earth and marks it with the boundaries and borderlines of the architectonic; the *Third* undertakes to dig up the foundations for a "last" look, a final test.

With this "last" test, we might ask, with Deleuze and Guattari, "what does an alcoholic call the *last glass*?" *(MP 438)* The "last" forms a limit, a break in a series and the incipience of a threshold, which, in the case of the alcoholic, is marked by the continuation of the series following the limit, the last glass, and the "'I'm going to stop', the theme of the last glass" (Ibid). In like fashion, critique never stops: just as, in Lyotard's *Libidinal Economy*, Little Girl Marx reproaches Old Bearded Prosecutor Marx for never quite completing the case against capital,[6] so the delirial Jacobin-Revolutionary Kant and the strict, sober and just Prussian-Reformist Kant are caught in the critical machinations of endless cycles of de- and re- territorialisation, of increasing intensity.

From the case of enthusiasm, we proceed to that of the Sublime, or the threshold of critique's becoming-delirial that sets all its borders and careful deliniations oscillating wildly. As we said, the excavators of the *Third Critique* set to work on the liminal coded space of the tribunal. What the *First Critique* did to history, the third does to space. Nothing illustrates quite so clearly these indissociable circuits of de- and re-territorialisation as does the Sublime, the aesthetic judgement of which, Kant writes, "contributes nothing to the cognition of objects; hence it belongs only to the critique that is the propaedeutic to all philosophy - viz., the critique of the judging subject" *(CPJ Ak.194)*.

Judgement Deranged

Just as Kantian theatrics delimits the specular space of derealised conflicts, the topological series which figures in both the first and second introductions to the *Third Critique*, delimits the field of the concept, bounded by the inaccessible field of the supersensible, and subdivides the former field into territory, domain and residence. The purpose of this conceptual geography is both to reassert the critical conquest of speculation, or the prohibition of undertaking perilous voyages on the unbounded ocean, "native home of illusions", in theoretical reason, and to (provide the incentive to "occupy (*besetzen*) (the supersensible) with Ideas", to invest in this unbounded field with neither territory, domain nor residence *(CPJ Intro.II, Ak.174-5)*. As Kant says, the critique of the power of judgement bears precisely on placing the claims made by the various powers or faculties "within the boundaries of their rightful (use)" *(Ak.176)*. Judgement, meanwhile, has itself no domain nor field, its task being "*to have already explored*" the terrain "supporting the edifice" of metaphysics, to establish and secure "the first foundation of our power of principles independent of experience" *(Ak.168)*. Judgement, both primary and parasitic, territorialising and deterritorialising, a supplementary power par excellence, "may be annexed to (theoretical or practical reason) as needed" *(Ak.168)*.

Having no proper field, then judgement remains the war-machine[7] of critical philosophy: the Tribunal's "judicial sentence" not only "strikes at the very root of conflicts" and thus "secures an eternal peace", as in the *First Critique (A752/B780)*, it revivifies these conflicts as spectacle, and consumes them in a state which "borders on enthusiasam" *(KH p.144)*. Judgement can find no residence in the liminal fields of critique, and its mercenary annexation to one or the other of the realms of reason, theoretical or practical, far from establishing and securing the terrain upon which the edifice of metaphysics is to be constructed, intensifies their disjunct spontaneity, mobilizes and agitates the "permanently armed state" occupied by critique.

Judgement remains nomadic, both critical and sceptical: it circulates both inside the pre-critical spaces *deranged* or perverted by desire, or, as the Anthropology has it, fragmented by the "intrusion of a disturbed power of judgement *(gestorte Urteilskraft: APV s52, Ak.215)*; and outside, "uninvolved", looking peacefully on from the "safe seat of the critic" *(CPR A747/B775)*. Similarly, it is in the "state of nature", a "state of violence and injustice", in the "absence of critique", that war as opposed to the lawsuit provides the only only means to "establish and secure" the claims of reason *(CPR A751-2/ B779-80)*.

It is particularly striking that what was the "boundless ocean" and the "native home of all illusion in the *First Critique (A235-6/B295)*, has become, in the conceptual geography of the *Third*, an unhabitable realm, but a field nonetheless. There is a geological acceleration of the becoming-land of the ocean, at the same time as there takes place in the Judgement of the Sublime, a becoming liquid of the affect, as the *Anthropology* puts it. The one deterritorialises the other, but neither can reterritorialise on the other. Deleuze and Guattari are only partially correct then when they write that with the Copernican Revolution, Kant establishes a "direct relation between thought and the earth" *(QP p.82)*. All this changes with the Third Critique. The earth prepared for the Tribunal and its liminal spaces enters, with the nomad power of judgement seizing on the affect of the Sublime. As affect, it "works like water that breaks though a dam" *(APV s74, Ak.252)*. Here, in the Sublime and in enthusiasm, we catch a glimpse of the delirium that drives critical philosophy, an obsessional relation to the becoming liquid of the earth, or as *The Anti-Oedipus* puts it, "the greatest danger would be yet another dispersion, a scission such that all the possibilities of coding would be suppressed: decoded flows, flowing on a blind, mute deterritorialised socius - such is the nightmare" that critical philosophy, as opposed to the "primitive social machine", cannot exorcise." *(A-Oe p.153)*

There is also an intensive relation; the circuits of the affect increase in intensity with the Sublime, since the latter is "a pleasure that arises only indirectly: it is produced by the feeling of a momentary inhibition (*Hemmung*: the text has Freud's word) of the vital forces followed immediately by an outpouring of them that is all the stronger" *(CPJ s23 Ak.245)*. This is indeed the desirerevolution that Deleuze and Guattari ascribe to Kant;[8] the sublime effects an absolute deterritorialisation that brings the critical cycles of deterritorialisation and reterritorialisation to its peak of intensity all the way to a draining that brings it to its base =0, or the critical Body without Organs.

Since philsophy is a majoritarian, molar, institutional discourse that still adheres to the "tedious lingring method" that Hume was so bored by, opening a discourse on intensities is a tricky business. Thus Lyotard in *'Notes on the Return and Kapital'*:
From the moment we begin to speak here we are in representation and theology. The walls of Cerisy-la-salle are the walls of a museum, i.e. the setting aside of affects and the privilege of exteriority accorded to concepts; intensitiesare placed in reserve, made quiescent, and thus put on stage. (...) Weakening, the loss of intensity, old age and normalisation sustain representation. Even if we suppress these castle walls, even if we held this discourse in the subway, it would remain corrupt as Nietzsche said. The condition of representation is internal to philosophical discourse.[9]

The deduction of volume, the theatrical *dispositif*: the institution puts intensities on stage. We find the same thing in Kant. Faced with the ennervating spectacle of the French revolution, unfolding "on a stage more than a hundred miles away", critique machines these errant intensities and regicidal desires into signs, into an index of progress. We find the same thing in Freud. Dreams, as the "royal road to the unconscious",[10] take place on "another scene or stage *(ein andere Schauplatz)*";[11] here too the displacing and condensing intensities of the primary processes are molded into signs to be decoded, indices of what Deleuze and Guattari call a relative deterritorialisation, or a transcoding and reterritorialisation.

Thus the theatrical apparatus: the body at the centre of a concentric organisation of spaces, the institution shares its walls with the auditorium. Hence Freud's regal quost, and hence Kant's regicidal enthusiasm: there was quite a different scenario when Queen Metaphysics was gleefully deposed and butchered by nomads, sceptics and anarchists, as Kant relates in the preface to the *First Critique:*
Her (metaphysics') government, under the administration of

the dogmatists, was at first despotic. But inasmuch as the legislation still bore traces of the ancient barbarism, her empire gradually through intestine wars gave way to complete anarchy: and the sceptics, a species of nomads, despising all settled forms of life, broke up from time to time all civil society. (...) And now... the prevailing mood is that of weariness and complete indifferentism - the mother, in all sciences, of chaos and night. (...Such indifference) is a call to reason to (...) institute a tribunal which will assure to reason its lawful claims, and dismiss all groundless pretentions, not by despotic decrees, but in accordance with its own eternal and immutable laws. This tribunal is no other than the critique of pure reason. (CPR Aix-Axii)

Here regicide was a pretext for (and Kant is uncertain) either "approaching reform and restoration" or "a single and sudden revolution"; if not to reassemble, revive and reinstate the Queen, then to reterritorialise her in the new earth's bureaucracy, to frantically guzzle at her remains in order at least to renew the savour of her "strict, just and sober" prohibitions, in the face of the manifest indifference currently regining over the battlefield of metaphysics. "We have hung the Queen, so we must hang her portrait". The first Critique is resonant with the building of a severe architecture, which has as its purpose to prepare the ground for the assembly of a new organism. There is a redrawing of borders, a redrafted statute of rights of way, and, when all the limits have been established and are adequately policed (as Kant has it, "to deny that the service which the Critique renders is positive in character, would thus be like saying that the police are of no positive benefit" *(CPR Bxxv)*, they produce a skeletal proto-interiority, a maquette of pure reason. Deleuze and Guattari have provided a machinic portrait of the Kantian Body without Organs, the exquisite corpse of critique:

"We could imagine", write Deleuze and Guattari, "a machinic portrait of Kant, illusions and all:
1.- the "I think", the sonorous cow's head which endlessly repeats Ego = Ego. 2.- the categories as universal concepts (4 great headings): extending and retracting shafts that follow the circular motion of 3. 3.- the mobile wheel of the schemata.

4.- Time, the shallow streaming gutter, as form of interiority into which the schemata-wheel plunges and resurfaces. 5.- Space as form of exteriority: shores and beds. 6.- the passive Ego on the stream-bed as the juncture of the two forms. 7.- the principles of the synthetic judgements that sweep space-time. 8.- the transcendental field of possible experience, immanent to the I (plane of immanence). 9.- the three Ideas or illusions of transcendence (circles turning on the absolute horizon: Soul, World and God)." *(QP 57)*

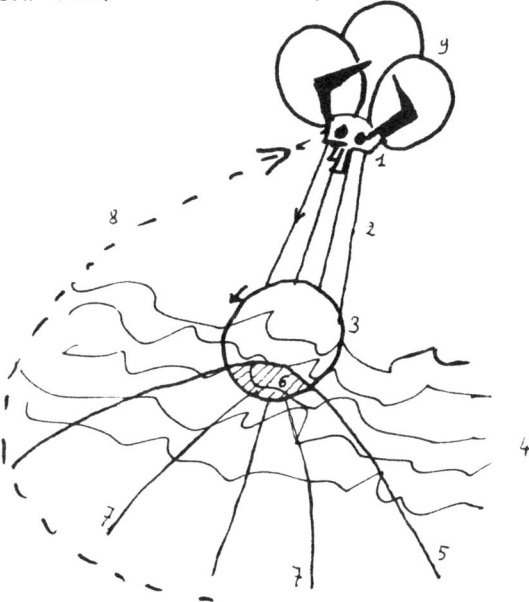

("Machinic Portrait of Kant" by Deleuze & Guattari)

What sort of space does critique inhabit? Kant, of course, delineates a series of sites for critique: the *Kampfplatz*, the "other scene" (the French Revolution), the island-dominion of the pure understanding, surrounded by the "native home of illusion", the wide and stormy ocean, and the "realm of the concept", subdivided into territory, domain and residence. What is crucial in each space is its intensity: the degree, according to what Deleuze and Guattari accurately designate as Kant's "profoundly schizoid theory" *(A-Oe 19)* of space, according to which "matter that has no empty spaces" is filled up with intensive qualities. Liminality, circumscription and border definition are crucially important to the critical revolution, not just because they define boundaries and prohibit transgressions, but because they annihilate interiority/exteriority in favour of intensity and extension. Critique, like the unconscious, is constantly condensing and displacing. Although this is most tangible in the *Critique of the Power of Judgement*, it flows wildly through the *First Critique*. All critical space is "precipitous space", and as such, according to Sun-Tzu,[12] must be avoided. These ancient Chinese military codes revolve around the measured accumulation of "All-Under-Heaven" with minimal losses. Sun-Tzu advises that as much be left intact and unchanged as is militarily practical. Critical combat, however, while modelling its spectatorial core on the sceptical model of "shadow warriors" and "mock conflicts", is engagaed in what Lyotard has called "populocide":[13] propelling even the remnants of an irrelevant humanity to the farthest reaches of the earth, Dr. Kantenstein redistibutes its organs in a way that neither Wolff nor Napoleon could hitherto manage.

This is no mere provisional occupation, schizoanalysis cannot but invest in the critical *Kampfplatz*, albeit in the name of "a race oppressed, bastard, inferior, anarchic, nomadic; irremediably minor" *(QP 105)*, in the name of those pack animals that consume the obsessional deliria collectively known as Kantianism: "Schizoanalysis must devote itself with all its strength to the necessary destructions. Destroying beliefs and *representations,* theatrical scenes. And when engaged in this task, no activity will be too malevolent." *(A-Oe, 314, emphasis added.)*

Just as the theatricised spectacle of regicide on the French scene made Kant feverish and delirious with enthusiasm, so we greet the demise of representation with a sly grin as we pull the trigger. And let's face it, after two centuries of Kantianism, philosophers are well prepared for a bullet in the brain. In the corridors of every institution, we can still here them chant: "Our age is, in especial degree, the age of criticism, and to criticism everything must submit" *(CPR Axiin)*. We can practically see them, head on the block, gazing into the basket, wetting themselves with excitement over fulfiling the duty of their excremental fatality as the chair starts to hum, as water mixes with gas, as the blade falls.

"Critique", writes Marx in the 'Contribution to a Critique of Hegel's Philosophy of Right',[14] "is not a scalpel; it is a weapon": even the butchered corpse of the socius lying on the operating table expends its last strength nodding in agreement. We might have read this in Kant: critical philosophy is indeed forever brandishing arms, arms which, as Lyotard claims, "reflection", in Kant's third *Critique*, "seems simply to dispose of altogether".[15] We have our doubts: reflexion, as Derrida says, is a "barricaded street"[16] not a rest home in the midst of the battlefield. Unable to cope with the eerie silence reigning over the battlefield, critique, desperate for renewed slaughter, baits a trap to draw its enemies out of the shadowplays:

They wish to prove, very well then, let them prove, and the critical philosophy will lay down its weapons before them as victors. Since they do not actually wish to prove, presumably because they cannot, we must again take up these weapons... (CPrR, Preface, 5)

In spite of the challenge and the intimation of conflict ("They wish to prove"), they remain silent ("they do not actually wish to prove"), but are cut down anyway; their silence even *impels* ("we must again take up these weapons") critique to war, to nature, to a renewed scepticism, anarchism, despotism and nomadism.

Notes

1.   *References to Kant's texts are as follows:*
CPR: Critique of Pure Reason, tr. N.K. Smith (London: Macmillan, 1929)
CPrR: Critique Of Practical Reason, tr. L.W. Beck (Indianapolis: Bobbs-Merrill, 1956)
CPJ: Critique of the Power of Judgement, tr. W. Pluhar (Indianapolis: Hackett, 1987). Although Pluhar's translation is simply entitled The Critique of Judgement, this ignores the Kraft in the German title, Kritik der Urteilskraft; I

have ammended this in accordance with Pluhar's own
practise in rendering Vermogen.
APV: *Anthropology from a Pragamatic Point of View*, tr. V.L.
Dowdell (Carbondale: Southern Illinois UP, 1978)
KH: *Kant on History*, ed. & tr. L.W. Beck (New York:
Macmillan, 1963)
2.   References to Deleuze and Guattari's texts are as follows:
A-Oe: *Anti-Oedipus*, tr. H.R. Lane, R. Hurley and M. Seem
(London: Athlone, 1984)
MP: *A Thousand Plateaus*, tr. B. Massumi (London: Athlone,
1988)
QP: *Qu'est-ce que la philosophie?* (Paris: Minuit, 1991)
3.   Arnaud Villani, 'La Geographie physique de Mille plateaux', *Critique*, 1985, p.333.
4.   Jean Tinguely's *Vittoria-machine* (Piazza Duomo, Milan,
28th November, 1970) shows the stages of increasing delirium
that disrupt the critical Tribunal. Tinguely reports that he was to
build "a large white machine that would turn itself intoa large
black machine and drive away" (Jean Tinguely andPontus
Hulten, *A Magic Stronger than Death* (London: Thames & Hudson, 1987), p.196): "A gigantic gold phallus, about ten metres
high (...). Smoke rose from the tip of the phallus. Some of the
explosions were extremely loud; a few of the rockets seemed
to reach around 250m. The testicles were adorned with gold
plastic bananas and grapes. The man (Kant?) who turned the
big wheel to set the huge internal machinery going wore a
shiny silver asbestos-lined suit. (...). It lasted about half an
hour." Tinguely has also engineered several other machines,
amongst which the 'Study for an End of the World' series (1: 'le
monstre- sculpture- autodestructive- dynamique and aggressif':
2:
'L'Opera- Burlesque- Dramatico- Big- Thing- Sculpto-Boum')
highlight the Kampfplatz and the theatrical aspects of critical
terrain. Deleuze and Guattari discuss his 1989 retrospective
show at the Centre Pompidou, Paris, in QP, pp.55-6.
5.   David Hume, *Treatise of Human Nature* (Oxford: OUP,
1896),Introduction, p.xx.
6.   Jean-Francois Lyotard, *Economie libidinale* (Paris: Minuit,
1974), pp.117 ff.
7.   In the 'Treatise on Nomadology: The War Machine',

Deleuze and Guattari indicate that although "the despot and the legislator" (...u)ndoubtedly stand in opposition term by term, (...t)he two together exhaust the field of the function. They are the principle elements of a State apparatus that proceedsby a One-Two, distributes binary distinctions and forms a milieu of interiority. (...) It will be noted that war is not contained within the apparatus. Either the State has at its disposal a violence that is not channeled through war - either it uses police officers (cf. CPR Bxxv - IHG) and jailors in place of warriors, has no arms or no need of them, operates by immediate, magical capture, "seizes" and "binds", preventing all combat - or, the State acquires an army, but in a way that presupposes a judicial integration of war and the organisation of a military function. (MP 352). The war machine remains "irreducuble to the State apparatus (ibid).This model is also employed in the kantian division and reterritorialisation of theoretical and practical reason; these latter also exhaust the field, leaving judgement, like the war machine, in the Third Critique, with neither "territory", "domain" nor "residence" within critical philosophy.

8.   Discussing the "traditional logic of desire", Deleuze and   Guattari draw attention to the fact that "Kant... must be credited with effecting a critical revolution as regards the theory of desire, by attributing to it "the faculty of being, through its representations, the cause of the reality of these representations (CPJ Introduction s3, Ak.177-8)" (A-Oe 25).

9.   Jean-Francois Lyotard, Des dispositifs pulsionels (2nd Edition. Paris: Christain Bourgois, 1979) p. 291). See also 'Notes on the Return and Kapital' tr. R. McKeon Semiotext(e) 3:1, 1978, p.44.

10.   Sigmund Freud, The Interpretation of Dreams, tr. and ed. J. Strachey. Penguin Freud Library 4 (Harmondsworth: Penguin, 1975), p.769.

11.   Ibid., p. 684ff.

12.   Sun-Tzu, in The Art of War, tr. S.B. Griffith (New York: OUP, 1971), Ch.IX v.16, classifies five "precipitous torrents": Heavenly Wells, Prisons, Nets, Traps and Cracks.H e w r i t e s : "You must march speedily away from them. Do not approach them." (See also Ch.X v.1, 6).

13.   Jean-Francois Lyotard, Le Postmoderne explique aux

enfants (Paris: Galilee, 1986), p.40.
14.   Karl Marx, 'Contribution to a Critique of Hegel's Philoso-phy of Right', in Early Writings tr. R. Livingstone and G. Benton (London: Penguin and New Left Review, 1975), p.246.
15.   Jean-Francois Lyotard, Lecons sur L'Analytique du Sub-lime (Paris: Galilee, 1991), p.47.
16.   Jacques Derrida, La Dissemination, (Paris: Seuil, 1972), p.299: "...la marche barre d'une telle reflexion." B. Johnson's English translation gives "the impeded march of any such reflection" (London: Athlone, 1981).*

Iain Hamilton Grant
May 1992

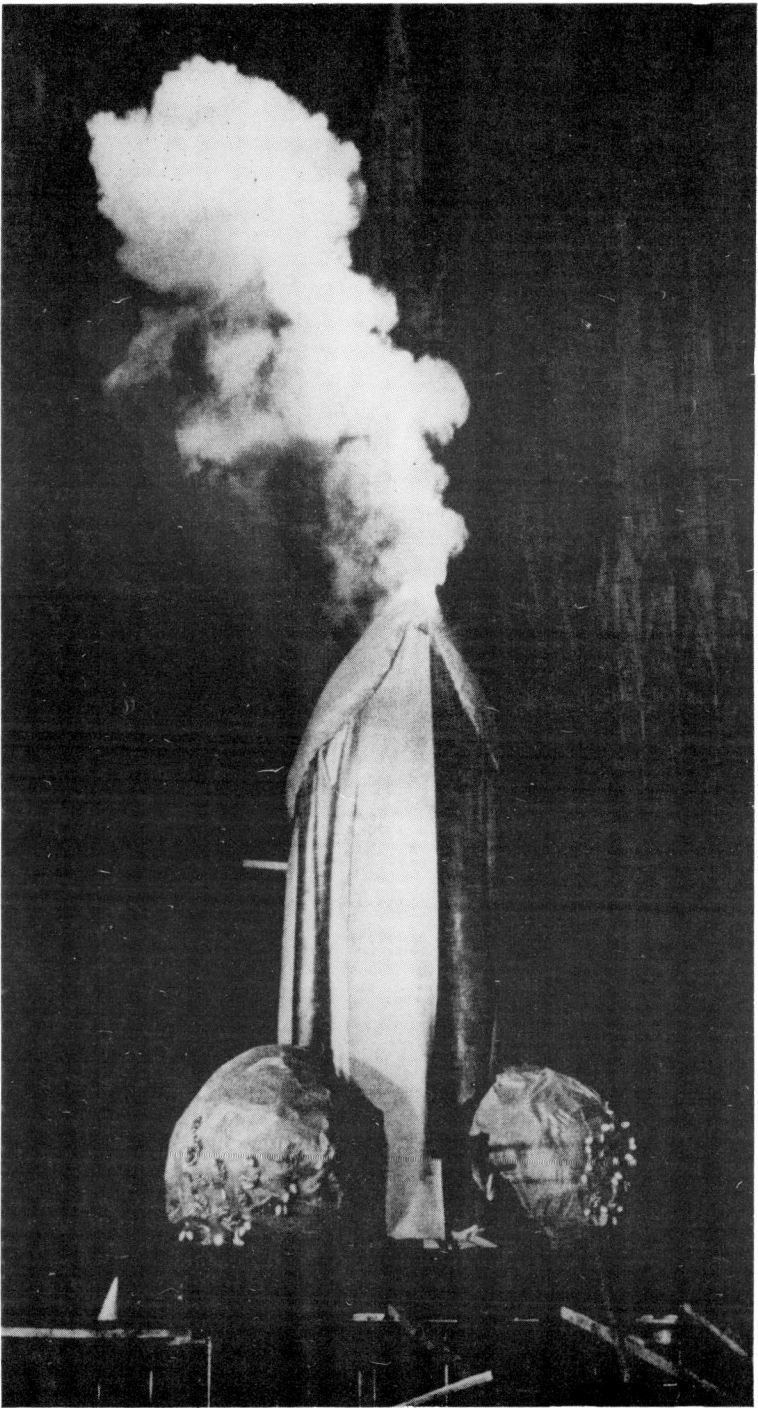

JAMES WILLIAMS

Monitoring vs *Metaphysical Modeling: or, How to predict the future of the postmodern condition*[1]

Everything in the world may change its appearance, because everything is capable of Increase and Diminution; and from this Rule even Kingdoms that seem the best established are not exempt. It is the part of every wise man therefore to prevent such declensions, as the Fortune of Men, more than Governments, is liable, without waiting till a sudden Turn comes, to give him a severe Demonstration of it. Adversity is, as it were, the natural Situation in which everyone, sooner or later, and by one means or another, is sure to relapse; unless he takes care in time to cut off the occasions of it.[2]

I. Positive and negative views of the postmodern condition

Fear of a prosperous stability is a surprising factor to have emerged in philosophy and literature. In particular, when such stability is associated with liberal democracy and a highly, or even astoundingly, successful economic system. What has become of the more comprehensible fears of apocalypse associated with nuclear armageddon and the dominance of neo-fascist or communist ideologies? Have philosophers and writers turned sour at the thought of a peaceful and comfortable future -- the **New World Order**? Or is the new tack of their thought spurred on by a sense of their redundancy in a world where all problems have become technical?

Take the recent world best selling high-brow novels **Vineland**

and **Immortality** by Thomas Pynchon and Milan Kundera, respected and widely read essayists with a proven track record in social critique. The former has further refined his theory of entropy to create a vision of a world where social intercourse is dominated by media images and where dissent and difference is being eliminated more thoroughly than ever. Pynchon's world is populated by schizophrenics mesmerized by a flow of television images that disturbs their thought patterns -- tube intoxication. Under the influence of media images, these people are incapable of revolt:

"Easy they just let us forget. Give us too much to process, fill up every minute, keep us distracted, it's what the tube is for, and though it kills me to say it, it's what rock and roll is becoming -- just another way to claim our attention, so that the beautiful certainty we had starts to fade, and after a while they had us convinced all over again that we really are going to die. and they've got us again." It was the way people used to talk.[3]

The latter has developed the category of kitsch so now it can map all current politics, ethics and aesthetics; for Kundera, the world is stuck in absolute denial of shit through the management of mass taste. This is his account of the kitsch effect in aesthetic interpretation:

The Kitsch-interpretation is a seduction that has come from the collective unconscious; an injunction from the metaphysical prompter; a permanent social requirement; a force. That force goes beyond the frontiers of art and aims at reality itself. Kitsch-interpretation throws the veil of the commonplace over the present instant and hides the face of the real.
So that you may never know what you have lived.[4]

Both cases betray a will to portray the world as a stable, valueless system in which all sources of past worth have been persecuted or denied. They fear a spread of indifference caused by a massive exposition to meaningless images. The resulting absence of authentic variety allows any remnants of beauty or productive revolt to be wiped away without reactions or aftershocks.

Why have these authors chosen such scenarios when the economic and political success of our Western society allows greater individual freedom, greater wealth and more opportunities than ever before? "Just rejoice!" we feel inclined to shout when faced by their bad faith and negative attitude. It is not easy, however, to dismiss Kundera as merely a nostalgic aesthete -- although his reaction to the state of affairs resembles such a position; neither is it simply a matter of accusing Pynchon of revolutionary disenchantment -- although he does focus on the perdition of revolt in present Western societies. They cannot be so easily brushed aside because other thinkers have been coming to similar conclusions on a wider basis. Such thinking usually takes place around the study of the postmodern condition. It is not restricted to any particular academic discipline, it takes on many different forms and it cannot be associated with any particular political group. In the work thinkers of the postmodern such as David Harvey, Frederic Jameson and Jean-Francois Lyotard there is a deduction of the possible emergence of a stable society. This possibility gives rise to fear and foreboding.

Remarkably, these deductions have many things in common. The following points recur in all the studies, they can also be found as themes in **Immortality** and **Vineland**:

1. capitalism is undergoing a metamorphosis that has strong implications for the political and social nature of society;

2. the change in capitalism is mirrored in the changing cultural environment of society;

3. there is upheaval in the relation of time and space that constitutes our experience of the world;

4. ethical norms are disappearing in favour of practical economic rules;

5. dissent is becoming impossible.

Thus Frederic Jameson sees capitalism as entering its third stage, "late capitalism" or "a network of power and control even more difficult for our minds and imaginations to grasp: the whole new de-centred global network of the third stage of capital". A stage associated with the global market and the unpredictable -- but all- powerful -- flow of vast investment sums. This market works in tandem with technological media that control cultural changes and innovation. The role of historical time in the understanding of society has disappeared in favour of spatial differentiation; for example, the history of conflicts matters little when compared with the mediated presentation of present day differences. The human subject can no longer focus its own ethical norms, instead, these are replaced by transient rules communicated through the media and set according to their perceived profitability. Class con-scious dissent is no longer possible in a society that favours groups above classes, where new and old groups do battle in the media and through the markets. In Jameson's view, de-mocracy, the political system of the new order, merely fulfils the function of hub, bringing these different forces into con-tact and order.

Not only does Jameson note the disappearance of rational human values and with them the possibility of bringing about a society based on such values. He also notes that the postmodern period is one of transition where a steady dis-membering of the old order leads to a new form of society based on a new mode of production:

The postmodern may well be little more than a transitional period between two stages of capitalism, in which the earlier forms of the economic are in the process of being restructured on a global scale, including the older forms of labour and its traditional institutions and concepts.[5]

The older oppressed forms of labour will appear again, the underclass will grow, the power of capitalist bosses will in-crease. All this will take place on a backdrop where historical understanding gives way to media led spatial awareness, conflicts and differences can be recognised but their causes can no longer be identified. Thereby, the seat of power, the market, will be able to control cultural processes, the source of any potential revolt. These developments lead to the stable state described by Pynchon and Kundera. The bleak view is repeated in the work of David Harvey as he maps the shifts in capital ownership, working practices and patterns of poverty: the first toward supranational super rich investors, the second toward insecure hourly paid employment, the last toward a growing disenfranchised underclass:

The street scenes of impoverishment, disempowerment, graffiti and decay become grist for the cultural producers' mill, (...), not in the muckraking reformist style of the late nineteenth century, but as a quaint and swirling backdrop (...) upon which no social commentary is made. "Once the poor become aestheticized, poverty itself moves out of the field of social vision", except as a passive depiction of otherness, alienation and contingency within the human condition.[6]

However, if we return to the list of critical points, a very different interpretation can emerge contradicting thinkers such as Jameson and Harvey. The main operative points, the first three, remain unchanged. There is agreement on the metamorphosis of capitalism, the accompanying change in cultural environment and the upheaval in the relation of time and space (interpreted as the end to violent historical conflicts). But the value laden points become:

4. Ethical differences can be resolved according to practical economic rules.

5. All dissent is worked out through the democratic process and disappears.

What we are left with **then** is the highly positive politics of consensus or "culture of contentment". Society has become an economically successful, pluralistic and just system. A system based on the ability of late capitalism to incorporate difference and render it profitable, and on the ability of world-wide democracy to cushion conflicts into consensus. Stability to be sure, but it is eminently valuable rather than fearsome.

II. The postmodern dilemma

Are we on the verge of a stable and steadily more affluent consensus, or, a new all-powerful and rigid system of oppression? A crucial question to those who recognise the moment as one of perhaps irreversible change. Any answer to it must be two-fold: first, we have to determine whether we are indeed on the verge of a stable world order; second, we have to gauge as to the nature of that order. The writers and thinkers mentioned above make claims as to the unfurling of world history based on the observation of cultural, economic and technological changes. Their findings may be convincing at first sight. However, when we consider the abstract question of an analysis claiming to have the last word on the present state of world-wide economics and culture, "total critique", philosophical experience in the fields of epistemology and critique leads to a sceptical response. A convincing social commentary does not add up to a true scientific or critical analysis.

The point of this article will be to respond to this problem of evaluating the claims of total critique in the light of the problematics given above. I will study the works of thinkers close to Kundera and Pynchon, Guy Debord and Deleuze and Guattari, and I will contrast their work and the theories put forward by Jameson and Harvey. Kundera's development of the aesthetics of kitsch rejoins Debord's analysis of the society of the spectacle. Pynchon's ode to revolutionary politics and marginal societies is steeped in Deleuze and Guattari, from implicit connections such as the machine-like hook up to television analyzed in **Mille Plateaux** and experienced by Pynchon's characters, and up to the point of a veiled humorous hint:

Fortunately Ralph Wayvone's library happened to include a copy of the indispensable **Italian Wedding Fake Book**, by Deleuze and Guattari (...)[7]

Deleuze and Guattari and Debord offer new and powerful theories submitting changes in culture, economics, ethics and politics to general principles: the axioms of Schizo-analysis (Deleuze and Guattari) and the rules of the Spectacle (Debord). To help to isolate these principles, the study will go through the first three points associated with the postmodern condition to see how they are covered by Deleuze and Guattari. The way these points are handled by the thinkers will allow us to determine whether the thinkers are in a position to make ethical and political judgements on the postmodern condition, the topic of the last two themes. The point of the study will be to isolate some of the problems and solutions involved in the total critique of the postmodern condition.

III. The metamorphosis of capital

Whatever the actuality of the immanent form, third generation modern States do restore the most absolute of all empires, a new "mega-machine". They do this by realising an axiomatic that functions as much by machine enslavement as by social subjection. Capitalism has woken the Urstaat and given it new forces.[8]

In a book entitled **The Society of the Spectacle**, I showed what in the modern spectacle was already in essence: the auto-cratic reign of the market economy which had acceded to an irresponsible sovereignty, and the totality of new techniques of government which accompanied this reign. (...) the spectacle has thus continued to gather strength; that is, to spread to the furthest limits on all sides, while increasing its density at the centre. It has even learnt new defensive techniques, as powers under attack always do.[9]

Debord and Deleuze and Guattari observe a change in the nature of capitalism or, at least, in the relation of capital to society. They make their observations on the back of meta-theories that stands independent of any particular manifestation of capitalism. Deleuze and Guattari use of the axioms of their "machine" theory as the basis for their study, Debord appeals to his analysis of the society of the spectacle, that is, "the reign of the market economy". These meta-theories allow them to predict the future of capitalism from observations of its present state. What is the nature of their prediction? Can we study their meta-theories in detail?

To start with Deleuze and Guattari. The central theory depends upon an opposition drawn up between **States**, that is, machines of organisation and normalisation, and **Nomadic War Machines**, that is, machines that function as destroyers of norms and organisations through the creative disturbance of organised space. If States can be seen as bureaucratic organisers of well defined identities, spaces and functions, nomadic war machines can be seen as machines designed to sack such spaces, dissolve any identity and break the functions. States and nomadic war machines operate against one another and with one another: they are fundamentally opposed and yet when states go to war or require internal changes they must function with a nomadic war machine to liberate creative forces of change and conflict. Deleuze and Guattari start with an absolute distinction based on two fundamentally different types of machine; one can only preserve, the other can only destroy and create. They must function together whenever there is preservation **and** creation, order **and** radical change, for example, when a state is at war or when a nomadic machine must determine or preserve its identity.[10]

Existence is constituted by the opposition of nomadic war machine and State. The nomadic war machine destroys the State as a nomadic invader from without or as a rebellious force from within. The essential enterprise of the State therefore is to conquer the nomadic war machine, to capture it and use it for its own purposes: war against other States. The most successful State is one that captures external and internal nomadic war machines in order to turn them against its enemies. The final moment of this war of states will be fascist total war where the full forces of each state are brought into the war effort. After fascist total war an **Empire State** or "mega-machine" emerges, it has rid itself successfully of competing states and can turn its attention to using nomadic war machines in the consolidation of the State, that is, putting forces of liberation and creation to the service of organisation and planning. The stage of "mega-machine" corresponds to the focus of this discussion, the stage of late capitalism:

This world war machine that "returns" from the States in some way has two successive figures: first that of fascism making war into a movement without limits with no goal other than itself; but fascism is merely a trial, and the post-fascist figure is that of a war machine taking war directly as its object as the peace of Terror or Survival. The war machine forms a smooth space anew, one that claims to surround the earth in its entirety. Total war is itself overtaken, towards an even more terrifying form of peace. The war machine has taken upon itself the goal of world order, and States are now only the objects or the means appropriate to that new machine.[11]

This is Deleuze and Guattari's deduction of the new world order of late capitalism: a world capitalism, or capitalist nomadic war machine, dedicated to the consolidation of capitalism, or the capitalist world state. The capitalist "mega-machine" is thus particularly powerful because it **combines** nomadic machine and state machine instead of facing them up to each other in conflict. In this way, Deleuze and Guattari have a meta-theory that deduces the stage of late capitalism observed in the postmodern condition. The deduction is a logical step in the history of the appropriation of nomadic war machines by states. Deleuze and Guattari will interpret the results of that step by studying the axioms that map the flows of energy from the nomadic machines of capitalism to its state machines and back again. In an inversion of Clausewitz's famous statement, they say: "Politics becomes the continuation of war; **it is peace that liberates technically the limitless material process of total war."**

Guy Debord shares Deleuze and Guattari's interest in the role of war or conflict in the analysis of late capitalism -- he also shares their interest in Clausewitz's theories. For him, though, the current war does not oppose a machine-like state to nomadic war machines. Debord sets up an opposition of the state, defined as the society of the spectacle, and reason, given as the capacity of logical reasoning to determine truth. The society of the spectacle, the market economy and associated systems of government, seeks to increase its power by eliminating any source of critical questioning that may give rise to alternative forms of power. Thus the enemy of late capitalism is critical reason:

We have dispensed with that disturbing conception, which was dominant for over two hundred years, in which a society was open to criticism or transformation, reform or revolution. Not thanks to any new arguments but quite simply because all argument has become useless. From this result we can estimate not universal happiness, but the redoubtable strength of tyranny's tentacles.[12]

The stage of late capitalism, or integrated spectacle, has been reached when the spectators have been so mesmerised by the spectacle that opposition to it has all but disappeared, "the spectator is simply supposed to know nothing, and deserve nothing. Those who are always watching to see what happens next will never act: such must be the spectator's condition":

Once it attains the stage of the integrated spectacle, self-proclaimed democratic society seems to be generally accepted as the realisation of a **fragile perfection**. So that it must no longer be exposed to attacks, being fragile; and indeed is no longer open to attack, being perfect as no other society before it. (...) the commodity is beyond criticism: as a general system and even as particular forms of junk.[13]

The integrated spectacle has five principle features: incessant technological renewal; integration of state and economy; generalised secrecy; unanswerable lies; and an eternal present. Debord deduces the emergence of the integrated spectacle by observing the war that brings it up against its main enemy, critical reasoning; as reason is defeated, the integrated spectacle becomes more permanent. The pattern of the conflict is not ruled by the internal necessity of the spectacle or Reason, like the conflict of state and nomad, instead, the traditional rules of war hold true. Debord uses the great theorists of war and intrigue Clausewitz, Sun Tsu, Gracian and others in a more traditional understanding of tactics and strategies where war has a logic independent of the nature of the protagonists. Unlike Deleuze and Guattari, he does not need to subsume the rules of war to the logic of machines. For example, in order to understand the ruthless efficiency of capitalist expansionism in present conflicts, Debord uses Clausewitz's principle, **knowledge must become power**, and his distinction between "tactics, as the use of forces in battle to obtain victory, and strategy, as the use of victories in battle to attain the goals of war." Translated by Debord Clausewitz's principles become:

A general working rule of the integrated spectacle, at least for those who manage its affairs, is that in this framework, **everything that can be done must be done**.[14]

Any new discovery must be put on the market at any cost. Any advantages gained in the market place must translate into market share and political power.[15] For Debord, a great power has been emerging whose power depends on the elimination of critical reason. The logic of war dictates that this power will use all the means at its disposal to eliminate its foes. The observation of the battle field indicates that the integrated spectacle is close to overall victory.

Thus Deleuze and Guattari and Debord deduce the metamorphosis in capital on the basis of similar but not identical meta-theories. They share an interest in war-like power struggles, but where Deleuze and Guattari depend upon a metaphysics of the interaction of two machine types, Debord falls back on the canonic laws of war and intrigue. The former are in the lineage of Freud and Marx, the latter follows on from Sun Tsu, Gracian and Clausewitz. This does not mean that they do not borrow from one another's lines, Clausewitz features strongly in Deleuze and Guattari as does Marx in Debord. What it means is that the fundamental logic seen as governing the conflict is different.

IV. Changes in the cultural environment

Debord and Deleuze and Guattari apply their meta-theories on the metamorphosis of capitalism to the cultural environment. This allows them to interpret cultural changes in the light of changes in capitalism, thereby offering a test of the theory and the opportunity to demonstrate the relation of culture to capital. This application holds great advantages over the approach of other thinkers on the topic of postmodern cultural shifts. Because they do not start with an fixed overall theory, thinkers like Jameson and Harvey observe cultural changes and then try to work out their significance: a method dependent on answering questions such as "What is cultural postmodernity?" This method encounters grave difficulties due to the wide-ranging nature of the cultural field and because of the variety and variability of cultural products. Whenever a trend has been detected by the cultural critic, that trend is liable to alter or disappear. To put much weight on the significance of a film type such as the Cyber-Punk film **Blade Runner** by Ridley Scott, as Harvey and Jameson do, is to become hostage to the vagaries of cultural fashion; it may even be to become part of that fashion.

What we find in the postmodern cultural environment is a great ability to change the form and content of works of art, architecture, urban planning, etc. We even find that this ability to change is often applied as a reaction to cultural criticism -- for example, it is possible for postmodern architecture to adopt the form of modern architecture once the hegemony of modern architecture has been eliminated, the result is a postmodern modernism, a style among many shifting and contradictory styles. It is almost impossible, then, to draw lasting or significant conclusions from the monitoring of cultural trends in art or architecture; these trends will shift as the ink dries on the critic's page. A consequence of this is that any wider conclusions drawn from the cultural study will also fall prey to the rapid shifts in the cultural environment. To avoid the problem of building cultural obsolescence into theory it is necessary, first, to eschew the making of predictions concerning the form and content of cultural trends, and second, to come to the cultural field armed with a wider theory that allows the thinker to make sense of the rapid cultural shifts without having to fix them according to type. This amounts to refusing to give any priority to the cultural environment when trying to understand the postmodern condition. Deleuze and Guattari and Debord give weight to the mapping of conflicts instead of the monitoring of cultural changes.

In the **Postmodernism, or, the Cultural Logic of Late Capitalism**, Frederic Jameson encounters a particular problem in the interpretation of cultural products. What he notes is that concepts such as anxiety and alienation no longer have any import in the judgement of cultural products. This is because the viewer has been subjected to such a quantity, mix and variety of cultural products that there no longer appears to be a core of experience left that could be called authentic. Not only does this leave Jameson bereft of concepts for judging cultural products, it leads him to deduce the fragmentation of the human subject as a result of the changes in the cultural environment. The subject required a sense of identity through time in part given through cultural experience; in effect, now, changes in the nature of that experience have split the subject:

All of which suggests some more general historical hypothesis: namely that concepts such as anxiety and alienation (...) are no longer appropriate in the world of the postmodern (...) This shift in the dynamics of cultural pathology can be characterised as one in which the alienation of the subject is displaced by the latter's fragmentation.[16]

This train of thought leads Jameson on to his wider theory on the role of shifts in space and time in the fragmentation of the subject. The problem is, though, that there is no guarantee that cultural production will have such an effect of fragmentation; it may indeed lead to the constitution of a subject -- either through a conjunction of the various cultural products (the creation of the Yuppie, for example), or through the development of a subject able to take account of the fragmenting cultural bombardment. The effect of fragmentation may be a passing phenomenon linked to the shift from modern to postmodern world and Jameson must wait for these developments because his theory depends upon generalisations based upon them. Thus his approach leaves him far too exposed to cultural developments in a world that is arguably built on cultural development. This is also true of Harvey and others a fact that must have serious consequences for their ability to define the postmodern condition and predict its future developments.

Deleuze and Guattari, on the other hand, have a meta-theory that explains processes of subjectivisation and de-subjectivisation (leading to the unified and fragmented subject) without having to take recourse to particular instances of that process. Subjectivisation is a result of machine processes on other machines -- not on men as such. The modern human subject is the product of the state's capture of the human machine; this is one among many processes of subjectivisation including the counter possibility of de-subjectivisation:

If capitalism appears as a world-wide undertaking of subjection it is by constituting an axiomatic of decoded fluxes. Except that social subjection, as the corollary of subjectivisation, is much more apparent in the models that realise the axiomatic than in the axiomatic itself. It is in the frame of the nation state, or national subjectivities, that the processes of subjectivisation and the corresponding subjections appear. The axiomatic itself, that the States are the models of realisation of, restores or reinvents, in forms that have become technical, a whole system of machine enslavement.[17]

If motive machines have constituted the technical machine's second age, cybernetic and data processing machines form a third age of generalised enslavement: reversible and recurrent "man-machine" systems replace the old relations of enslavement, non reversible and non recurrent in the relation of the two elements; the man machine relation is achieved in terms of mutual internal communication and in terms of use or action.[18]

The advantage of the Deleuze and Guattari approach is that it allows for an understanding of the main events in the advent of the postmodern condition, for example the effect of the growth in the role of mediated images: the television-man machine studied by Pynchon. It does not, though, get caught in the situation of having to constantly chase developments in the man and media relation. Where Jameson has to wait for the next technical or social development, Deleuze and Guattari are in a position to use their meta-theory in order to make judgements and predictions independent of particular events. Events are the opportunity to put the theory to the test but the theory does not have to deduce a trend from the profusion of events.

Changes in the cultural environment are given weight in theories of the postmodern condition because they are said to mirror changes in the nature of capitalism. However, the thinkers who develop this view from the **monitoring** of the cultural scene soon find themselves hostage to fortune. This is because the dominant quality of the cultural aspects of the postmodern condition is unpredictability -- or even, unpredictable changes driven by the emergence of predictable patterns. Whenever they try to fix the nature of postmodern culture it slips away from their findings. This unpredictability cancels out their statement of the mirroring of culture and capital because theorists no longer know the nature of the first term. For the same reason, cultural change also cancels any value judgements made upon the nature of our postmodern culture. The attempt to generalise from observation fails on two counts: it is incapable of relating the main points of the postmodern condition, culture and capital; it is incapable of judging cultural developments. However, this postmodern Catch 22 can be avoided if we take on board the findings of Deleuze and Guattari and Debord. They do not start with an observation of the cultural realm, they start with a meta-theory which they then **illustrate** by applying it to that realm. In this case, the consideration of cultural changes can begin to convince us of the accuracy (or inaccuracy) of the meta-theories but cultural change alone cannot disprove the theories. These stand or fall as working hypotheses subsuming the five main points of the postmodern condition and not as models developed from an monitoring of the postmodern condition in cultural, economic or social fields.

V. Spatio-temporal upheaval

I want to suggest that we have been experiencing, these last two decades, an intense phase of time-space compression that has had a disorienting and disruptive impact upon political-economic practices, the balance of power, as well as upon cultural and social life.[19]

The main theory to have evolved from the observation of the cultural and economic postmodern is that of spatio-temporal upheaval. This involves the thought that the relation of time and space is changing, for example, that spatial differences understood in terms of time in the past -- "it takes four days for a letter to get there" -- are now merely spatial differences independent of any measure of time -- "I will fax it to you now". What is interesting is that this theory plays an important role in the work of most postmodern thinkers (Jameson, Harvey, Lyotard, Deleuze and Guattari, and Debord, for instance). Furthermore, if we observe the different treatments of the theory we note that the findings of the previous section find further support: the thinkers dependent on the observation of postmodern societies for the basis of the theory encounter difficulties that the meta-theoreticians avoid.

Once again, the starting point for the theory of spatio-temporal upheaval, or time space compression, is the monitoring of the disorientation of the subject. Rapid advances in technology and fundamental changes in business practice have changed the world in such a way as to make the subject lose its bearings. It is difficult, perhaps even impossible, to maintain a sense of authentic identity in a world governed by rapid fashion changes and a multiplication of cultural references (David Harvey, for example, cites the number of food styles available in any Western market and the number of architectural references on show in any Western capital.) What is important, here, is to realise first that this proliferation does not offer the genuine article but a simulacrum manufactured in order to give the illusion of authentic Greek food or Renaissance architecture, and second that the goods on offer are never the same, so that the consumer is always faced with new choices across the board rather than with an addition to a familiar set of products. The subject is disoriented because there is no consistency or authenticity in the proliferation of styles, a point made brilliantly by Italo Calvino:

(...) the true journey, as the introjection of an "outside" different from our normal one, implies a complete change of nutrition, a digesting of the visited country -- its fauna and flora and its cultures (not only the different culinary practices and condiments but the different implements used to grind the flour and stir the pot) -- making it pass the lips and down the oesophagus. This is the only kind of travel that has a meaning nowadays, when everything visible you can see on television without rising from your easy chair. (And you must not rebut that the same result can be achieved by visiting exotic restaurants of our big cities; they so counterfeit the reality of the cuisine they claim to follow that, as far as our deriving real Knowledge is concerned, they are the equivalent not of an actual locality but of a scene reconstructed and shot in a studio.)[20]

The disorientation of the subject due to environmental changes, in urban planning and technological innovations in the media, for instance, is understood by thinkers such as Jameson and Harvey in terms of the compression of time into space. They note that the bewildering proliferation of choices and styles in the market place has been made possible by technological advances shortening distances to the point where time has no bearing on them. All differences, then, have become spatial and this in turn leads to the disorientation of the subject because of the need for time in the organisation of an authentic subjective identity. We need time to establish who we are; it is time that the postmodern world deprives us of thereby causing our disorientation:

(...) this latest mutation in space -- postmodern hyperspace -- has finally succeeded in transcending the capacities of the individual human body to locate itself, to organise its immediate surroundings perceptually and cognitively to map its position in a mappable external world.[21]

The intensity of time-space compression in Western capitalism since the 1960s, with all its congruent features of excessive ephemerality and fragmentation in the political and the private as well as in the social realm, does seem to indicate an experiential context that makes the condition of postmodernity somewhat special.[22]

Thus the theory of time space compression is follows two independent observations, the first is of the disorientation or fragmentation of the subject in the postmodern world, the second is of the compression of time into space in the postmodern market place, made possible by advanced technology and new marketing, distribution and production techniques. The theory goes beyond the level of observation in the linking of these two factors: time space compression is the cause of subjective disorientation. This important deduction allows Harvey and Jameson to begin to understand and criticise developments in the postmodern world in so far as they are now in a position to predict the outcome of certain commercial and technological developments in terms of the disorientation or fragmentation of the subject. For example, the developments in news media leading to the broadcasting of a confusing and eclectic series of snapshots of events from around the world can be linked to the subject's loss of historical and spatial awareness due to a lack of in depth coverage of events and to the juxtaposition of events from distant and unrelated regions.

However, the deduction lacks credibility once we try to apply it as a general rule. The linking of subjective disorientation and time space compression is circumstantial. As in the case of the cultural postmodern, Jameson or Harvey cannot guarantee that time space compression will lead to disorientation. It is possible, for example, that the changes in the relation of time and space will lead to novel forms of subjective identity based on a new perception of time and space. This type of transformation has already taken place in the case of motorised transport and telecommunications where the subject took on board new possibilities and became modern, that is, aware of a range of choices in terms of where to live, where to work, who to live with, etc... There is no reason to believe in the impossibility of such a transformation now. Jameson and Harvey can always bemoan the passing of some "authentic" identity, they cannot predict the passing of identity in general. Again, the first remark can be based legitimately on monitoring but the second demands an account going beyond that. There has to be a non empirical basis to their remarks if those remarks are to make predictions that run into the future. Jameson and Harvey do not provide such a basis.

This is not to say that the theory of time space compression has no merit. Rather, it is to question the validity of versions of the theory based merely on the observation of two parallel trends, the disorientation of the subject and the compression of time into space. In the works of Deleuze and Guattari and Debord, on the other hand, the theory is integrated to an overall meta-theory. There, it takes on a much more complex form eschewing the simplistic association of subjective disorientation and compression of time into space. For Deleuze and Guattari, time and space are thought of together in terms of two types of space, smooth space and striated space:

Smooth space and striated space, -- nomadic space and sedentary space, -- space where the nomadic war machine develops and space instituted by the machine of state, -- are not of the same nature. But sometimes we can note a simple opposition between the two types of space; sometimes we must indicate a much more complex difference implying that the successive terms of the operations considered do not coincide completely. Sometimes we must remember that the two spaces only exist in combination (...)[23]

Striated space is regular, well ordered and measurable; it is possible to situate any of its points with respect to any other, it is also possible to define a path from one point to another. Smooth space, on the other hand, cannot be ordered in its totality; position only makes sense in it in a specified neighbourhood, the situation of a point is forever changing and cannot be determined according to any particular system of measurement, instead, such systems rapidly gain or lose validity. Striated space has a universal system of orientation, smooth space is such that such a system is impossible. However, the boundary between the two spaces is unclear and subject to change. For example, in specific neighbourhoods, smooth space is similar to striated space and furthermore it is difficult to determine the boundaries of such neighbourhoods. Striated space can lose its means of orientation and become a smooth space; this can happen once the means of measurement or orientation break down -- because of the relation of space to the things that occupy it.

Deleuze and Guattari relate space to the other main factors of their philosophy. First, smooth space is related to the nomadic war machine and striated space is related to the machine of state. This explains the close interaction of smooth and striated space as the two are caught up in the complex conflict of the two machine types: the State seeks to order space and thereby extend its power of organisation and stratification, the nomadic war machine seeks to disturb such ordering so that it may unleash its destructive and creative powers on a space free of restrictive measures and boundaries. Second, space is associated with the movements of subjectivisation and desubjectivisation; the subject is linked to striated space where the point of origin coincides with a subject from which the rest of space can be measured and oriented. Smooth space, due to its lack of order and measure acts to disturb and disorient the subject, disrupting its role of origin and making its powers of orientation redundant. Thus smooth space and striated space, subjectivisation and desubjectivisation, the machine of State and the nomadic war machine are included in an account where each of the terms is a factor in the alterations undergone by the others. No factor is given priority in a chain of causality such that this factor can be seen as the key to all subsequent effects or events.

For Deleuze and Guattari changes in the spatial environment are one element in a complex interaction of different processes. For them, time space compression is an important factor, as it is for Harvey and Jameson, but it cannot be separated from a theory encompassing the conflict of machine structures and the constitution and erosion of the human subject. They recognize the change in contemporary spatial relationships, the role of capitalisme in that change, and its effect on the constitution of the human subject:

Surplus labour and the capitalist organisation as a whole proceed less and less through the space-time striation corresponding to the physicosocial concept of labour. It is as if human alienation in surplus labour has been replaced by a generalised "machine enslavement", in such a way as to mean that we give surplus value independent of any given work (the child, the pensioner, the unemployed, the television watcher, etc.) Not only does the user become an employee but capitalism works less on a quantity of labour than on a complex qualitative process involving modes of transport, urban models, media, the leisure industry, ways of perceiving and feeling, all semiotics.[24]

Yet they do not make the tempting but simplistic move of fixing all these changes in a specific space time relationship such as David Harvey's compression of space into time:

At the outcome of the striation that capitalism has been able to take to a peerless point of perfection, it is as if circulating capital necessarily reconstitutes a sort of smooth space where the fate of men is played over once again.[25]

In the late-capitalist or postmodern world, striated and smooth space have come to resemble one another and it is more and more difficult to tell them apart. Capitalist technological progress allied to the commercial need for greater information and organisation of markets has lead to an over organised and measured space, a homogenous striated space accompanying the world capitalist mega-machine. Paradoxically, this surfeit of organisational information transforms a striated space into a smooth space in an effort to rid the world of smooth spaces. This contradictory effect comes about due to the need for the invention of ever more complex forms of striation involving nomadic war machines, and hence smooth space, in their creation:

Multinational companies manufacture a sort of deterritorialised smooth space where points of occupation as well as poles of exchange become highly independent of the classic means of striation.[26]

The explosion in the production of striation has required machines dependent upon smooth spaces and the appearance of smooth space has necessarily accompanied striation. For instance, the need for ever increasing capital to finance states and companies has brought about vaste flows of capital that move about the world at great speed; this capital occupies a smooth space and is very difficult to control and organise because it involves such great sums and because it can move so fast: a nomadic war machine has evolved out of the need for growth of machines of state. Thus smooth and striated spaces cannot be distinguished simply in terms of how they come about, their appearance is complex because the machines they are associated with are in a complex relationship: a mega-machine, the joining of the machine of state and the nomadic war machine. This analysis contradicts the more straightforward version of time space compression. David Harvey and Frederic Jameson have observed a series of events but this monitoring lacks an overview of the relation of time and space that would allow for the kind of predictions they hope for. Deleuze and Guattari provide such an overview but its results do not allow for the separation of two different types of time-space relations and the consequent criticism of time-space compression.

Conclusion: the loss of ethical norms and of the possibility of revolt

Behind the question of whether it is possible to predict the future development of postmodern societies lies the aim to control that future. In turn, this aim involves an evaluation of the values prevalent in postmodern societies allied to a wish to replace them with superior ones. When analyses of the postmodern condition fail in the attempt to gauge its evolution they also lose hope of successfully changing that evolution and of providing an alternative set of values: it is difficult to justify political action on the basis of poor knowledge of the terrain on which one must act.

The natural reaction to a state as complex and confusing as the postmodern condition, to a state that defies set traditional methods for the analysis of states, is to redouble ones efforts of observation. Philosophers such as David Harvey and Frederic Jameson have set out to observe the main aspects of postmodernity in order to make sense of them. However, what I have found is that this push in the direction of the objective assessment of the postmodern condition encounters great difficulties once it tries to shift from the mode of monitoring to that of prediction or even to that of the understanding of the various aspects of the postmodern condition in unison.

In contrast, philosophers like Debord and Deleuze and Guattari, who come ready armed to the analysis of the postmodern condition, manage to offer a convincing unifying account of the various aspects of the postmodern condition. They do this by testing an overarching meta-theory, or metaphysics, on the different aspects of the postmodern condition. For the moment, only they are able to take the next step and make judgements in terms of the values of postmodern societies and recommendations in terms of the political steps necessary to bring about change. If you are prey to the sense of disquiet and fear mentioned at the outset of this article, I want to suggest that the most profitable course of action lies in the direction of the evaluation or emulation of philosophies such as those presented by Debord and Deleuze and Guattari. The objective assessment of the postmodern condition has lead nowhere, instead, we must proceed to the creation and evaluation of metaphysical systems.

NOTES

1 Dr James Williams, University of Dundee, 31 July 1992

2 Balthasar Gracian, **The Hero**, Edinburgh, 1748, p.113

3 Thomas Pynchon, op.cit, p. 314

4 Milan Kundera, ˮA la recherche du présent perduˮ, **Infini**, no.37, Spring 1992, p.12.

5 Frederic Jameson, **Postmodernism, or, the Cultural Logic of Late Capitalism**, London, Verso, 1991, p. 406.

6 David Harvey, **The condition of Postmodernity**, Oxford: Blackwell, 1990, pp. 336-337.

7 Thomas Pynchon, **Vineland**, London: Minerva, 1991, p. 97.

8 Gilles Deleuze and Felix Guattari, **Mille Plateaux**, Paris: Minuit, 1980, p.574. (All translations from this work are mine)

⁹ *Guy Debord,* **Comments on the Society of the Spectacle,** *London: Verso, 1990, pp.2-3.*

¹⁰ *But because the war machine is a form of exteriority it only exists in its metamorphoses; it exists just as much in an industrial innovation, a technological invention, a commercial channel, a religious creation, in all those flows and currents that are only appropriated by the state secondarily. It is not in terms of independence, but in terms of coexistence and competition,* **in a field of perpetual interaction,** *that we must think exteriority and interiority, metamorphosising war machines and identifying state apparatus, gangs and kingdoms, megamachines and empires.*
Deleuze and Guattari, op.cit., p.446.

¹¹ *Deleuze and Guattari, op.cit., p.525.*

¹² *Guy Debord,* **Comments on the Society of the Spectacle,** *London: Verso, 1990, p.21.*

¹³ *Guy Debord, op.cit., p.21.*

¹⁴ *Guy Debord, op.cit., p.79.*

¹⁵ *According to the basic interests of the system of domination, the dissolution of logic has been pursued by different, but mutually supportive, means. Some of these means involve the technology which the spectacle has tested and popularised; others are more linked to the mass psychology of submission. Guy debord, op.cit., p.27.*

¹⁶ *Frederic Jameson, op.cit., p.14.*

¹⁷ *D&G, op.cit., p. 572.*

¹⁸ *ibid.*

¹⁹ *David Harvey, op. cit., p. 284.*

²⁰ *Italo Calvino, "Under the Jaguar Sun", in* **Under the Jaguar Sun,** *London: Cape, 1992, p. 12.*

²¹ *Frederic Jameson, op. cit., p. 37.*

²² *David Harvey, op. cit., p. 306.*

²³ *Deleuze and Guattari, ibid., p. 593.*

²⁴ *Deleuze and Guattari, op. cit., p.613-614.*

²⁵ *Ibid.*

²⁶ *Ibid.*

ANDREW GOFFEY

The Cruelty of the (neo-) Baroque

For Valere Noverina the world is a problem to be treated with caution. Like any good story it is worth repeating, but being a fiction, a battleground to treat suspiciously. At the beginning of his *Discours aux Animaux* he remarks "Je recommencerai toujours le monde avec l'idee d'un ennemi derriere moi" and that if one does "crache toutes ses pensees par terre, d'ou vient qu'elles tombent rien qu'en paroles ?"[1].

Appropriately enough, the *Discours* is itself a fiction, or rather a series of eleven fables bearing witness to a journey across the interior surfaces of Noverina's being. But it is never an easy 'journey', for just as in the determined animal discourse there is always the idea of an enemy behind, so always in front of the determining subject. "Je poussais mon melodique en chant idiot. Sur ce, trois cents convives subrepticement s'installerent autour de moi affames et joyeux"[2]. Quite besides being populated with a vast array of 'base' creations, the *Discours* is permeated by an atmosphere of terror and joy. The music of Noverina's strange speech resonates with the madness of his ideas as if (along with earlier works such as 'Drame de la Vie') some long lost Thermidorian passion had been awakened.

In another context, Gilles Deleuze approaches a similar difficulty. Towards the end of his study of Leibnitz and the Baroque, *Le Pli*, Deleuze states that "le question est toujours d'habiter le monde"[3]. The statement is left hanging, and the 'question' is not posed. Now whilst, as Deleuze has repeatedly shown, the questions a philosophy asks are not the same as the problems which determine it, one wonders how this question might make itself heard, if at all.

The choice of the Baroque is propitious though. Here the problem of the world is an acute one, for as Alexander Koyre has shown, for the general outlook of European thought, from

Nicholas de Cusa through Giordano Bruno to Leibnitz and Newton, there was a shift from the 'Closed World to the Infinite Universe', the role of the Divine Artifex came under considerable strain as the world lost its centre. Likewise, as a recent commentator has noted in a discussion of the Baroque arts, there was a shift in conceptions of artistic practice towards the immanence of creation and away from the notion of divine inspiration[4]. At any rate, it is in the Baroque Modern that the infinite appears as someting so near and by a cruel paradox, that which is most distant. A discussion of the Baroque in the context of Le Pli will provide a first approach to the 'problem of world', as it might be called.

The first point to be made here about Le Pli is that it is not in any simple sense a book of the history of either philosophy or art. Deleuze argues that it is a matter of giving the Baroque the concept it 'lacks'. It could also be suggested that it is a kind of genealogy of the modern in a Foucauldian sense, or even better, a stratum in the 'geology' of the present (the continuity and discontinuity of the Leibnitz series, its connections with various scientific, architectural, artistic series, and so on...)

However one decides to classify Le Pli in terms of possible disciplines, it remains that its value lies in its applicability in 'this world', for as Deleuze will say, 'only the present exists'.

The most succinct formulation of the relations between the Baroque and the present would be that 'the Baroque thinks in us'. Quite contrary to what say, an art historian might argue, the Baroque in contemporary culture has less to do with some kind of nostalgia for the past, and far more to do with a possibility endemic to, and perhaps unrealisable in, the present. If 'we' are Baroque it is because the perennial, and deepening crises of 'late' capitalism require faster and faster circulation, more and more artifice to realise value and secure its subjects. Which is not a way of saying that the Baroque is either 'good' or 'bad', since such quick judgements tend to confuse as much as they may clarify.

For the Baroque, a central concern was the new, as indeed it was for Leibnitz, according to Deleuze. As cultural historian Jose Maravall has argued, this concern was rather limited : "Baroque declarations in favour of the new were no less fervent than those of the sixteenth century, but to the extent that they were to be limited or permitted they were to be limited to poetic game playing, literary outlandishness and trick effects machinated on stage, which evoked wonder in and suspended the depressed psyche of the sixteenth century urban inhabitant"[5]. Besides a characteristic emphasis on motion - a man(sic) never being 'so similar to himself as when he is in movement, according to Bernini, there was a tendency to use science and technology to 'extrarational' ends" (Lewis Mumford). Perhaps more significant was a preponderance of violence and cruelty. Apart from noting that the Baroque marked the 'psychotic episode' in theological reason, a crisis which asked "y a-t-il moyen de sauver l'ideal theologique a un moment ou il est combattu de toute part, et ou le monde ne cesse d'accumuler ses "preuves" contre lui, violences et miseres... "[6], Deleuze makes little of this predominant aspect. Rousset, on the other hand, has detailed extensively manifestations of the macabre in literature of the period, and Maravall argues that in the social, the 'savagery' of Baroque spectacles was a way of instilling a Hobbesian sense of all against all, a subjectivity primed for the developing market mentality.

Such, in brief, is the Baroque, one has the sense that it secured at least in part, and by the most artificial of means, a 'new world order'. A recent study of the 'Baroque State' has suggested the extent to which it marked a passage towards a state system, which could gather all the differences between cities.[7]

A writer of the time remarked that "the desire to know about new, strange and amazing things, and enquire into their causes, is natural in everyone"[8]. A better example of the naturalisation of the cultural (or, perhaps vice versa) could not be found. It is the law, with no mistake. Deleuze argues that it is a necessity of the law that the world be put in the subject, in order that the subject 'be' for the world. But as he shows, this is exactly where the problem lies, for 'il faint mettre' can always also mark the law's failure. As a first explanation of this argument of Deleuze's one may suggest as an initial gloss on this argument the following can be suggested : the world, pace Heidegger, is the 'truly transcendent', and this is for Leibnitz as much as for us. For the established sentiments (whether Leibnitz's or ours) the truly transcendent is God (ditto for Deleuze the implicit anthropomorphism of Dasein). In order that the subject 'be', it must include the world. And as commentators on Leibnitz do not fail to point out, his work was a kind of reconstruction of the new universe discovered by science, on the basis of a set of principles which would retain a divine centre to the agency of the world. Likewise one might recall that after all, Bernini did decorate the insides of churches! However, since the Baroque to which Leibnitz pertained, and the material universe more generally, is permanently becoming, and since all monads, in all possible worlds (even those incompossible with the one God has chosen) strive for existence (which is the same thing), then this imperative to 'include' will always fail. At moments of particular crisis such as that of the Baroque, where everything is in movement and there is a crisis of property relations, this problem of inclusion will inevitably become more extreme. Hence, perhaps, the cruelty of the culture. To use some slightly older Deleuzian terminology, deterritorialisation is compensated for by reterritorialisation of a more and more artificial type. As will be seen, it is the eye which forms the material part most heavily inscribed as a territorial locus of inscription.

If the Baroque thinks in us by means of the simultaneous mechanism of the en-closure of and opening onto a world, the same, it may be said, is true of Leibnitz, his is a kind of phantom presence in contemporary thought. How can this be the case ? Firstly, insofar as he may be said to be Baroque. The 'and' in Leibnitz and the Baroque is not a dialectical relation but one of 'compossibility' between two worlds at least. The fold, as in the folded fabrics of Baroque still life, or in the folds of St. Teresa's clothing, appears in Leibnitz as an example or analogy frequently. In the Monadology, Leibnitz remarks that the "soul can only read in itself what is distinctly represented there; it canot develop all the things that are folded within it, for they stretch to infinity" (9). Secondly, because despite the efforts of Christian Wolff to save the most 'acceptable' aspects of the Monadology - by denying the crucial claim that even animal and plant monads were capable of perception (implying dubious morals on Leibnitz's part), it is this 'molecular aspect of Leibnitz's work that has survived on today. Mandelbrot and Prigogine both acknowledge the importance of Leibnitz in their works, his 'analysis situs' has become topology, and finding in Rene Thom an influential proponent. And despite what Prigogine and Stengers may have said about Leibnitz in 'Entre le Temps et Eternite', Leibnitzian arguments about incompossibility may still offer a way to think about self-organising systems, Benard instabilities and so on. How exactly DO scientists deal with perceptual events ? A closer examination of Deleuze's Leibnitz will aid in deciphering the claim that 'we remain Leibnitzian' and how this can help in the 'problem of world'.

Calling out to the 'animal of time' the narrator of the *Discours aux Animaux* offers the following piece of advice : "Meme si les corps ont disparu, la tombe repond toujours a nos questions et nous lisons encore les pierres des noms des chutes des spheres et les sons des tombes. Arpente, garcon !"(1O).

This is precisely the sort of advice that Deleuze seems to have taken in his re-reading of the Leibnitzian 'oeuvre'. Whilst it must be recognised that dead philosophers can always offer the occasion for a ritual exhumation of their bodies, even if their corpus does live on, the body's unity must be something of a phantasm, since its matter will long since have passed into the earth. However, Deleuze thinks it possible to find the actuality of Leibnitz across his work. Now this is not a matter of 'patching up' his system, as if in so doing it might work 'better' than that of Hegel (Belaval registers a certain amount of suspicion on the part of 'French Hegelians' towards Leibnitz). Nor is it a matter of 'commiserating' with Leibnitz for his failures (the universal characteristic, the alchemy, Harz mines, and so on) and then selecting his 'successes' (what criteria ? those of logical atomism ?) Rather, Deleuze treats all the failures with the utmost seriousness, such that one may say that they all offer some way into the secret life of Leibnitz. For example, Leibnitz's notion of cryptography, which is the "art of inventing the key for an enveloped thing"(11). This key is, in the domain of Leibnitz's mathematics, the process of extracting an irrational number,

the number which 'contains' a whole seies of rational numbers, or as in the analysis of existants, the sphere of contingent
truths, the extraction of a differential relating incommensurable series and contained under 'a certain potential'.

Deleuze argues that these two domains of knowledge can be
grouped together, suggesting that in the former case, analysis
determines predicates as requisites, in the latter, as 'world'.
Requisites are that without which a thing can neither be nor be
conceived. Reading Leibnitz to the letter Deleuze finds in his
work numerous examples of a root or differential which brings
together incommensurable series. Leibnitz's use of the Neo-
Platonic triad of explication-implication-complication already
demonstrate the sharing of a common root - pli - a substantive
and verbal morphological form. This fold can certainly be
conceived, since it has its requisites in, for example, the discussions of the folds of the ground revealed to Leibnitz in his work at the
Harz mines, or in his calculator which was to perform feats of
multiplication. A kind of delirium of analogy permeates Deleuze's
reading of Leibnitz in so far as he 'replicates' Leibnitzian principles to
extend his claims beyond the limits he had established for them
himself. The rule about existent things or possible existences is that
they may be 'actualised' in so far as they imply no contradiction, and
all monads strive for existence, it is one of their basic characteristics
as 'drive'. The fold is one such notion, and Deleuze argues that since
it implies no contradiction it is indeed possible. One might also add
that it is a simple term (simplicity usually being argued to be at the
base of any monadic substance), a 'primitive simple notion' which
cannot be defined - as with Leibnitz's own understanding of these
terms - without presupposing a matter form which it can be deduced.
In other words the 'fold' is susceptible of real definition (which shows
its possibility) but only in so far as one can 'work back' to it from the
causal infinity of time, number, matter and so on.

However, despite Deleuze's convincing demonstration that this new
concept is possible in Leibnitz, allowing him to re-read his work in a
new light, this concept remains there in Leibnitz's work under a
certain potential, and was not of course realised by Leibnitz himself.
Clearly the notion of 'incompossibility' may help. Paraphrasing Deleuze
somewhat this can be explained as follows. Leibnitz has advocated

God, but the contrary of this proposition, Leibnitz non-advocate, is not impossible or contradictory in itself (as would be 2 and 2 are not 4). This is the property of propositions of existence. To explain why Leibnitz non-advocate is not contradictory in itself, another relation is needed, but not between the two Leibnitzs, rather between Leibnitz non-advocate and the world where Leibnitz 'has advocated'. Now one would indeed fall into a contradiction if one failed to recognise that this world where Leibnitz has advocated is included in Leibnitz, it is included in an infinity of other monads also. The non-advocating Leibnitz must be excluded form the world in which he has advocated, and as a consequence the two worlds are in a relation of incompossibility - a world in which Leibnitz does not advocate cannot pass into existence at the same time as the world of advocacy. Consequently one can suggest that a Leibnitz that does not conform to the established sentiments is perfectly possible (it implies no contradiction) but that it requires another world in which to be realised.

The concept of the fold, which would give us a new Leibnitz is thus incompossible with the 'original' Leibnitz. Incompossibility, although a 'great mystery in God's understanding', occurs, according to Deleuze, when 'series' diverge in the 'vicinity of a singularity'. That is, when the predicates of a subject imply a contradiction, one finds oneself, in so far as that subject exists, in the presence of another world. However this is not an easy argument to make with regards to Leibnitz. For as long as one treats a philosopher, implicitly or explicitly, according to the usual notions of a substance, as having one or two essential attributes (thinking and or extended substance) all other determinations of his/her existence would refer to accidents, contingent occurences which do nothing to alter the essence of that substance, in this sense, failure is a permanent possibility and extra-philosophical activities are to be maintained in strict separacy. However, if one were to follow Leibnitzian notions about a compound substance being composed of a multiplicity of monadic substances, and being defined in terms of existence as a unity of movement and change, one could treat the singular predicates which define his notion as relations to world and not at all to essence. So, for example, one would have a Leibnitz constituted around a number of 'pre-individual' singularities : to work for the king; to study mathematics; to write philosophy; to advocate God. Then one can add a fifth singularity : to transvalue all values. Clearly, between the fourth and the fifth there is a relation of contradiction. However, in so far as these can be determined as world - relations to existence - it may be suggested that the world in which Leibnitz transvalues and the world in which he advocates, are in a relation of incompossibility. A transvaluing Leibnitz is not contradictory in itself ! Thus there would be two diverging Leibnitz series, and Leibnitz can live on after the death of God. The reason for this divergence, as was suggested earlier, is a mystery in God's understanding. Clearly, as this example tends to suggest, God will not be in a position to allow those worlds to pass into existence which threaten his own !

Deleuze argues that a singularity (such as to create one's own values) is always surrounded by a number of ordinary `points'. So in the case of transvaluation, which is actually the same thing as the notion of a perpetual folding, one would have such examples as the one earlier from the Monadology, which thus signal the presence of a singularity. Deleuze finds, in his reading of Leibnitz in terms of a determination of predicates as world, relations to existence, a set of roots or differentials, such as the term `pli', discussions of the history of words and their inflexions, and so on. The fold, besides being a theme of Baroque art, can also be `seen' moving across the surfaces of the multiple subject `matters' of the Leibnitzian oeuvre, the `visible traces' of which Leibnitz talks'in his `New essays on the Human Understanding', the crucial feature of the `Universal Characteristic'.

Deleuze's analysis suggests that if Leibnitz `lives on' today, it is through an event extracted from the crypt of Leibnitziana. The fold is the `law' of the Leibnitz-Baroque series, or rather its law in this world, because in the world Leibnitz advocated, folding as relation to existence, whilst explaining how Leibnitz was `for' his world, was nevertheless incompossible with that world in so far as it implied values incommensurate with those of the established sentiments.

Leibnitz's work can continue to think in us because it contains in it under a certain potential, an 'understanding' of this relation to existence, being for the world, as the infinite movement of folding as the perfect co-incidence of transcendence of world, immanence of subject.

It is now possible to return to the Baroque and the initial problem of 'the world'.

As Bernini recognised, a crucial mark of the culture in which he lived was its frenetic motion, and for Gracian movement was the 'definition of life'. As has just been suggested, it is precisely this movement which is for Deleuze central to 'being for the world', the movement being implied in Leibnitz's work and offering a 'key' to its unity. Such movement also problematises the very efficacy of the law, because the 'il faut' which marks its necessity, securing its subjects also necessarily fails. By examining the genesis of this strange mechanism, it will be possible to assess more precisely the machinations of the (neo)Baroque.

Leibnitz is well known for his argument that all predicates are in the subject, an argument which some have claimed makes him a forerunner of modern subject-predicate logic. However it must be noted that the subject-predicate argument also works at a metaphysical level, supporting the deterministic argument that a monad only ever unfolds from a 'complete individual notion' contained in God's under-standing.

Deleuze uses this argument to follow through the idea that all analysis is infinite, and particularly the analysis of existants in terms of the actually infinite (as opposed to infinite in itself, by cause, or in terms of the internal convergence of series). At this point the notion of synthesis is left in abeyance, but if there is to be a secret life of any substance, Leibnitz included, one can see immdiately that it must involve a relation with the outside, for how else would a world escape God's understanding? A most elusive synthesis indeed.

For all predicates to be included in the subject means the same thing as saying that the world is in the subject. Deleuze suggests too that in the analysis of predicates as the requisites (see above) one determines predicates according to the idea of closure and internal limits, giving us a 'pleonastic' perception of things, their texture and their 'reality', but in such a way as to tell us several things at once. The subject is not yet truly an 'individual'. However it is this idea of closure and intrinsic, finite limits, which (according to the idea that the monad has no windows) gives the condition of being for the world. However Deleuze suggests that this notion of limit and closure leaves an 'objective uncertainty'. That is to say, do the differential relations which constitute the requisites of a thing find their limit in the subject or beyond it ? Are the converging series which a subject includes, making up the texture of its world in it or in the actual infinity outside ?

Deleuze suggests that this closure opens up the subject onto the world such that the world is indeed the truly transcendent, and the law of its series is extrinsic to it. This being the case, it becomes possible to say that the subject includes the world as the law of its determination, but only in so far as this law is repulsed into the 'transfinite unity'. So taking the previous of 'pli', the Leibnitz series can only include this Baroque event in so far as it develops in formal continuity with the exterior. Leibnitz thus produces what might be called an 'individuation' of things, deduced from the analysis of the requisites of the notion of the fold. An infinite movement contained in the subject virtually or under a certain potential. The ambiguity of the 'il faut' is now easily understood - one is only for this world because one goes beyond it...

But, as has been stressed repeatedly, only under a certain potential. This is not Leibnitz's 'failure'. The 'production' of the infinite movement which Deleuze discerns in Leibnitz is not realised in his world. Here is the cruel movement of the world. The institutions of the established remained intact, and this having been the case, curbing the liberty of movement and securing subjectivity for the world of God remained the imperative. To repeat: more and more deterritorialisation calls for more and more reterritorialisation. Arbitrary measures by 'the state'. Maravall's observations concerning the function of novelty are now clear, but to understand the importance of the visual and the savagery of Baroque spectacles will require a brief discussion of the differential theory of perception which Deleuze analyses.

The differential theory of perception in Leibnitz works on two stages. In the first place, the world is an hallucination, a multiplicity of unintegrated little perceptions and affective inclinations, anti-molecular monads striving for existence, each of which including a possible world in some capacity or other. Following God's law the only perceptions which can pass into existence are, of course, those which are compossible with his world, by means of the differential relations discussed earlier under the rubric of 'requisites'. Michel Serres has discussed this in terms of what he calls the 'cribratio', or filtering system which 'leads' to clear and distinct perceptions (or ideas, little matter the difference here). At/on this stage they remain without object (hallucinatory in this sense), but conform to matter by a process of ressemblance. that is to say, little perceptions ressemble vibrations in matter, macro-perceptions, or clear and distinct perceptions, their 'conformity to an organ'). Ressemblance, or rather ressembling (an ordering, and not ordered relation) works according to the model 'we' have of matter, a model God provides. The conformity of perceptions to a body of matter with organs is a 'consequence' of the transcendental model God provides, whilst the passage from one perception to another is determined by the appetitive striving at the 'molecular' level. Thus, in terms of perception one can say that being for the world is secured by the conformity of the anonymity of the actual infinity of little perceptions, with some 'thing' in matter (my perception). (It should be noted here that the perceptual unity thus conferred on the subject indicates a 'failure' on Leibnitz's part. In his correspondence with the Jesuit Scholastic, Des Bosses, Leibnitz 'conceded' the existence of a substantial relation, the 'vinculum substantiale' which unified multiple monads under the relation of a dominant one. The important point to note about this is that, although Leibnitz was in a certain sense conforming to the established..., this notion also testified to a relation outside the subject, and in so far as relations are predicates, acknowledges a synthetic relation...)

In the final chapter of his study, Deleuze discusses the Baroque unity of the arts. Sculptures, he suggests, overflow their 'usual' ornamental space and become architecture, paintings, as in the *trompe l'oeil* likewise seem to come out of their frame. One need only look at one of Bernini 's extravagant Gesamtkunstwerks to see how the law of a perceptual series ('contained' within the space-time frame of a 'subject'), the world it envelops, cannot be held within, precisely the representational content of that world. It is as if the Baroque realise that, the world being an hallucinatory presence, a fiction, true being for the world requires a realisation of perception precisely AS fiction, without the false transcendence a divine model in matter supply. What reasons could God supply for believing in this world ?

One can now 'see' why the eye which should have been the most heavily inscribed as organ in the Baroque. Perhaps in spite of the Baroque unity of the arts and the pleasures of say, Bernini's St Teresa of Avila [12], public spectacles still bespeak what Maravall has called the 'Baroque pedagogy of violence'. It is perhaps here that the 'objective uncertainty' of which Deleuze speaks finds its greatest significance - the events of perception, do they find their law in the intrinsic, intensive limits of the subject, or in the extrinsic limits of the individual as/ individuation of world ? One can never be quite sure whose world this is a being for...

Deleuze is thus perfectly correct to state at the end of *Le Pli* that the question is always one of inhabiting the world. The world is an anonymous pre-individual field, transcendental, and the secret synthesis of the outside, the determination of predicates as world, the extrinsic substantial relation of world, cannot be determined in advance. Only deduced 'Nachtraglichkeit', to pinch from Freud.

Noverina knows this too. In the cruel world of the *Discours aux Animaux*, the 'monde immonde', Noverina is lucid in the middle of his madness. The determining subject, the enclosing 'moment' of world is always the idea of an 'enemy behind'. When it is the 'detemined' individual, one recalls that this individuation can always be an 'idiot's song.'

NOTES

(1)   *Valere Noverina : LE DISCOURS AUX ANIMAUX (Paris P.O.L. 1987)*

(2)   *ibid p.24*

(3)   *Gilles Deleuze : LE PLI : LEIBNIZ ET LE BAROQUE (Paris Minuit, 1988) p.189*

(4)   *see Giancarlo Maiorino : THE CORNUCOPIAN MIND AND THE BAROQUE (Manchester M.U.P. 1988)*

(5)   *Jose Maravall : THE CULTURE OF THE BAROQUE (Manchester M.U.P. 1986) p.227*

(6)   *Deleuze p.71*

(7)   *see the review by Anne-Marie Lescourret : L'ETAT ET LA MUSIQUE CRITIQUE 469-70 (Paris Minuit 1986)*

(8)   *Suarez de Figueroa q.p.225 Maravall*

(9)   *Gottfried Leibniz : MONADOLOGY 61 in Loemker : LEIBNIZ PHILOSOPHICAL PAPERS AND LETTERS (Dordrecht Reidel 1969)*

(10)   *Noverina p.163-4*

(11)   *Leibniz cit Deleuze p.6*

(12)   *cf. Jacques Lacan : SEMINAIRE XX : ENCORE (Paris Seuil 1975)*

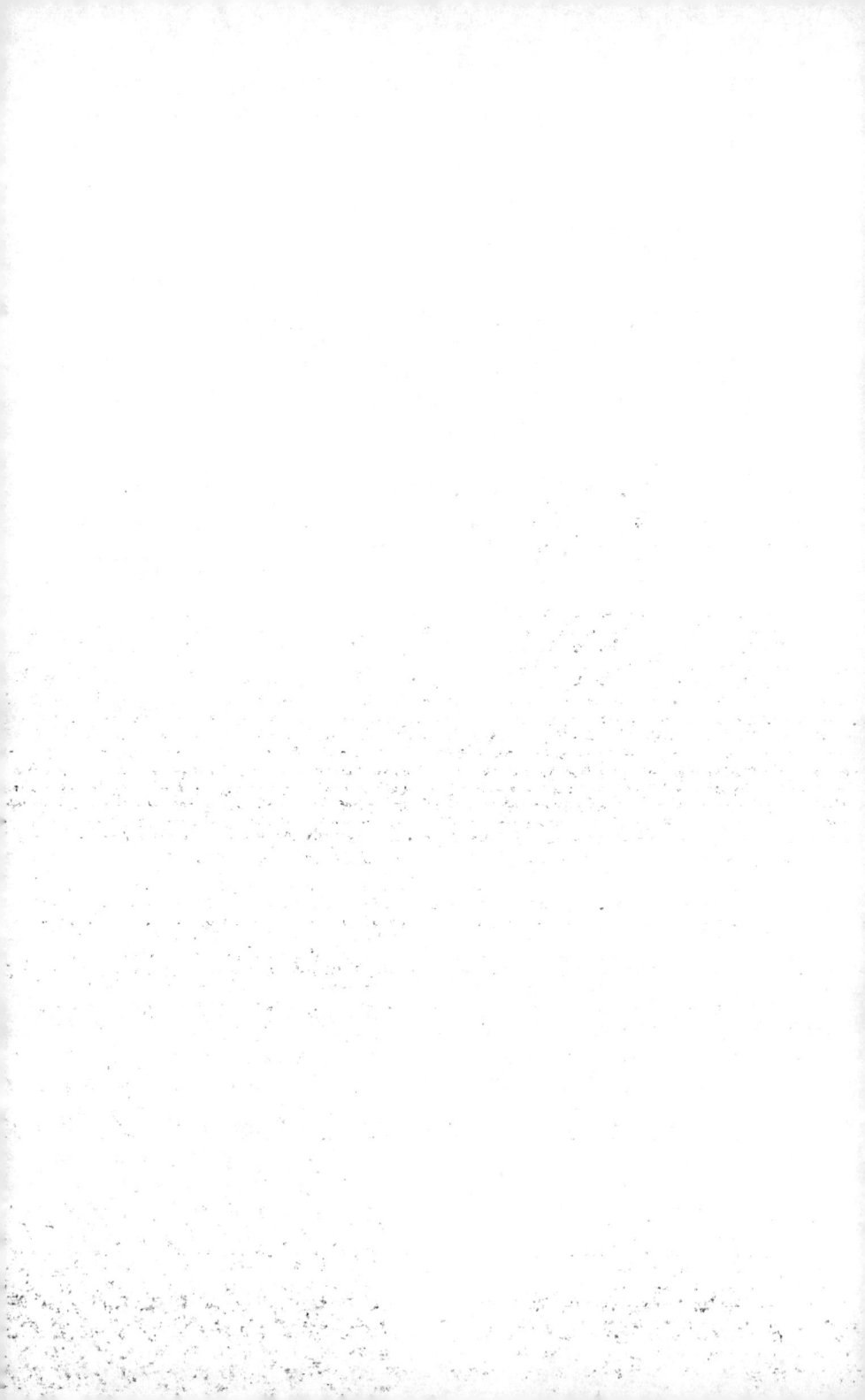

NICHOLAS BLINCOE

Deleuze & Masochism

When Aristotle states: "Man is by nature a Political animal." [1], it is often ignored that the "Political" describes a relation before it reflects a nature; it is, as Aristotle argues: "a common interest uniting master and slave" [2]. The "Political" gains its supremacy only by virtue of philosophical reflection, a reflection that casts the relation between master and slave as an essential principle. Deleuze's essay on the relation between sadism and masochism, *Coldness and Cruelty* (CC. Deleuze, Zone Books, NY 1991) concludes by stating: "The genius of Sade and that of Masoch are poles apart; their worlds do not communicate." (CC 133). If Masoch does not speak to Sade, if there is no relation between the slavish and the masterful, then perhaps there is no "Political" realm. Although by no means an apolitical philosopher, Deleuze seems to have abandoned politics: the idea of a space of communication, a space assuring the circulation of discursive relations, a transcendental realm uniting common interests.

Such a realm underpins Kantian critique. Whilst Kant provides an account of a whole variety of empirical relations, a field of relations he terms a "commercium", he insists that any reflection upon this field take place at a higher level, under a non-empirical form. For Kant, the role of transcendental reflection, or "Critique", is to institute a Political space. He views "Critique" as a demand, stating: "It is a call to reason to undertake anew the most difficult of all its tasks, namely that of self-knowledge, and to institute a tribunal which will assure to reason its lawful claims, and dismiss all groundless pretensions, not by despotic decree but in accordance with its own eternal and unalterable laws. This tribunal is nothing other than the critique of pure reason." [3]

When Kant considers specious ideas, illusions of pure Reason, he will not abandon this central idea: a Political space. He argues that Plato's *Republic*: "is at any rate a necessary idea, which must be taken as fundamental not only in first project-ing a constitution but in all its laws." (Kant, A 316)

Despite the necessity of this idea, its constitution is not assured. For Kant, the idea of the "Political" at times seems specious, but nevertheless exerts a regulative effect on thought. He states: "The *Republic* of Plato has become proverbial as a striking example of a supposedly visionary perfection, such as can exist only in the brain of the idle thinker. ... We should, however, be better advised to follow up this thought, and, where the great philosopher leaves us without help, to place it, through fresh efforts, in a proper light, rather than to set it aside as useless on the very sorry pretext of impracticability." Kant A 316

Kant's tribunal is built upon uncertain ground. It has no consti-tution as such, it exists by virtue of principles that exert only a regulative effect and that might at times be found wanting. For Kant, discussion, even in its failures, institutes a tribunal, a space of open and free consideration of principles. Or does so in reflection, through a transcendental reflection upon discursive relations and their excessive or straitened claims.

Deleuze never rejects "Critique". In *Coldness and Cruelty,* he states: "Philosophical reflection should be understood as "tran-scendental", that is to say concerned with a particular kind of investigation of the question of principles." (CC 111). The twist lies with the word "particular". Deleuze will not follow a line that returns, circuitously or uncertainly, to a defence of the "Political". He will not institute a juridical tribunal. He be-lieves, in fact, that: "Philosophy is not particularly communi-cative" [4].

Speaking, in *Coldness and Cruelty*, of experience, and hence of the empirical, Deleuze defines the term "principle": "What we call a principle or a law is, in the first place, that which governs a particular field". (CC 112). In reflecting upon these principles, Deleuze will not make the mistake of assuming that behind the empirical field lies another realm, a "Political" realm assured by "eternal and unalterable laws". Certainly not a space uniting the common interests of master and slaves. Deleuze states: "The concurrence of sadism and masochism is fundamentally one of analogy only; their processes and their formations are entirely different; their common organ, their "eye" squints and should therefore make us suspicious." (CC 46). Here, the term "eye" refers to the way in which philosophical reflection might speculate upon a link between the one perversion and the other. Above all, in the context of *Coldness and Cruelty*, it refers to a sign of conservation, to a value sanctioning a measure of pain for the sake of unity, to the institution of the "super-ego" and to the work of the "reality principle". Deleuze abandons all these different transcendent signs of political unity. *Coldness and Cruelty* considers two ways in which such a sign might be abandoned: once in sadism, once with masochism. It is however, the more interesting because it does not take the part of the sadist but that of the slave, the hero of Hegelian dialectics and the figure that, after his own *Nietzsche and Philosophy*, Deleuze might be expected to ignore.

* * *

The French philosopher Vincent Descombes brackets Deleuze under the term "Mad Black Hegelians". His interest in Deleuze arises solely from this relation to Hegel. Specifically, from the way he and the other Mad Black Hegelians turn Hegel's idea of Political Sovereignty into a principle of destruction. Descombes' interest in Deleuze is symptomological, seeing Mad Black Hegelianism - a term describing Klossowski, Blanchot, Bataille, Deleuze and early Lyotard - as symptomatic of a peculiarly French problem. Speaking of Habermas' exasperation at these philosophers, Descombes argues that it is inadequate to see them simply as misguided. It is not that they casually betray the political projects of the Enlightenment. They symptomise French problems with the whole Enlightenment project. He states: "The french perplexities have another origin./ Speaking in very general terms, we do not reason, in France, through a perspective opened up by a modern Project. We reason through determining ourselves after a modern Work. We reason after the Revolution, the which heritage profoundly reunites us before it settles our divisions. Now, this intimates only one thing: we reason after the failure of the (french) Revolution to liberate humanity." [5]

Following Habermas, Descombes notes the distinction between conservative Hegelians and Left or neo-Hegelians before speaking of a third trend. He states: "a third current breaks away, sustaining an untoward position: the real must be criticised not because it lacks rationality, but simply because it is too rational. Habermas presents Nietzsche as the founder of a philosophical heresy: the real is the rational, the real must be denounced for the "reason" that it is rational." (Descombes, 69)

Descombes notes Habermas' surprise that Nietszche should fuel a philosophy with radical pretensions. However, where Habermas is scornful of attempts to turn Nietssche over to the Left, Descombes takes this "third current", which is primarily Hegelian and only secondarily Nietszchean, to highlight the changes and disillusionments that characterise the French Left. In France, as Descombes argues, the Left at one time tended to be Nationalistic; liberties were to be protected through the revolutionary state. The Left only began to view its agenda as internationalist in the twentieth century, partly in response to fascism and partly in response to Soviet communism. As a result, the Left began to have problems placing the Revolution, or its promise. Further, with the emergence of an anonymous Mass alongside postrevolutionary democracy, working on behalf of totalitarianism or for consumer capitalism, it seems the promise of Revolution is simply to degenerate into impersonal "Mass" movements. For Descombes, Mad Black Hegelianism symptomises schisms beneath the surface of postrevolutionary France. He states: "How might the collective system of representation which disposes the French to identify as French Citizens accommodate itself to the schism between the promise of revolution and subsequent experience. A schism already plain to contemporaries and from which the more level headed had drawn the lesson of sociology: one may not construct the social through political operations." (Descombes, 72)

Here, Descombes' sympathies are clear, one may still talk about the social; indeed, one should. Mad Black Hegelians are interesting only as regards the fact that political opera-tions threaten rather than construct the social sphere. How-ever, the fact that the Social is deconstructing, and in particu-lar deconstructing because of its relation to concepts drawn from a sociopolitical "reserve" and originally intended to construct a new revolutionary politics, implies only that some-thing very like the "Political" continues "en passant".

Descombes' level-headed sociology depends upon its politi-cal deconstruction in order to reflect a social logic at all.

Descombes' account of the socio-political sphere has the virtue, over Habermas', of treating the Mad Black Hegelians as real symptoms. In consequence, he does not simply erase the violence to which they attest in favour of an enlightened and "Modern" project. The explanation for their reality, however, redounds back upon a socio-political formation. In Descombes' work, or through his philosophical reflection, their mutant, anarchic politics become symptomatic of a social problem. Although he states that the social is not con-structed through political means, it is clear that in its deconstruction, as it confronts wayward symptoms of dissipa-tion and violence, a discursive, communicative realm contin-ues to be sustained. Here, Hegelianism becomes the sign for a lively, if abused, tradition.

Why should Descombes appeal to Hegel, rather than to Kant? In Kant, as has been seen, the empirical and its principles, devolve onto the transcendental and its principles. However, in Kant, the process of instituting a political tribunal through reflection does not depend upon experience or its principles, reflection finds only regulative principles in a discussion that has already begun to circulate in a reasonable, juridical manner. In a sense, then, this "transcendental" tribunal is groundless because it is only regulated, not constituted, by reflection. There is no Political constitution, as everyone in Britain knows. The Political is instituted obliquely, by a kind of ruse; a ruse that lives through other processes, other forms of negotiation; through scientific or commercial projects, self-interest, perhaps even an "invisible hand". Kant's *First Cri-*

tique appeals to Plato's *Republic* as a regulative principle, thus leaving the question of its constitution open. His *Second Critique,* as Deleuze himself makes clear in both *Coldness and Cruelty* and his earlier *Kant's Critical Philosophy,* leaves the idea of a constitutional form open but empty. In practice, reason invents or appeals to regulatory principles but never succeeds in justifying any activity because of the emptiness of the constitution. An emptiness that suffuses every action with a suffocating sense of guilty responsibility. His *Third Critique* notes that personal tastes divide rather than unite a community but ends by arguing the failure to impart partisan tastes itself works on behalf of an idea of uncertain but lively debate. In short, all three Critiques appeal to the notion of a tribunal, a place where debate or discussion is enabled through regulative principles, but a realm which - although "Political" - remains both open and groundless. The virtue of Hegel's *Phenomenology* is to bring these three facets of discourse together, explicity, as a Political realm. Hegel argues the principle of sovereignty is already impotent, that personal tastes flee into the world of alienation or "culture", but finally argues that alienation itself entrains the growing pains of modern political sovereignty. In short, Hegel makes explicit that underpinning Kant is an idea of conservation, of unity, and of suffering on behalf of the advent of an ideal that remains groundless. What is strange about Descombes' account of a third stream of Hegelianism is that it need not depend upon Hegel at all. After the French Revolution, one need only draw from Kant the compulsive and groundless instituting of tribunals and align this with Sade's work. Specifically, with the idea that Political institutions produce the secondary effect of relating suffering to the preservation of authority, but primarily indulge in a wilder passion for destruction. A destruction carried out in cold blood, beyond anything related through present experience.

* * *

The fallacy inherent in Descombes' account of the Mad Black Hegelians is that whilst he recognises the reality of the passions they evince, he makes them symptomatic of a discourse that, although groundless, continues to live through its deconstructions, or its flirtations with violence. Here, Descombes appeals to Derrida; arguing that Derrida's logic explains the inner-limit of every deconstructive negotiation with violence (Descombes, 90). Violence is experienced but only as it is negotiated or mediated through suspensions, deferrals or differences. The fact is, the inner-limit to deconstruction should be abandoned. As Deleuze states of the insecure symbolic world of the Masochist and its own deconstruction: "It would be "wild" psychoanalysis to favour this breakdown of his defences by mistaking the "protest" from external reality for the experience of an inner reality." (CC 65)

Which is to say, to take disruption and violence, in all its reality, as possessing a symptomatic power only by virtue of the way in which such symptoms are put back into circulation for the sake of a socio-political discourse, is in itself "wild". This may be taken in two ways; as a wild mistake, a flight of fancy, or as wild in the sense that no socio-political sphere exists, only a wilderness. The irony of Deleuze's account lies in the fact that he means both. He criticises a fallacy as apparent in current french philosophy as in psychoanalysis. He does not, however, make such positions disappear through a rationalisation. Such positions become wild as they project the emanations of external reality onto an inner-form that has become "wild", unhinged, a fantastical perversion of a demented psyche.

Descombes is right to cite Derrida as the proponent of the "inner-core" of a French Hegelian tradition. Derrida frequently places Hegel in opposition to exemplars of Descombes' Mad Black Hegelianism. More than anyone, Derrida invests in the idea of a "third current" that breaks with a Hegelian tradition. As, for instance, in *From a Restricted to a General Economy*, where he places Hegel opposite Bataille. Wherever there is little hope of communication, and Derrida emphasises every symptom of silence, a kind of non-symmetrical relation remains in force; a relation characterised as one of suspension, or deferral. The idea of a dissymmetrical relation, as the inner-limit of deconstruction, allies every wayward symptom with an apology for a notion of the "Political". A notion Deleuze abandons.

Deleuze' work could have been aligned with a Sado-Kantian tendency before Descombes dreamed up the notion of Mad Black Hegelians. *Coldness and Cruelty*, however, is significant because it places him on the side of negotiation, of dialectics and of the slave. There is this whole other side to Deleuze, a side that brings out the "wildness" of every philosophy that seeks to institute a notion of discourse, negotiation and debate on exactly the kind of terms set out by Kant. A humorous side, insofar as it ridicules his contemporaries, but a humour that contains a serious philosophical point insofar as it recognises that the terms of debate do not lead to communication but to separate, partisan worlds with their own different imperatives.

What, then, is the difference between the master and the slave? In order to speak of this difference in detail, it will be necessary to again stress the role of Revolution, which as Descombes argues, lies at the bottom of the French tendency to reflect upon Kantian principles as though they were political imperatives. And secondly, to look again at the groundlessness that characterises the transcendental political realm in Kant. Deleuze stresses that revolutions underpin both Sade and Masoch's work but, crucially, different revolutions, different causes and different ideals: "Sade's ironic attitude to the 1789 Revolution is that the Revolution would remain sterile unless it gave up making laws and set up institutions of perpetual motion; it is paralleled by Masoch's humorous attitude to the revolutions of 1848 and the pan-Slavic movement: he suggests that contracts should be drawn up with a terrible Tsarina, thus ensuring the most sentimental but at the same time the coldest and severest law." (CC 93)

Sade's irony resides in his fidelity to the principles of the French Revolution, but only in order to urge a principle of destruction that is exacerbated rather than stabilised by the institutions of that revolution. Masoch's humour resides in his selfish espousal of a cause for his own ends, but only to make himself more obviously and agonisingly revolutionary, with all the more cause to feel unworthy, devious and, of course, betrayed.

In the espousal of these revolutionary aims, Sade and Masoch must appeal to ideals that exceed any possible experience. Sade appeals to institutions of terror, Masoch to the idea of a contract. Like Kant's tribunal, these ideals are intended to be socially inclusive, to either enfranchise or mobilise different peoples. Deleuze, however, stresses that these ideals are not communicative. They do not reflect back onto social discourse but break with any pre-extant social order. As ideals, they are unapologetically untoward and utterly groundless. He states: "Both sadism and masochism imply that a quantity of libidinal energy be neutralised, desexualised, displaced and put at the service of Thanatos." (CC 110)

In the case of Sade, these depersonalised, cold impulses are framed as an idea of institution that demands utter identification. In Masoch's case with the ideal of a contract that brings one personally into the presence of the unfeeling Tsarina. However, both ideas, in their transcendence, annul the possibility of sexual or social intercourse in favour of another power that no longer knows the laws of inclusion, enfranchisement or purposeful mobilisation. In the langauge of Freud, Deleuze states: "Beyond Eros we encounter Thanatos; beyond the repetition that links, the repetition that erases and destroys." (CC 114)

Eros would reflect the transcendental aspect of the possibility of building alliances, inclusive groupings, and so on, that seems to lie at the base of every uncertain attempt to conserve the status quo, or preserve a certain amount of suffering for the sake of a stronger social order. Thanatos reflects another form of repetition, one that is never betrayed in experience but, rather than reflect social continuation or growth, reflects only cosmic disorder. As Deleuze states, repetition is the crucial point, transcendence does not countermand empirical reality, the value of the empirical realm is reflected through the repetition of effects and the principles of probability, of expectation etc. However, repetition can also go beyond anything of empirical validity. It can create wildness. As Deleuze states:

"This is the essential point: pain only acquires significance in relation to the forms of repetition which condition its use. .../ Such a conclusion would nevertheless seem to be disappointing, insofar as it suggests that repetition can be reduced to a pleasurable experience. There is a profound mystery in the *vis repetitia*. Beneath the sound and fury of sadism and masochism the terrible force of repetition is at work. What is altered here is the normal function of repetition in its relation to the pleasure principle: instead of repetition being experienced as a form of behaviour related to a pleasure already obtained or anticipated, instead of repetition being governed by the idea of experiencing or reexperiencing pleasure, repetition runs wild and becomes independent of all previous pleasure." (CC 120)

As regards the ideals or idealised principles produced in the work of Sade and Masoch, what is brought out by transcendental reflection, of the Deleuzian kind, is precisely how mad each is. This madness, this coldblooded perversion, could never be redeemed on behalf of a socio-political realm that survives its endless deconstructions. Deleuze states: "In sadism and masochism there is no mysterious link between pain and pleasure; the mystery lies in the desexualisation process." (CC 120-121)

Taking these desexualised, desocialised ideas in turn, beginning with Sade, it is certainly true that sadism is manifested by acts of cruelty, but this cruelty does not testify to a relation between torturer and sufferer. Deleuze argues: "The acts of violence inflicted on the victims are a mere reflection of a higher form of violence to which the demonstration testifies." (CC 19)

Indeed, everything in Sade is spoken as though through the mouth of the abused. It is not the description of torture that is important but the way the descriptions combine with imperatives of violence to project a cold, transcendent idea of an institution that ceaselessly demonstrates violence, and in this demonstration reflects a cosmic force which has no interest in what might be related of pain or of suffering, and of their pleasures. Deleuze states: "Secondary nature is bound by its own rules and its own laws ... In opposition to this we find the notion of primary nature and pure negation that override all reigns and all laws, free even from the necessity to create, preserve or individuate. Pure negation needs no foundation and is beyond all foundation, a primal delirium, an original and timeless chaos solely composed of wild and lacerating molecules." (CC 27)

This theme is repeated later in terms of the mother and the father. Deleuze argues the mother reflects an idea of socio-political continuation for Sade, and states: "Although parricide occurs as frequently as matricide in the works of Sade, the two forms of crime are far from equivalent. Sade equates the mother with secondary nature, which is composed of "soft" molecules and is subject to the laws of creation, conservation and reproduction; the father by contrast only belongs to this nature through social conservatism. Intrinsically he represents primary nature, which is beyond all constituted order and is made up of wild and lacerating molecules that carry disorder and anarchy: *pater sive Natura prima*. Therefore the father is murdered only insofar as he departs from his true nature and function, while the mother is murdered because she remains faithful to hers." (CC 59)

Turning now to masochism, it is impossible to ignore the impression of "softness", the aesthetic effeteness of Masoch, that owes much to socio-cultural notions of feminity. But again, femininity is not recast in a way that allows for discursive negotiation. It is a pure form. Deleuze states that: "Formally speaking, masochism is a state of waiting; the masochist experiences waiting in its pure form." (CC 71)

This waiting, Deleuze argues, is: "the messianic idealism of the steppe." (CC 54). When Deleuze associates Masoch's russophilia with judaism, his strategy is plain. He is aligning masochism with a kind of Levinassian messianism which also finds an expression in Derrida's espousal of deferral, of waiting or, more recently, adjournment in his "La democratie ajournee". Again, Masoch's effeteness anticipates french philosophy's championing of the otherness of women. Above all, Masoch is a dialectician whose love of dialectics finds its transcendental expression in suspense. In Masoch, the dialectic is desexualised, desocialised, primarily and formally concerned with suspense not movement. Deleuze states: "Masochism is above all formal and dramatic; this means that its peculiar pleasure-pain complex is determined by a particular kind of formalism, and its experience of guilt by a specific story." (CC 109)

Which is to say, he experiences the story of the dialectic, the story of how the slave suffers alienation in order to preserve a socio-political realm and gains a secondary pleasure from this story that is entirely adequate to the dialectic. Primarily however, his idealisation of the dialectic abandons the story in favour of suspense. Or, rather, narrative is frozen, suspense takes over. This frozen moment, as has been said, is reflected upon as a contract. Deleuze argues that: "To imagine that a contract or quasi-contract is at the origin of society is to invoke conditions which are necessarily invalidated as soon as the law comes into being. For the law, once established, violates the contract in that it can apply to a third party, is valid for an indeterminate period and recognises no inalienable rights." (CC 92)

Which is to say, socio-political realities determine that the contract is a failure. If, in its failure, it represents the basis for Society (which, since Rousseau, French thinkers like Derrida are prepared to countenance), it does so by regulating kinds of communication that the law apparently ignores. It makes possible dissymmetrical relations where differences in power are seemingly settled for the sake of an extant social order. Where for instance, state power or the power of the mass market seems to brook no kind of negotiation. It is entirely possible to posit these dissymetrical relations, however to do so does not countermand power. To take the inevitable protest of the State or the Market as a reflection of an inner reality is wild. Is, in fact, fantastical. Thus, Deleuze states: "the law transcends the contract but leads us straight into ritual and myth ... The law now ordains what it was once intended to forbid; guilt absolves instead of leading to atonement, and punishment makes possible what it was intended to chastise." (CC 102)

Masoch, in a strange alignment of real revolutions with revolutionaries that exist only within his own fictions, disavows the very real fact that forces exist which are capable of ruthlessly stamping upon any transgression. In his dream world, as Deleuze states: "What remains is a strange and oppressive atmosphere, like a sickly perfume permeating the suspense and resisting all displacements." (CC 34)

Masoch courts failure in order to conjure himself as a genuine product of revolutionary times with his own revolutionary zeal. Deleuze states: "The contract represents a personal act of will on the part of the masochist ... The situation that the masochist establishes by contract, at a specific moment and for a specific period, is already fully contained timelessly and ritually in the symbolic order of masochism." (CC 102)
Which is to say, the masochist never knows his obliteration because any suffering experienced reflects only aesthetic preferences, refined "feminine" tastes, and an ego created for art's sake with no reference to institutionalised, socialised ideals.

* * *

Descombes, like Derrida, reifies a "Hegelian" tradition because it appears to offer continuation; in effect a discursive, dialectical tradition, where none exists. If, as this paper argues, Deleuze involves himself thoroughly in this tradition, and does so - via Masoch - as a kind of idealised dialectician, he does not thereby fulfill, revitalise or deconstruct the dialectic. As he states: "Dialectic does not simply mean the free interchange of discourse, but implies transposition or displacements ... a scene being enacted simultaneously on several levels with reversals and reduplications in the allocation of roles and discourse." (CC 22)

Through Masoch he gives an account of a slave who is in

control, but only in control of personal, partisan aims and, crucially, rejoins a "transcendental" topography in such a way that negotiation is no longer possible. It is not possible to debate with Masoch, it not worth speaking to such fantasists at all. Mikhail Bakunin, a contemporary of Masoch and an enthusiast of both the pan-Slavic movement and the Revolutions of 1848, wrote: "Unfortunately, there is still a multitude of people who in fact, in their innermost hearts, do not believe in freedom. And so, for freedom's sake, it is worth our while to concern ourselves with these people. They are of very different kinds./ First of all we encounter high-placed, aged, and experienced people who in their youth were themselves dilettantes in political freedom - a distinguished and rich man takes a piquant pleasure in speaking about freedom and equality, and so doing makes himself twice as interesting in business. .. There is no profit in speaking with these people: they were never serious about freedom and freedom was never for them a religion which offers the greatest pleasure and the highest bliss only by means of the most extreme conflicts, of the bitterest griefs, and of complete, unconditional self-denial." [6]

Bakunin, was the first, perhaps the only Mad Black Hegelian. However, to argue solely that Deleuze ridicules effete dilettanteism, as opposed to engaging with it, ignores the fact that he gives a positive account of Masoch. He joins Masoch on his wilder course. He explains, for instance, why, as he states: "Sadism is hostile to the aesthetic attitude." (CC 134). Or why Bakunin should highlight dilettanteism as an evil that, lost in its own musings, is incapable of manifesting a total identification with Revolutionary struggle. Deleuze echoes this when he says of Sade and Masoch: "We cannot ... say they are exact opposites, except insofar as opposites avoid each other and must do so or perish." (CC 68). But he does something else. One of the mysteries of the anarchist movement is that, at precisely the same time, it brought figures like Bakunin alongside others like Oscar Wilde or the Pointillistes whose extreme aestheticism, and slogan of "art for arts sake", seemed to lack any political principles. In fact, there are a variety of ways to abandon the idea of a Political space and any hope of discursive debate without diluting the anarchism of Revolution.

It all, finally, depends upon the weight placed upon the resexualisation that succeeds the desexualisation of transcendence. If resexualisation means re-socialisation, a return to social intercourse, one can still appeal to something like Adam Smith's "Invisible Hand" or Derrida's "Other hand" that writes the text of a politics upon Kantian terms. Against this notion of re-socialisation, Deleuze gives us a notion of resexualisation that promotes partisan themes only as it pursues the anarchism of Revolution.

It is easy to see which course is the more perverted. Plato and Aristotle explicitly hold, and this has become implicit in other philosophers, that relations are discursive insofar as everyone is capable of reflecting upon relations as though they were a philosopher. Sure, reality protests to the point of abusing their inner worlds, but this proof of the existence of murderous powers is utterly disavowed. Here, a professional philosopher is one who professes that reality intrudes only so that it might be negotiated, or socialised, within a debate. This is ludicrous. Philosophy is a thing few people do. Philosophers, like any other professional, pursue a partisan approach to questions with a fervour that seems perverse to those who do not share their bents. Where debate has been raised as an imperative, to be bent seems to be culpable. In the ensuing paroxysms of guilt, the intrusion of reality - the failure of debate - is awaited like an avenging angel. Failure, or its expectation, is projected onto society as though to be slightly bent is both a shared responsibility and an occasion for plea bargaining.

This fantasy solidifies with the belief that all forms of professionalism work on behalf of centralised power structures. Unfortunately, in French universities, positions are confirmed by the government, heightening this sense of pimpery. In conse quence, certain philosophers deny that the vagaries of the State relate to anything other than the field of negotiation, of enlightenment, of juridical participation. The collapse of government, either its pure collapse or its collapse into totalitarianism, is expected as a juridical decision, as a meet punishment for post-revolutionary perversions. There is, however, no need to be ashamed of professionalism unless that's how one gets one kicks. This is a passage from another professional, Dr Hunter S Thompson: "Did you have fun?" asked the bell captain, as he opened the driver-side door for me./ "Are you crazy?" I said. "I have a serious deadline to meet. We've been at the tattoo parlor all night. It was the only way to do it."/ "What?" he said. "You got yourself tattooed?"/ "Oh no," I told him. "Not me." I pointed to Maria, who was already far into the lobby. "She's the one who got the tattoo," I said. "A huge black and red panther between her shoulder blades."/ He nodded slowly, but I could see that his face was tense. "What do you mean?" he said. "You made that poor girl get tattooed? Just for a newspaper story?"/ "It was the right thing to do," I said. "we had no choice. We are, after all, professionals." [7]

NOTES:

1: Aristotle: Politics. *Penguin, Middlesex, p. 28.*

2: ibid, p.26

3: Kant: Critique of Pure Reason. *A xi*

4: Magazine Litteraire, *entretiens avec Gilles Deleuze. Special Issue: Deleuze 1990.*

5: Vincent Descombes: Philosophie par les gros temps *(Descombes). Gallimard, Paris. pp. 71 - 72.*

6: Mikhail Bakunin: The Reaction in Germany. *(Deutsche Jahrbuchert fur Wissenschaft und Kunst, 17-21 October, 1842) trans. Mary-Barbara Zeldin. Russian Philosophy Vol. 1: The Westernisers. ed. Edie, Scanlan, Zeldin & Kline p. 385*

7: Hunter S Thompson: Gonzo Papers Vol 11, *Generation of Swine. Picador, Pan, London. 1988. p. 15*

LORNA CAMPBELL

Anteros and Intensity

For too long discourses of desire have been frozen in a dream of the most illusory kind. Desire has become a freeze frame of the screen dream which characterises much of psycho-analysis. Desire has been projected only through the classical projector on to a single screen, the black and white Oedipal screen. It has been abstracted from the psycho-social world in which, in reality, it circulates, and fossilised as polar images/ projections of love and hate, or lost in a morass of coded words: sadism, masochism, narcissism, love, eroticism, hatred. My feeling is that this Freudian psychoanalytical interpretation of desire is too polarised. Surely what characterises desire is that it is a fluid system constantly interconnecting with other surfaces and economies. In the words of Deleuze: "desire does not designate another 'economy', another 'politics', but rather the libidinal unconsciousness of political economy as such."

And what of the fluctuating nature of the component drives which make up the economies of desire? I can not believe that desire can be nailed down every time to the solid statuesque figure of Oedipus. The psychoanalytical paradigm has not explained to me why the desire to love someone can so quickly become the desire to hate them.

This frozen molar confusion can be glimpsed in the works of Julia Kristeva. Although she has approached the problematic relationship of love, hate and desire, I believe that she has a fatal flaw in her understanding of the machinations of desire. In *Histoires D'Amour* Kristeva has identified and characterised several different drives of love; Eros, Agape, Narcissus, the romantic, impossible love of Romeo and Juliet and the male libidinal love of Don Juan. For Kristeva, these individual figures inhabit only the amorous imagination, they are purely mythical with no past, present or future. These individualisations of

Kristeva's are static figures without any trace of figural move-ment. It is impossible to see how they relate to each other, all are quiescent and codified, with little relation to any external forces or realities. There are no connections, nothing moves.

Admittedly Kristeva does clearly identify the love-hate duality and acknowledges the destructive face of her 'love quest' through the words of Shakespeare's Juliet: "...my only love, sprung from my only hate." However, although she is lucidly aware of the interplay of these two pulses, Kristeva also suc-cumbs to the fatal polarity that has resulted from the paradig-matic confusion of the screen dream. She believes that, although love and hate can both be projected on the same screen, they can not come together, to be alternative faces of a single one, as they are by their nature essential opposites.

This confusion arises primarily from the fact that Kristeva reads Freud *psycho-analytically,* through Lacan. Freud does ob-serve the dialectical relationship of the psychic drives of de-sire, the life instincts and the death instincts, where negativity is surpassed and absorbed in a cumulative movement towards synthesis. At the same time however Freud denies the interac-tive role of Eros and Thanatos stating that they are qualita-tively differentiated instincts. Freud's initial hypotheses of de-sire have been distorted on the classical Oedipal screen by those who in the words of Felix Guattari: "have tried to drag them back , handcuffed, to the familial and social norms of the establishment." The classical paradigm of Eros and Thanatos was originally introduced by Freud in order to insert his theories into a philosophical and mythical tradition of wider scope. However rather than allowing the further reach-ing combinations of particles and intensities as Freud intended, the classical paradigm has been used to individualise and personalise the psychic drives of love and hate, the life and death instincts. Eros and Thanatos have become individual actors on opposite poles of the screen and as a result they have become disengaged from the myriad economies and networks of connections which make up the psycho-social world. The actors are standing against a blurred screen of illusory mental images. They do not inhabit the sexual, political and social worlds of circulating economies which constantly collapse and are resurrected.

Like Freud, Kristeva does initially perceive the fluctuating nature of the intensities that are desire. Life and art she poetically describes as: "works in progress capable of self-depreciation and of resubmitting themselves to the flames which are without distinction the flames of language and of love." However I feel that because of the psychoanalytical paradigm in which she is trapped, she fails to recognise the forceful economy which produces this resubmission. And more disturbingly she plays down and refuses to address the importance of the role of histories in the formation of theories of desire. Surely all theories of desire are socially and politically conditioned through the discourses of the societies across which they circulate. Could a form of love as rarified and obscure as courtly love really function in a capitalist western society today? Perhaps Kristeva is too wrapped up in her mythical worlds where desire is static and not subject to the powerful forces which shape our psycho social world. She has completely divorced social formations from those of the unconscious. What Kristeva has not recognised is that desire produces the real equation where desire becomes energy through the social and through power. In the words of Deleuze and Guattari: "If desire produces, its product is real. If desire is productive it can be productive only in the real world and can produce only reality... The real is the end product, the result of the passive synthesis of desire as autoproduction of unconscious desire."

She has captured and embalmed in mythology the economies of desire and broken them down into distinct parts which must be static and authentic. Where people, particularly the mother and father figures, lack distinction society becomes baroque and perverse, people are masked, contamination abounds and essential authenticities are hidden. I find that the writing of Kristeva is pregnant with words such as "essential", "distinct" and "authentic." The actors on the screen must play one role only, no faces or expressions can change. I can not help feeling that Kristeva's distrust of the mask is all the more curious as one of the classical attributes of Eros is that he is often portrayed as a masked god who shoots his arrows blindly and wildly.

*

I want to move away now from the entrenched mythical world of psycho-analysis to an alternative discourse of desire which will produce the real and which will perhaps elucidate the confusing interactions of love, hate and desire. This is the dialogue of schizo-analysis as proposed by Gilles Deleuze and Felix Guattari in *The Anti-Oedipus* and *Mille Plateaux*. In the rapidly shifting worlds of desire schizo-analysis may succeed at the very point where psycho-analysis has failed. The fundamental failure of the screen dream of psycho-analysis has been that it has tried to block the connections of particles which constantly flow across the surfaces of desire. The result has been a fossilisation of the passage of intensities which are currencies of economies of desire. However it is this specific diagram of moving flows and schizes which is the most basic condition of the being of schizo-analysis. There appears a discourse based entirely on connections; connections of desiring machines, assemblages and rhizomes and connections of signs and sensations which are the schizes. Against the Oedipal screen dream, Deleuze has set up the programme dream or machine dream as outlined by Roger Dadoun in *Les ombilics du reve*. The machine dream is purely productions of desire. Its operation is to establish connections of circulating flows at the vanishing point where libido is engulfed and deterritorialised.

I feel that Deleuze's most convincing break down of the stationary structural opposition of Eros and Thanatos, the two main actors of the screen dream, appears in his exposition of sadism and masochism in *Masochism:Coldness and Cruelty*. Here he proposes that the distinctive characteristic of masochism and sadism are respectively disavowal and negation. For Deleuze disavowal is the point which contests the validity of that which is, which suspends belief in and neutralises the given in such a way that a new horizon opens up beyond the given and in place of it. This horizon is the horizon of the machine dream which goes beyond that of the inert Oedipal screen dream. It is this Deleuzian concept of disavowal which I would like to extend to all the faces of desire, not simply masochism, to draw a map on which the circulating intensities of desire can be traced.

However disavowal alone can not explain exactly how the pulses of desire can so quickly mutate across the plane of consistency which is our psycho-social world. Why can love so quickly become hatred? What causes the metamorphosis of masochism into sadism? And why do writers such as Turgeniev, to whom Sacher-Masoch was often likened, warn us to: "…. beware the love of women, beware that ecstasy, that slow poison."?

At this point Deleuze argues directly along with Freud that Eros and Thanatos can not transform directly into one another and he specifically warns against the illusory dangers of 'transformism'. Deleuze progresses his argument by suggesting that although Eros and Thanatos are indeed different psychic drives, the combining intensities of the life and death instincts can freely mutate through the process of de-sexualisation and re-sexualisation of libidinal energy. It is at this point, the vanishing point of disavowal, that the crucial production and re-production of energy takes place. The moment of de-sexualisation projects libidinal energy forward to a new dimension of reality, the movement is always forward and recurrent. Both fission and fusion occur at a single point of deterritorialisation. Intensities combine and split apart each time causing a displacement of energy leaving a trace upon the libidinal surface that is the Body without Organs. The de-sexualised elements are both re-sexualised and retained but retained in a different form as a kind of distorted refraction. It is as if the excess libidinal energy has bounced off the surface of a prism and been refracted at a new frequency. The new horizon has been opened and the repetitive process of the transferance of libidinal energy can proceed, causing not only liberation and *jouissance* but also failure. Just as when the Body without Organs, which is desire, destratifies too suddenly or proliferates into cancerous stratum creating black holes and masochistic and fascistic bodies without organs. The deterritorialisation is not always positive but there is always movement and production and reproduction of energy. We are no longer the passive audience of the screen dream with its static Oedipal method actors. We have now been drawn into the program of the machine dream where the only projections are momentary flickering intensities against a background of multiplicities of human, social and technical machines. Schizo-analysis is the link which connects the psychic drives of desire with the libidinal world of flows and connections. It frees the flow.

*

Schizo-analysis has succeeded in dissolving the stationary polarity of Eros and Thanatos, replacing them with an assemblage of libidinal connections, with a socio-historical machine extracted from the segmentary regime that is capital. But what of the force which controls the deterritorialisation of libidinal currencies across the general economies of desire?

I want now to return to the classical psychoanalytical paradigm, not to reinforce the stasis but to try to subvert it with an injection of the excess libidinal energy produced at the point of resexualisation. To unchain the Freudian handcuffs as mentioned by Guattari and turn on the lights dissolving the images of the screen dream.

Here I will introduce the diagram of Anteros. Anteros, a figure occluded from the psycho-analytical territorialisation of classical mythology is the avenging Eros, the *deus ultor*, the god who punishes those who do not return the love of others, those who don't connect their desiring machines to an assemblage. However it is not my intention that Anteros should simply become another frozen psycho-social individualisation of the forces of desire. Instead Anteros occupies the Deleuzian middle ground as a diagram of interaction of the psychic drives of love and hate. Here is the mid line of the rhizome where intensities gather speed. Neither the beginning or the end but the central lines of escape through which all circulating intensities must flow, the line of deterritorialisation and becoming. If disavowal is the result and re-sexualisation the impetus and movement then Anteros is the plane of consistency upon which the traces of intensities which are desire, are inscribed. Anteros is pure surface.

*

Finally I would now like to return, with Anteros, to the somewhat stagnant position which Julia Kristeva appears to have been drawn into. As I said before, I do believe that Kristeva is aware of the fluctuating passage of intensities which constitute the surface of desire, but because of the Freudian Lacanian discourse in which she operates she has failed to make the connections across the surface and failed to mobilise the flow. Kristeva's dilemma has been clearly pin-pointed by Cornell and Thurschwell who also recognise Kristeva's fear of separatism and abstract negation; while observing that it is the very Lacanian framework of her discourse which: "... permits the expression of the longing for a relation beyond the dictates of the Oedipal narrative, but which can not completely escape its spell." Perhaps this is why she has attempted to supplant Oedipus with Narcissus, Romeo and Juliet and Don Juan. However, all are still understudies to the divas of Eros and Thanatos on the screen dream. Kristeva is still chained to the screen of psycho-analysis where all is negativity and lack. Worse still, because of her rigid adherence to the Lacanian framework, where the solidified sexualisation of discourse obscures the reality of the Real as itself, she feels it necessary to present, in her paper *Women Can Never Be Defined*, such bewildering statements as: "...because of the decisive role that women play in the reproduction of the species and because of the privileged relationship between father and daughter, a woman takes social constraints even more seriously, has fewer tendancies towards anarchism, and is more mindful of ethics."

Had Kristeva been less concerned with these ethics of maternal nurturing and more aware of the circulating passage of intensities through Anteros, which are desire, she may have understood more fully what causes the resubmission of her "works in progress", life and art. Rather than vaguely suggesting that this conflagration is caused by the flames of language and love, she might have connected her desiring machine to the assemblage of libidinal unconciousness of the psycho-social world. And had Kristeva been less mindfull of her Lacanian maternal ethics and more in tune with the surface which is Anteros she may have begun to understand why, in *Venus in Furs*, Wanda is drawn to warn Severin: "..beware I may grow to enjoy it."

TEXTS USED

Freud, Sigmund The Ego and the Id
Kristeva, Julia "Women can never be deprived" Histoires d'amour - Love stories *in conversation with Rosalind Coward ICA documents esire 1983/4*
Cornell, Druscilla & Thurshwell, Adam "Feminism, Negativity, Intersubjectivity" *from* Feminism as Critique
Deleuze, Gilles and Guattari, Felix "Balance Sheet Program for desiring-machines" Semiotexte 1973

TIMOTHY S. MURPHY

The Theatre of (the Philosophy of Cruelty) in Difference and Repetition

In giving his essay on *Difference and Repetition* the title "Theatrum Philosophicum", Michel Foucault emphasized something that many of Deleuze's other readers have overlooked: the performative or theatrical quality of his texts, the manner in which they dramatize their own productions and deployments of concepts. But although Foucault stages his account of Deleuze's "multiplied, polyscenic, simultaneous theater"[1] according to the logic he finds in Deleuze's texts, he does not, strictly speaking, explicate this theatrical logic, neither by discussing Deleuze's ontological use of theatrical terminology nor by relating this "dramatic ontology" to Deleuze's own textual practice. Even if Foucault's text dramatizes Deleuze's thought quite well, which I believe it does, the task of explicating the strict terms and development of this thought as they are embodied in Deleuze's own writing remains. I would claim that Deleuze's critical and ontological philosophy is staged according to his own logic of dramatization; the exposition of this logic is one of the achievements of *Difference and Repetition* and the text explicitly dramatizes it. Because of the limited space and time at my disposal, however, I must restrict myself here to discussing only a section of *Difference and Repetition*, the highly structured third chapter entitled "L'image de la pensée".

The third chapter of *Difference and Repetition* follows a lengthy introduction to the problematic and two chapters covering, respectively, "Difference in itself" and "Repetition for itself" in the history of philosophy, and is followed in turn by chapters delineating the "Ideal Synthesis of Difference" and the "Asymmetrical Synthesis of the Sensible" that constitute Deleuze's ontology. "L'image de la pensée" is concerned, as it admits from the start, with "the problem of beginning in philosophy"[2]. This problem may seem a bit out of place at this juncture in the book; why begin a critique of beginnings in the middle? As we will see, the question of beginning (as repetition) can only arise in an opening between the past's hold on the present, in this case the history of philosophy, and the future, Deleuze's own ontology as it develops in the fourth and fifth chapters. Thus it is appropriate that an investigation of the difficulties of beginning in philosophy finds its place at the (material if not conceptual) centre of Deleuze's text, following the more historical exposition of the problem in the first two chapters. We must remember, however, that Deleuze does not begin any text, including the one under discussion, in the phenomenological manner of the Kantian tradition; to begin in this fashion would be to make the crucial mistake of assuming what one seeks to explain, of transferring a conditioned empirical figure, in this case the subject, onto the transcendent conditions that render it actual, thus inverting their relation[3]. Rather, like Spinoza, he begins with the infinity of virtual conditions, with axioms and definitions that will appear wholly abstract to thinkers in the Kantian tradition but that are commonplace in the Scholastic tradition, for example[4].

The chapter itself is highly structured, as a glance at the analytical table of contents shows: it is comprised of six sections which group the eight "postulates" that constitute Deleuze's critique of what he calls the "dogmatic[5] or orthodox" image of philosophy (172). "Each postulate has two figures...because it is once natural, once philosophical; once in the arbitriness of examples, once in the presupposition of essence" (217). Under this double aspect, each postulate is paired with a brief but detailed refutation, not of the contents of the postulate per se, but of its relation to the transcendent condition it purports to describe on the basis of conditioned empirical cases; thus what is refuted in each case is not the postulate but rather its pretension to exhaustive validity as an explanatory principle. Deleuze does not try to deny the limited descriptive power of the dogmatic postulates, but rather to unmask the prescriptive nature concealed by their apparently neutral establishment of norms. The first postulate, the "principle of the cogitatio natura universalis",follows immediately from the posing of the problem of beginning and is addressed within it. The next three postulates, the "ideal of common sense", the "model of recognition" and the "element of representation", are grouped together around a critique of Kant; this leads directly into the third section of the chapter, which departs from the presentation of postulates in order to outline a "differential theory of the faculties" (181) which acts as a "caesura" and provides the creative break necessary to carry out the construction of the rest of the chapter (and perhaps the book). The fifth postulate, the "'negative' of error", is treated separately as befits an ahegelian philosophy. The sixth and seventh postulates, the "privilege of designation" and the "modality of solutions", are grouped against a discussion of sense and the category of problem. The last postulate, the "result of knowledge (savoir)", gives way to a meditation on the signification of learning. As even this brief outline suggests, the chapter has two overlapping structures: a symmetrical arrangement of doubled postulates centered on the axis of the differential theory of the faculties, and an asymmetrical arrangement of discrete blocks of text eccentrically coordinated by the differential theory. This redoubled structure is a crucial element in the staging of Deleuze's thought, so I will attempt here to lay out its relevent parts in some detail.

As I noted above, the differential theory occupies the place of a dramatic "caesura" for both aspects of the double structure, but this needs to be understood in the sense Deleuze gives the term earlier in *Difference and repetition*. In a commentary taking as its points of departure Hume's associationism and Bergson's duration as well as Marx's reflections on historical repetition in the *Eighteenth Brumaire* (in chapter 2, "Repetition for Itself"), Deleuze elaborates the three syntheses of time (already sketched out in *Proust and Signs*[6]) within which repetition takes place. The first is the passive synthesis of the living present which contracts all of the past and the future, allowing time to pass unidirectionally (under the sign of Hume's theory of habit); the past and future belong to this pregnant present, "the past to the extent that the preceding instants are retained in contraction(,) the future, because waiting (l'attente) is anticipation within this same contraction" (97). The past and the future are merely dimensions, perhaps even modalities, of the present. The second synthesis is the active synthesis of the pure past in memory that represents the old past and the current representation of that past (under the sign of Bergson's intensive theory of memory); "(t)he old and current presents are thus not like two successive instants on the timeline, but rather the current one necessarily carries a dimension more by which it represents the old one, and in which it itself is represented as well" (108-109). In this synthesis, the pure past is the a priori, the general element that founds representation and that coexists with every current present as its constitutive and normative myth. The third and final synthesis is the static synthesis of the pure and empty form of time which displaces the relation between the others to create a differential repetition, the future (119-120); this last synthesis leads to Deleuze's definition of the "caesura", and can best be understood by explicating this term.

The caesura is the dramatic space of the time between the other times, the time within which beginning and end, past and present cease to coincide, within which repetition breaks out of the Same to create the new future; as such it is "pure and empty" because it is a logical time within thought, within the repetitive structure of every present, and can only be localized or exemplified allegorically. Therefore, in a move with important ramifications for his own later work, Deleuze explicates the caesura by considering the structures of *Oedipus* and *Hamlet* (120-121,123-125). The readings are not quite orthodox: Deleuze claims that the first part of each play is lived in the contracted present under the symbol of the pure past, of an action too great for the actors (though not for all that an action yet to come, for Oedipus has already acted), until the caesura, the pure and empty form of time, marks the actors' becoming-equal to the action and heralds the arrival of the future which shatters the actors into a thousand pieces and gives birth to the multiple and depersonalized Overman. The time between, the caesura, is the time that Hamlet says is "out of joint"; time is no longer subordinated to the cardinal points by which pass the movements that time measures, and no longer submits to circular repetition (119-120).

In terms of Marx's distinction between tragedy and farce in historical repetition ("All great historical events and characters are repeated twice...the first time as tragedy, the second time as farce"), the third disjointed synthesis comes between the productive tragic repetition and the later comic repetition as a sort of opening that goes beyond them: a dramatic repetition in which something new is produce Against the apparently retrograde movement of repetition from tragedy to farce in Marx's model, Deleuze claims that the true sequence manifest in Oedipus and Hamlet goes from comic (Oedipus' inquiry, the murder of Polonius) through the caesura (the revelation of Oedipus' inquiry, Hamlet's sea voyage) to the tragic repetition, the movement of metamorphosis (123-124). The blinding of Oedipus and the death of Hamlet are not tragic events in the traditional Aristotelian sense, cathartic purgings of pity and fear, but in the Marxist sense, inventive and historically novel: they stage the unmaking of the subject. Marx's model of regression, according to Deleuze, is valid only when repetition becomes involuted and fails to create by virtue of the abstraction of its elements into genres. The crucial displacement here is the reading of the earlier parts of the plays as repetitions of what comes later, rather than the reverse, which would take place only within consciousness: *"Repetition is a condition of action before being a concept of reflection"* (121, Deleuze's italics). Repetition is anticipatory and active, in the other, theatrical sense that the word has in French: "rehearsal". The caesura is thus the crucial displacement that, in breaking time free of its measured bonds and repetition free of the Same, allows the future to come and repetition to create or rehearse the new. Deleuze's conception of drama appears to owe little to the domestic character studies so beloved of Freud that he built the unconscious around them; Deleuze returns rather to Artaud's theatre of cruelty, without texts or actors but only "a language which speaks before words, gestures which are elaborated before organized bodies, masks before faces, spectres and phantoms before characters" (19), even when reading the classically Freudian texts of Oedipus and Hamlet.

Deleuze's critique of the first four postulates in this chapter, like the first sections of Oedipus and Hamlet falls under the sign of the pure past, more specifically under the history of philosophy, which "exercises an obviously repressive function in philosophy" like the Oedipus complex in psychoanalysis[7]. The first four of the eight postulates occupy only twelve pages of this fifty-page chapter, almost all of it given over to exposition of their influence in philosophy. The polemics are relatively subdued, indeed repressed: they can only arise from under the floorboards, like Dostoyevsky's Underground Man, to sneer at the common sense and good will of the dogmatic thinker. Deleuze's counter-formulations in this section, when they occur in direct juxtaposition instead of being deferred to the caesura, remain for the most part allusive or assertoric and thus undeveloped. In a word, the critique of the first four postulates falls under the sign of ressentiment, even down to its ultimate image of difference crucified on the branches of the Cogito (180); Nietzschean critique constantly faces this danger of falling into the reactive position, and in this section of the chapter Deleuze seems to succumb. Let us consider this danger in more detail.

If beginning signifies eliminating all presuppositions, then a critique of philosophical beginnings must begin with a meditation on the forms of presupposition. The most general rubric under which presuppositions are smuggled into philosophy takes the form of the assertion "Everyone knows..." or "No one can deny...". In the dogmatic tradition, this ploy is dramatized in the figure of the natural idiot who is opposed to the artificial pedant. In appearing to begin with the lowest common denominator, the *cogitatio natura universalis*, it covertly conserves what is essential: the good will and will to truth of the philosophical labourer (the first postulate under its "natural, exemplary" figure), and the innateness of this form of thought even in the idiot (the same postulate under its "philosophical, essential" figure). Dogmatic thought assumes the subject. To this image of the thinker, Deleuze opposes the singular thinker of ill will who does not just "happen" to think but who must always confront a fundamental inability to think: the aforementioned Underground Man (171). It is important to note that this personification of the malefic thinker is not intended as a phenomenology but as a stage direction, as when Deleuze explicates Kierkegaard's claim that "the knight of the faith resembles...a bourgeois in his Sunday best(:) it is necessary to take this philosophical indication as a director's remark, showing how the knight of the faith must be *played*" (17, Deleuze's italics).

The second, third and fourth postulates are grouped together, and it is possible to see the fourth, the element of representation, as the culmination of the first stage of Deleuze's critique, not only because of the explicit statements to that effect (179-180) but also because this section of the text leads up to the "caesura" marked by the differential theory of the faculties. The second postulate of the "ideal of common sense" follows from the *cogitatio natura universalis*, as the two forms of facultative convergence necessary for the production of universality: the objective or "natural" "concordant exercise of all the faculties on an object supposed to be the same", and the "philosophical" or "subjective principle of the collaboration of the faculties", a *concordia facultatum* identical for everyone (174). The first figure Deleuze calls good sense, and the second common sense; together these mirror images form *doxa*. The "model of recognition" (the third postulate) is, in a sense, the tautological inversion of the ideal of common sense: if common sense allows us to exercise our faculties in concert with the norms of the empirical world and of all other subjects, then recognition allows us the opportunity to verify our common sense recursively by repeating exactly a prior instance of facultative convergence. Thus recognition functions as a model against which all our facultative operations must be checked: we recognize the external, "natural" object and simultaneously we recognize the "philosophical" form of convergence of our faculties.

There are two objections against recognition as a model: the way it denies specificity to philosophy by submitting it to the conformist demands of quotidian common sense; and the way it obscures the issue of values through its constant reinforcement of established values, behind the mask of pure science (17&177). Here Deleuze asks a very Nietzschean question that bears strongly on my task in this essay, a question to which we will return: "What is a thought which would do harm to no one, neither to the one who thinks, nor to others?" (177). Lest we think that this questioning of the relation of thought to established values is merely a form of historical relativism, Deleuze insists that the difference between established values and new values is formal, a difference in nature, since "the new remains always new" and "the established were established from the start, even if a little empirical time was necessary to recognize it" (177). As we saw above, the question of time appears to be internal to thought; this issue will take on greater importance as this chapter progresses as well.

The preceding points define the world of representation in general; the fourth postulate, the "element of representation", refers simply to the harmonious cooperation of the first three in thought and politics. Deleuze summarizes the fourfold structure of representational determination (identity in the concept, opposition in the determination of the concept, analogy in judgment and resemblance in the object) in order to resituate it within the problematic of the first four postulates of philosophical dogma:

The *identity of the concept* as such constitutes the form of the Same in recognition. The *determination of the concept* implies the comparison of possible predicates with their opposites, in a regressive and progressive double series....(of) *memory* and...*imagination.. Analogy* bears on the highest determinable concepts, or on the relations of determinable concepts with their respective objects, and makes appeal to the power of distribution in *judgment. As for the object of the concept,* in itself or in relation with other objects, it refers to resemblance as to the requirement of continuity in *perception.* Each element thus specifically solicits a faculty, but is also established from one faculty to another in the midst of a common sense...The "I think" is the most general principle of representation, that is to say the source of these elements and the unity of all these faculties: I conceive, I judge, I imagine and remember, I perceive--like the four branches of the Cogito. And precisely on these branches difference is crucified. (180, my italics)[8]

Under this dogmatic image of thought, which is based primarily on the phenomenological subject, difference can only be grasped as subordinate to the hegemony of conservative, exact repetition of the Same as principle, what Deleuze calls elsewhere "naked repetition" (37); the I brings all the faculties into agreement through the force of the four representational principles of similarity. The space and time available to difference within this tradition have been derived from these four categories and have always returned to them. But his critique will not escape from them unless he can pose it in constructive or productive terms which avoid the reactive pathos of "cruci-fied difference".

At this point, Deleuze's text breaks off from its enumeration and critique of the presuppositions of philosophy to venture into more productive territory. The "differential theory of the facul-ties" occupies the position of caesura (as I described it above) in this chapter, perhaps in the whole book, and it does in fact bring about a stylistic and polemical shift in the text. Like the critique of the first four postulates, this theory occupies twelve pages of text, but they are written in a somewhat different style: more measured, less hostile, even prepared on occasion to note precedent movements toward the discordant theory among the "moral dogmatists" like Plato and Kant. The differential theory explicitly contains Deleuze's counterformulations of each of the first four postulates, but in positive rather than reactive form. More importantly, with the differential theory of the faculties Deleuze begins to construct his own alternative ontology within the very space (though not the time) marked out by the dogmatic representational tradi-tion.

He begins his account of the faculties with a consideration of Plato's distinction, in the *Republic*, between things that leave thought tranquil (objects of recognition), and those that force thinking. But these objects that force thinking are not objects of uncertain recognition, nor hypothetical objects (ultimately it will become clear that they are not "objects" at all?); concepts such as these only designate possibilities for thought, and lack the absolute necessity of a violent encounter to bring thought out of its "stupor" of naked repetition and into actuality. "What is first in thought is breaking in, violence, it is the enemy..." (181). Deleuze here makes a clear statement of purpose: "The conditions of a true critique and a true creation are the same: destruction of the image of a thought which presupposes itself, genesis of the act of thinking in thought itself' (182). These conditions represent the refusal of the first postulate of dogma, the *cogitatio natura universalis*. The first character of the encounter, this violence, can only be sensed, but this is not a sensible quality, which refers back to the exercise of the faculties in common sense, but a sign. "It is not a sensible being, but the being *of* the sensible. It is not the given, but that by which the given is given. It is as well the insensible in a certain fashion...from the point of view of recognition " (182, Deleuze's italics). In this sign, this sentiendum which can only be sensed but not represented under the convergence of the faculties within dogmatic time, sensibility finds its limit and is raised to its transcendent exercise, the "nth" power (in the sense of an exponential raising in mathematics), in pure and empty time. This exercise is no longer limited by common sense to convergent work under one dominant faculty or another; it enters into discordant, creative play, undoing the second dogmatic postulate of common sense.

Second character: what can only be sensed unsettles the internal accord of the "soul", perplexes it, and forces it to pose a problem, since this violence cannot be recognized as conforming to a memory, a perception or any other convergence of the faculties. This problem is related rather to the Platonic question of transcendental Memory which can only be recalled without ever having been seen, understood or imagined: the being of the pure a priori past, as I described it above under the second synthesis of time. Forgetting is thus what is addressed in addressing this Memory, and the memorandum is also unrememberable. This transcendent forgetting exists in the memory as the "nth" power, the limit of memory as a faculty, as that which could only be sensed formed the limit of the faculty of sensibility. Likewise, the third character of the encounter is that which can only be thought, the cogitandum or the Essence, which is not the intelligible which can be grasped in another mode than thought but rather the being of the intelligible. The faculties of sensibility, memory and understanding do not reach an accord under the alternating dominance of one of them within a living present frozen by the pure past, as they would have in recognition *a la Kant*[10], but rise to a discordant and paradoxical exercise, within the pure and empty time of the third synthesis or caesura, that explodes *doxa* (183-184); since such an exercise can only operate through the unconscious and not through a conscious subject, it explodes that subject as well.

Deleuze insists that his use of the term "transcendent" does not mean "otherworldly", but rather the world that concerns each faculty exclusively. Therefore it cannot be transferred to a traditionally-defined empirical world, which presupposes common sense, but to a "superior empiricism", a "properly transcendental empiricism" that discovers the lands beyond the convergence of the Same (186). These "what can only be...", of which *sentiendum, memorandum and cogitandum* have served as our examples, are not limited to the three faculties explicitly discussed; in fact it is in the case of the imagination that Kant prefigures a faculty freed from the form of common sense that he himself imposed upon them: this is the famous problem of the Analytic of the Sublime[11], where thought is faced with its own incapacity to resolve the conflicting exercise of its faculties of understanding and imagination in their wild flight toward their limits (187). The project of *Difference and Repetition* is not to found a doctrine of discordant faculties, but to determine its requirements. What is crucial to thought is its relation to nonthought, this encounter which forces sensing and which can only be sensed, and not to what comes before thought, as phenomenology tends to suggest; the things thought encounters here are not orderly gods of continuity but demons, forces of the leap and the interval. Paradoxically, this encounter that guarantees the necessity of the forcing to think is itself contin gent and can take many forms; there is no predestination (189).

There is an order and linkage of the faculties, Deleuze insists, but this does not imply a unity of object or subject. The linkage is forced, strained and broken because its usage is paradoxical:

the "discordant accord" (Kant's phrase remotivated by Deleuze) communicates only the violence of its difference from one faculty to another. Deleuze suggests that the name of Ideas should be reserved for these "agencies that go from sensibility to thought and from thought to sensibility, capable of engendering...the transcendent or limit-object of each faculty" (190). The Idea must be at once distinct and obscure (rather than clear), to mark its relation to the radical violence that comes from the outside of closed, dogmatic thought to unsettle it and create new, actual thought which, as we will see, has no outside since it is only outside (191):

The distinct-obscure is the properly philosophical drunkenness or dizziness, or the Dionysiac Idea...And perhaps Apollo, the clear-confused thinker, is necessary to think Dionysos' Ideas. But never are the two brought together to reconstitute a natural luminosity *(lumiere)*. They compose rather two ciphered tongues in philosophical language, and for the divergent exercise of the faculties: the disparity of style. (276)

The outside comes into thought, as into language, as the necessary torsion to which these activities submit in order to come into existence, in order to create; here Deleuze uses Nietzsche's categories for tragedy, formless Dionysiac delirium and formal Apollonian representation, to enact this point. Thus the asymmetrical relation of thought and its outside run together like two merging streams, though they do not form a resolvable dialectic, and together create the self-differenciation that is style, but a style that never returns to the Same.

Later Deleuze will amplify this point by saying that "style...belongs to people of whom you normally say, 'They have no style'...A style is managing to stammer in one's own language"[12].

The transition between the differential theory and the resumption of the critique of dogma is instructive: it turns around the correspondence of Jacques Riviere and Antonin Artaud, which dramatizes the conflict between a thought of common sense and good sense, born of doxa, and a divergent thought, born in the event of an encounter with the outside of thought. Riviere and Artaud function here as "dark precursors" (156) or "conceptual personages"[13] who act out the conflict between the dogmatic and generative forms of thought, as Deleuze's strict separation between the exposition of the first four postulates and his own differential theory acts out the same conflict. In the pages that follow, this conflict, which earlier appeared reactive or negative in Hegelian fashion, develops into a critique that is no longer oppositional (if it ever was) but productive. The organization of the chapter shifts. The last four postulates cover twenty-five pages, but the majority of that space is taken up by Deleuze's counterformulations that do not simply oppose the traditional structures of dogmatic philosophy but subsume those structures as specific cases within a set of conditions larger than the conditioned concepts and objects they explain. Let us see how this new strategy operates.

Under the dogmatic image of thought, the only "misadventure" to which thought is susceptible is error, which is nothing other than the logical negative of rational orthodoxy. This is the philosophical figure of this postulate:

(D)oes not error itself bear witness to the form of common sense, since it cannot happen to befall a faculty that is all alone, but to at least two faculties from the point of view of their collaboration, an object of one being confounded with *another* object of the other? (193)

For example, in misrecognition we mistake an object in perception for a different object in memory, and in misunderstanding we subsume an object in perception or memory under an inadequate concept. Dogmatic thought does not deny that thought is threatened by other hazards--madness, stupidity, wickedness--that are irreducible to error, but these threats are treated as facts external in their causality (and thus natural in figure), only affecting us insofar as we are not "uniquely thinkers" (194). But this is in fact to reduce them to error, since error is the sole way they can affect the interiority of thought. "From whence the hybrid character of this insipid concept which would not belong to pure thought if it wasn't delinquent from the *outside*, but which would not result from this outside if

117

this outside were not in pure thought" (194, Deleuze's italics) as Deleuze himself argues. Dogmatic philosophy has been able to multiply the forms of negative, but always under the rule of common sense and always on the basis of a logic of interiority.

The problem of stupidity *(betise)* is a much more fruitful object of inquiry, as non-dogmatic thinkers from Lucretius to Kierkegaard have realized, since it confronts thought with its inability to think and its "internal outside" in a particularly forceful way.

Cowardice, cruelty, baseness, stupidity are not simply corporeal powers, or facts of character and society, but structures of thought as such. The landscape of the transcendental livens up; we must introduce here the place of the tyrant, the slave and the imbecile--without making the place resemble that which occupies it, and without the transcendental ever being transferred onto the empirical figures it renders possible (196).

These "facts of character" or of characterization are not just negations of or failures to achieve the transcendental norm, nor are they forms of transcendental ego; stupidity is not the other of thought, but the object of a true transcendental question: how is stupidity (and not error) possible? It is possible due to the link between thought and individuation. This is more profound than the supposedly self-evident "I think"; the I (the subject) is only an index of species. The I is not a species, but it contains implicitly what species and genres explicitly develop: the recognition of specific forms subsumed under the rule of representation. Individuation has nothing to do with specification, though it renders specification possible and precedes it. Individuation, as a field of flowing intensive factors, cannot be separated from a pure backdrop *(fond)* [14]it brings up, a backdrop that is itself without form or figure; this backdrop is the undetermined Dionysos which continues to embrace Apollo's determination and specification. The I has no defence against the deforming and dissolving mirror of the rising backdrop, and must confront its own apparently internal relation to this radical outside. "Stupidity is neither the backdrop nor the individual, but this relation whereby individuation brings up the backdrop without being able to give it form... (....constituting the non-recognized of all recognition). All determinations become cruel and evil" (197-198). It is a question of seeing the formless behind every form, madness behind all reason, especially the subject's own form and reason, in other words of raising the faculties to their discordant exercise: when the factors of intensive individuation are taken as objects of the encounter with non-thought, the backdrop forces thought to take place in a theatrical mode and on a theatrical stage, not a proscenium stage but a cruel stage that dissolves both actors and roles. The subject's relation to the unthinkable backdrop is the violent cogitandum, in a certain sense.

Error and falsehood are relatively rare in what Deleuze calls the "homework *(devoir)*" of thought; they are far outnumbered by banalities, badly posed problems or those denuded of sense (198-199). It is the element of sense[15] that interests Deleuze as a displacement of the true/false dichotomy, just as useful as the question of stupidity above and for the same reasons: "We define sense as the condition of truth; but as we suppose that the condition has an extension larger than the conditioned, sense does not found truth without also rendering error possible" (199). Deleuze insists that there are two dimensions to every proposition: the Scholastic concept of expression, in which it states *(enonce)* something ideal [16], and designation, in which it indicates the objects to which this expression is to be applied. The first is sense, the second the domain of true and false, and it is to the second that the dogmatic image of philosophy owes its allegiance and its essential figure, even if it occasionally complicates the field by adding the third category of non-sense to the values of true and false.

Deleuze's goal here is to find an adequate, logically intrinsic genesis of sense as exteriorized relation rather than rely on a haphazard extrinsic conditioning; "Truth in all respects is an affair of production, not of adequation" (200), a matter of creation rather than the establishment of connections between propositions and extra-propositional states of affairs (the natural figure of this illusion). The relation of the proposition to the object it designates must be established from the point of view of sense, which does not allow the true-false relation to remain the same, since this relation is "backed *(fondé)*" by a "without-backdrop *(sans-fond)*". This "without-backdrop" forms the field within which the proposition is bound to its object as sense:

If sense is surpassed toward the object, this object can no longer be posed in reality as exterior to sense, but only as the limit of its process. And the relation of the proposition to what it designates, in so much as this relation is executed, is found constituted in the unity of sense, at the same time as the object which executes it. (200)

The proposition, apparently produced by and in a subject, finds its designated object at its own limit within sense rather than wholly outside itself; this formulation thus undoes the specular opposition of subject and object. Subject and object, inside and outside are only the arbitrary and convergent limits imposed by dogmatic thought on a process which would find its own divergent limit in a loquendum which could only be spoken (or silent) (186-187).

There is a difference between sense and signification as follows: "signification refers only to the concept and to the manner in which it is related to conditioned objects in a field of representation; but sense is like the Idea which is developed in sub-representative determinations" (201). The Idea, as we saw in the differential theory, however, cannot be reduced to sense, since it is non-sense (and the being of the sensible, of memory, etc.) as well. The proposition and its sense cannot both be formulated in the same utterance, since the proposition designates by convergence and sense expresses by divergence, but we can, like Lewis Carroll, make the sense of a first proposition into the object of another proposition, whose sense again could only be formulated in a third proposition, ad infinitun. The paradoxes of sense begin here, with the infinite proliferation of language. But this paradox can perhaps be escaped, if we suspend and immobilize the proposition in order to extract its double, not as a subject/object redoubling but as a dedoubling or splitting. This double, distinct from the proposition itself, from the one who formulated it and from the object to which it refers, does not exist beyond the proposition that expresses it but yet is the "first term of knowledge (connaissance)" (202). To distinguish the double from the object (a noun) and the proposition (a subject and predicate), we must say it in an infinitive or parricipial form-rather than "the sky" or "the sky is blue", we must say 'the being-blue of the sky". We can think of the double as the "text" of the Deleuzian drama, but a text deprived of subjects, both grammatical and phenomenological, and referential statements. This double "is an ideal event. It is an objective entity, but one of which we could not even say that it exists in itself; it insists, it subsists, having a quasi-being, an extra-being, the minimum of being common to real, possible and even impossible objects" (202). But it is also incorporeal, a phantasm playing at the limit of words and things; it has an Ideal sense but no propositional designation or signification, thus it gives rise to contradiction and idealism.

Perhaps the form of a question can offer a better alternative to the infinitive or participle, Deleuze suggests, as long as we can avoid the calculus of questions which anticipates the answers. Questioning is always done within the setting of a community, the natural figure of illusion: common sense, good sense. Despite this, questioning has an advantage as a model: it opens a new path that can lead to a more useful formulation, that of the problem. "A proposition conceived as response is always a particular case of solution...separated from the superior synthesis which related it with other cases to a *problem*...Interrogation...expresses thus the manner in which a problem is dismembered, short-changed, betrayed in experience and for consciousness" (204, my italics). Interrogation transfers the problems onto propositions within a context that presupposes convergence and uniformity, even though the Ideal expression of sense is carried in the problem, since sense is in every case an ensemble of questions and problems that changes nature when it is reduced to propositional logic. Platonism and its derivatives with their Socratic methods, even down to Anglo American analytic philosophy and German intersubjective communications philosophy, have not developed the discordant usage of the faculties, nor encountered the exteriority of thought.

What Deleuze means by "problem" is not be yet clear, nor is the relation between problems and solutions in the dogmatic image of thought, with its emphasis on the "modality of solutions". Problems are not simply given, like poll or exam questions, nor do they disappear in their solutions which would be true or false; "(t)his is an infantile prejudice, according to which the master gives a problem, our task being to resolve it, and the result of that task being qualified as true or false by a powerful authority...the problem as obstacle, the respondant as Hercules" (205). Problems are not all ready-made, but must be constituted and invested in symbolic fields which are their own. Foucault suggests that a problem is a "multiplicity of exceptional points, which are displaced as we distinguish their conditions and which insist and subsist in the play of repetitions" [17] More prosaically, the problem is the transcendent set of conditioned points that express the Idea's condition, and which only becomes a question in being represented on the basis of particular cases of solution that are treated as propositions divorced from sense. The problem is the demon of the encounter, as I noted above[18]. The Aristotelian method of Dialectic and Analytic, the production of propositions and the conclusion of syllogisms, then simply reproduces the structures of doxa : "prey to the philosophical illusion, it makes the truth of problems dependent upon commonplaces *(lieux communs)*, that is to say upon the *logical possibility* of receiving a solution (the propositions themselves designate the cases of possible solution)" (208, Deleuze's italics).

The philosophical figure of this privilege of solutions thus takes the form of a logically extrinsic variable rather than a necessary causality; and it is just this necessity the Deleuze seeks to recover. This characteristic of the problem is "the imperative interior element... which measures its power of intrinsic genesis: .. .the 'differential'. ...The problem is the differential element in thought, the genetic element in the true" (210). By this logic, the problem no longer depends on its possibility of solution, but rather the resolvability, like the solutions themselves, must be determined by the conditions of the problem. If sense is Ideal, then problems are (in) Ideas, and are bound as such to the differential theory of the faculties[19]: they provide the violence in which thought is engendered. The difference between a problem and a proposition is a difference in nature: a proposition is always particular, a determined response, even when it is part of a group of propositions which form the case of a general solution (as in algebra).

It is not the solution which lends its generality to the problem, but the problem which lends its universality to the solution. It is never sufficient to resolve a problem with the aid of a series of simple cases playing the role of analytical elements; it is necessary further to determine the conditions in which the problem acquires the maximum of comprehension and extension, capable ofcommunicating to the cases of solution its own ideal continuity...To resolve is always to engender discontinuities against the backdrop *(surfond)* of a continuity functioning as Idea. (211)

In the absence of the problem, the solution takes the form of propositions which are abstract and general, which are in a word designational. The problem must be reconstituted, but on the basis of the neutralized double of particular propositions and the empty form of general propositions (theorems, theories). The problem is universal as a pure virtuality, which expresses itself through the differentiating process of actualization; and "(t)o the relations which constitute the universal of the problem correspond the distribution of remarkable and singular points which constitute the determination of the conditions of the problem" (211). To resolve a problem so conceived is not to transcend it in Hegelian fashion, to sublate it into its solution, but to create differences and discontinuities that extend it.

These universal Ideas or problems that compel thought are not simple essences or Forms but dynamic multiplicities that complicate as they express themselves. Deleuze thus displaces the traditional opposition of possible/real, which conforms to the model of the Same since the real conforms to (a part of) the possible as a copy to its original, by means of the distinction virtual/actual:

(T)he possible is opposed to the real; the process of the possible is thus a "realization". The virtual, on the contrary, is not opposed to the real; it possesses a full reality itself. Its process is actualization. (In realization,) difference can no longer be other than the negative determined by the concept: either the limitation of possibles...in order to be realized, or the opposition of the possible with the reality of the real. The virtual, on the contrary, is the character of the Idea; it is from its reality that existence is produced, and produced conforming to a time and space immanent to the Idea.. In the second place, the possible and the virtual are distinguished further because the first returns to the form of identity in the concept, whereas the other designates a pure multiplicity in the Idea, which radically excludes the identical as preliminary condition. Finally, to the extent that the possible proposes itself to "realization", it is itself conceived as the image of the real, and the real as the resemblance of the possible. (273)

In his logic, the coupled terms virtuality/actuality do not relate negatively (by limitation or opposition) as do possible/real, nor identically, as a copy to its original, but instead relate through the multiplicity of affirmative and intense difference. The actual is the expression of the virtual, but it expresses the virtual by developing the difference internal to the virtual, by becoming different in actualizing:

(T)he actualization of the virtual is always done by difference, divergence or differenciation. Actualization breaks no less with resemblance as process than with identity as principle. Never do the actual terms resemble the virtuality that they : the qualities and species do not resemble the differential relations that they incarnate; the parts do not resemble the singularities that they incarnate. Actualization...in this sense, is always a true creation. It is not done by limitation of a per-existing possibility. (273)

Now that we have reached Deleuze's definitions of the virtuality and actuality, we can double back to clarify the difficult temporal syntheses that characterized the structures of Oedipus and Hamlet, and that also characterize the structure of Deleuze's own writing. The fact that we must leap forward in the text in order to double back is a paradox that should surprise no one who has followed the discussion this far. In the fourth chapter of *Difference and Repetition* "Ideal Synthesis of Difference", Deleuze extends and hones both his terminology and his logic in order to provide a further positive exposition of his ontology[20]. We have just seen that the virtual is real, but this must be specified further: he insists that "Structure is the reality of the virtual" (270) and thus the reality of the problem as Idea. Lest we take this as evidence that Deleuze owes some kind of allegiance to structuralism, we should recall a primary objection to structuralist analysis which is "founded on a distribution of differential characters in a *space* of co-existence" (1, my italics): its inability to account for temporaiity. This is just what Deleuze installs within the structure, and in so doing explodes the synchronic paradigm:

(E)very structure...possesses a purely logical, ideal or dialectical time. But this virtual time itself determines a time of differenCiation, or rather rhythms, diverse times of actualization which correspond to the relations and singularities of the structure, and which measure...the passage from virtual to actual. (272, my emphasis)

Instead of the Saussurean dialectic of synchrony/diachrony, Deleuze discovers a multiplicity of times by which a multiplicity of structures can be incarnated and transformed. These "diverse times of actualization" include the three syntheses we considered earlier[21], and provide a set of conditions that can determine both a return of the Same (the pure past) and the advent of the new future. The "differenCiation" of the structure in the process of being actualized in time follows from the internal "differenTiation" of the Idea as spatial structure and logical time: "While differenTiation determines the virtual contents of the Idea as problem, differenCiation expresses the actualization of this virtual and the constitution of solutions (by local integrations)...The T and C are here the distinctive trait or phonological relation of difference in person" (270). Difference too has an inaudible double figure, but this reflects an asymmetrical internal split rather than a symmetrical representational mirroring (as in the case of the dogmatic postulates); perhaps this helps to explain the asymmetrical textual displacement to which Deleuze submits the symmetrical arrangement of postulates in the third chapter[22].

Deleuze's ontology relies then on multiple dynamisms which "are no less temporal than spatial" (280) to avoid falling into the structuralist reduction:

(F)rom the point of view of actualization, if the dynamism of spatial directions determines a differenciation of types, the more or less rapid times immanent to these dynamisms found the passage from the ones to the others, or from one differenciated type to another, either by slowing down or by speeding up...The temporal factor renders possible, in principle, the transformation of dynamisms, even if they are asymmetrical, spatially irreducible and completely differenciated, or rather differenciating. (278-279)

The relations and articulations immanent to the Idea express themselves spatially but also temporally; temporality is a function of the Idea, not only as pure naked repetition of the Same (of which structuralism would be the latest great formulation) through the first two syntheses, but also as the virtual reality of novelty and creation in the third synthesis or caesura. Deleuze's ontology provides a principle for transformation while recognizing the critical force of structural analysis. The same point can be posed using the vocabulary of problem and question worked out above: "It is not wrong to say that only time brings its answer to a question, and only space, its solution to a problem" (280). This is because the problem, as transcendent Idea, is a spatial structure containing only logical time, while the question, which represents a fragment of the problem in the form of a proposition, expresses one of the diverse times within which the problem is actualized. The different forms of time make transformation possible, but only in principle, not necessarily in fact; in the dogmatic image of thought, this virtuality remains unactualized.

This formulation of problem and solution suggests what learning would mean in the context of a philosophy of difference and repetition:

The paradoxical usage of the faculties, and in the first place sensibility in the sign, refers therefore to Ideas, which run through all the faculties and awaken them in their turn. Inversely, the Idea refers to the paradoxical usage of each faculty, and itself offers sense to language. It amounts to the same thing to explore the Idea and to elevate each of the faculties to its transcendent exercise. These are the two aspects of *learning (apprendre),* of an essential apprenticeship (213, Deleuze's italics).

Learning is thus a singular practice rather than a repeatable method, a jurisprudence working on a case-by-case basis rather than the schematic conformity of precedent-based law. Learning to swim, Deleuze writes, is a process of "conjugating our body's remarkable points with the singular points of the objective Idea, to form a problematic field" (214). Learning always goes on in and by way of the unconscious, since it is also always a transcendent exercise of the faculties, an operation of encounter and the transmission of violence from one faculty to another, a pure event. "We never know in advance how someone will learn--by what loves one becomes good in Latin, by what encounters one is a philosopher, in what dictionaries one learns to think. The limits of the faculties fit together one into the others, under the broken form of what bears and transmits difference" (215). There can be no method in this, for method is the means of determining the correct subordination of the faculties and needs common sense and good will[23]; culture, in the Nietzschean sense, is rather the violent and cruel movement of the events of learning necessary to "breed a race of thinkers" (215).

The illusion of dogma is to see learning as the passage from non-knowledge to Knowledge *(savoir)*[24], to have learning vanish in its result. Knowledge of the transcendental obliterates the time it took to acquire, since it is only empirical time, while knowledge goes beyond time; Hegel for example claimed that the movement of Absolute Spirit becoming conscious of itself would finally transcend time, and that history would come to an end once Spirit reached its resolution. Plato, though, is the exception to this tendency: he refuses to reduce learning to the binarism non-knowledge/Knowledge, but relates it to the reminiscence, the memory of a time that was never present[25]. "A time is introduced into thought, not as the empirical time of the thinker submitted to conditions in fact, and for whom thinking takes time, but as time of pure thought or condition in principle (time takes thought)" (216). This is once again the time of the Idea, of the structure that differentiates in becoming actualized. Of course, Plato then submits this reminiscence to the myth of identity in the pure past, the Form of knowledge itself, but the thinker of difference and repetition must say rather: Knowledge is nothing other than an empirical, experiential figure, but "learning is the true transcendental structure, adding without mediation difference to difference, dissemblance to dissemblance, and which introduces time into thought, but as the pure form of empty time in general, and not as the mythic past" (216). Learning takes place exclusively within the third synthesis; it is the caesura. The eighth postulate, knowledge as a simple result, obscures this practice of learning as it banishes time and transformation from thought, and dismisses it from the dogmatic image.

We are finally in a position to address in its entirety Deleuze's dramatization, which is also his teaching, both as an ontological theory and a textual practice. I discussed above the spatiotemporal dynamisms that constitute Deleuze's response to structuralism, but they have a further dimension I have not yet explicated, a dimension that relates them to the question of dramatization:

The whole world is an egg. The double differenciation of species and parts always supposes spatio-temporal dynamisms. These are the dynamic processes which determine the actualization of the Idea. But in what relation are they with it? They are exactly *dramas,* they dramatize the Idea... (T)hey create, they trace a space corresponding to the differential relations and singularities to actualize. (279, Deleuze's italics)

The relation between the Idea and the processes which actualize it is dramatic, and we must recall here that for Deleuze, drama is the opening that allows comedy and tragedy to be staged[26]. The Idea is not simply a template or text on the basis of which the dynamisms actualize a structure, however; the dynarnisms do not reconstruct an already given space but create a new one. One must imagine a drama that changes with every performance even as it repeats, as Artaud demanded.

The world is an egg, but the egg itself is a theatre: theatre of staging *(mise en scene)*, where the roles get the better of the actors, the spaces get the better of the roles, the Ideas get the better of the spaces. Even more, by virtue of the complexity of an Idea and its relations with other Ideas, spatial dramatization is played on several levels: in the constitution of an interior space, but also in the manner in which this space spills over into the external extension, in occupying a region. (279, Deleuze's italics)

This notion of drama must be distinguished from Kant's schematism as a method for subsuming the singular under the universal: the schema operates by analogy, reducing the manifold of sensibility to the "naked repetition" of the Same as concept, while drama develops difference through what Deleuze calls "clothed or masked repetition *(répétition vetue)*", which we could also translate as "dressed rehearsal" (36-37). Again, as I said above, this form of drama is not classical or even representational; it is Artaud's cruel drama:

We distinguish the Idea, the concept and the drama: the role of drama is to specify the concept, in incarnating the differential relations and the singularities of the Idea...Every typology is dramatic, every dynamism is a catastrophe. There is necessarily something cruel in this birth of the world which is a chaosmos, in these worlds of movements without subject, roles without actors. When Artaud spoke of the theatre of cruelty, he defined it solely by an exteme "determinism", that of spatio-temporal determination insofar as it incarnates an Idea of nature or spirit, as an "agitated space", movement of turning and wounding gravitation capable of touching the organism directly, pure staging *(mise en scene)* without author, actors or subjects. (282)

It is not necessarily a drama of interiorized subjects designating their motivations propositionally, suitable as a model for a representational unconscious like Freud might have wanted. Under the dogmatic image of thought, however, this humanist theatre has been the normative stage for philosophy. On the basis of a broader theatre, a theatre of cruelty, one could also build a philosophy of cruelty, which is what a philosophy of difference and repetition must be. Here Deleuze alludes to his own earlier question which we discussed above: what is a thought that would do harm to no one? The repetition is not obscured by its mask or dress of difference: "What would an Idea be if it were not the fixed and cruel Idea of which Villiers de l'Isle-Adam speaks?" (283). The answer to both questions is the same: the thought that would do harm to no one would not be a thought, nor would the Idea that was not fixed and cruel be an Idea. The cruelty of which Deleuze speaks is not the empirical cruelty of subjects torturing one another, but the cruelty and violence of the encounter with the outside of thought that creates and inhabits thought, the transcendent cruelty that would provide the virtual conditions for the actualization of different forms of conditioned beings beyond the interiorized subject of dogmatic thought (and the static representational structures and institutions that accompany it). But cruelty alone is not sufficient to transform this thought and its institutions, since it is not predestined[27]; to gain its full extension, cruelty must be articulated with the other terms in its series, the terms of the second, creative half of this chapter: Idea, sense, problem, learning. It must be constructed through the labor of culture, through the material practices of a philosophy of difference and repetition.

According to Deleuze's ontology, the third synthesis of the pure and empty form of time is necessary to displace the living present and the pure past, and the caesura is necessary (in dramatic terms) to displace the weight of history and tradition that locks the present into "naked repetition". What is produced in these dramatic interventions is the future, not the telos of a Spirit, a subject, a nation or a text, but a becoming-unlimited, unlimited by the constraints of identity or representation. This is the key to the strategic placement and labor of chapter three in *Difference and Repetition* : it draws together the lines of the past, of the history of philosophy, the overcoming of which is a task too great for the actor/philosopher, and in the break that is produced by the differential theory of the faculties the actor/philosopher finds a new time and space, internal to the stasis of the traditional structure, which allows her/him to overcome the straighjacket of a certain tradition, disciplinarity and subjectivity. Hence its name is double like its structure, "the pure repetition of the old text and the current text *one within the other*" (5, Deleuze's italics): "L'image de la pensée" does not refer solely to the dogmatic image under critique but also to the new thought that is dramatized in and by the displacement of this image, the new thought that is the phantasmatic double, the sense of this image and of "images" in general. Perhaps this is what Deleuze means by the formula "thought without image" that brackets the chapter (173,217).

The caesura constantly displaces itself, however: I would argue that the chapter occupies the position of caesura within the book, but within the chapter the differential theory takes that position, and within the differential theory itself the encounter provides the break. As Deleuze shows, the caesura does not occupy an empirical space or an empirical time, though in traditional drama it can be represented and localized allegorically (as in *Oedipus* and *Hamlet*) and in a work of philosophy it can perhaps be distinguished formally or stylistically; the caesura instead occupies a logical time within thought, a transcendent time, in Deleuze's sense of the term, that has been frozen by the effects of *doxa*. This is the time that Deleuze attempts to revive against the representational history of philosophy, and it is precisely this dramatic notion of time and Its syntheses that, in differentially repeated forms, constitutes the leverage point of his later works[28]; it is also one of the notions that makes Deleuze's thought such an important tendency within the horizon of post-structuralism, as Jean-Francois Lyotard, like Foucault, has noted[29].

The task Deleuze sets himself is the determination of the conditions of a heterological, theatrical thought; that task reaches an important plateau in *Difference and Repetition* in which he explicitly and systematically deploys the ontology, ethics and practices developed in his earlier historical studies.[30] More dramatically than the earlier books, however, *Difference and Repetition* enacts in its very form and language the differences between "'the old style"' (4) of dogmatic thought and the new virtual realities Deleuze discovers in the temporal displacement of the third synthesis. There is a word other than "caesura" for this synthesis; "Following Nietzsche, we discover the *untimely (intempestif)* as more profound than time and eternity: philosophy is neither philosophy of history, nor philosophy of the eternal, but untimely, always and only untimely, that is to say 'against this time, in favour, I hope, of a time to come"' (3, my italics).

NOTES

I would like to thank Antonio Negri, Samuel Weber, Martin Januario and Harvey Rabbin for their suggestions regarding this paper.

[1]*Michel Foucault, "Theatrum Philosophicum"* in Language. CounterMemory. Practice *(Ithaca: Cornell University Press, 1977), translated by Donald Bouchard, p. 171; translation modified. Originally published in French in* Critique *282(1970), p.889.*

[2]*Deleuze,* Difference et répétition *(Paris: Presses Universitaires de France, 1968), p.169. All translations from this work (as well as ellipses and brackets within the translations) are my own, and further references to it will be specified in parentheses within my text.*

[3]*One could claim, on the basis of many assertions in this chapter and elsewhere, that this expansion of the transcendent condition beyond the apparent limits of its*

normative empirical cases remains Deleuze's initial assumption (see below, pp.15, 17).

[4]On Deleuze's "pre-Kantianism", see Michael Hardt, <u>Gilles Deleuze: An Apprenticeship in Philosophy</u> (Minneapolis: University of Minnesota Press, forthcoming), manuscript pp.86-89.

[5]Deleuze's use of the term "dogmatic" to designate, among other things, the Kantian tradition is rather ironic since the term is generally applied by that tradition to just the sort of thought that Deleuze seems to practice: thought that begins with abstract principles instead of the viewpoint of a subject.

[6]<u>Marcel Proust et les signes</u> (Paris: Presses universitaires de France, 1964,1970, 1976) also contains a chapter entitled "L'image de la pensée" which treats a number of issues also developed in chapter 3 of <u>Difference et repetition,</u> including the violent encounter with the sign and the divergent usage of the faculties (see below). The Proust chapter addresses the question of dramatization only implicitly, however, and since it forms the conclusion to the first edition of that text, it is less useful as a dramatic allegory of the caesura; in later editions (1970,1976) it is followed by chapters on machinic textual production and madness, which give it a dramatic relation to its context much more similar to the <u>Différence et répétition</u> case.

[7]Deleuze, "Lettre a un critique severe" in <u>Pourparlers 1972-1990</u> (Paris: Editions de Minuit, 1990), p. 14, my translation.

[8]On the subject of Deleuze's logic of determination, see Hardt's groundbreaking study of Deleuze's ontology, <u>Gilles Deleuze: An Apprenticeship in Philosophy,</u> cited above (note 4). Hardt takes seriously Deleuze's "hatred of Hegelianism" and explicates his logical alternative to Hegelian determination through readings of Deleuze's work on Bergson, Nietzsche and Spinoza, Hardt claims that Deleuze's alternative can best be understood as a modified form of Scholasticism "in which the discourse on causality is replaced with a discussion of difference" (manuscript p.21); this allows Deleuze to attack the external, haphazard nature of the Hegelian logic of being (dialectical negation) in favor of an immanent and expressive causality by which the internal differences of concepts generate only further differences as they express the univocity of being in

the material world. I will return to this point below, from a slightly different point of view.

[9]*See below, pp.17-18.*

[10]*See Deleuze, La Philosophie critique de Kant (Paris: Presses universitaires de France, 1963).*

[11]*Kant, Critique of Judgment, § 26-29.*

[12]*Deleuze and Claire Parnet, Dialogues (New York: Columbia University Press, 1987), translated by Hugh Tomiinson and Barbara Habberjam, p.4. Originally published in French in 1977 by Flammarion; see P.l0.*

[13] *"n conceptual personages", see Deleuze and Felix Guattari, Qu'est-ce que la philosophie? (Paris: Editions de Minuit, 1991), chapter III.*

[14]*The French word "fond" generally means "ground", though I do not believe Deleuze uses it in precisely this way, since this meaning can easily be recuperated into a Gestalt-derived dialectic of figure/ground. "Fond" also has a strong theatrical connotation, however, and can be translated as "backdrop" in that context; in order to emphasize this theatrical meaning and link it to the other uses of dramatic terminology in Différence et répétition I have opted to translate "fond" as "backdrop", and to translate its derivatives (like "fondé" and "sans-fond", below) on this basis.*

[15]*For an extended and stylistically distinct discussion of this entire problematic, see, of course, Deleuze, Logique du sens (Paris: Editions de Minuit, 1969).*

[16]*See Deleuze, Spinoza et le probleme de l'expression (Paris: Editions de Minuit, 1968).*

[17]*Foucault, op. cit., p.185 in the translation; p.899 in the original French.*

[18]*See above, pp.l²-l³.*

[19]*Foucault explains this eloquently: "Far from being the still incomplete and blurted image of an Idea that eternally retains our answers in some upper region, the problem lies in the idea itself, or rather, the Idea exists only in the form of a problem: a distinctive plurality whose obscurity is nevertheless insistent and in which the question ceaselessly stirs. What is the answer to the question? The problem. How is the problem resolved? By displacing the question" (Foucault, op. cit., p.185 in the translation; pp.899-900 in the original French).*

[20]Deleuze presented an earlier version of a substantial part of this chapter to the Societe francaise de Philosophie on January 28,1967 under the title "La Méthode de dramatisation" and which was published in the Societe's Bulletin (61:3 (July-Sept. 1967)). The presentation was extensively revised for inclusion in the chapter, the most important change being the abandonment of the term "method", which will be discussed below. The other terms remain unchanged between the two versions.

[21]See above, pp.3-4.

[22]See above, pp. 2-3.

[23]This is why Deleuze revises "La Méthode de dramatisation" and deletes the term "method" when he incorporates it into Différence et répétition ; see above, note 20.

[24]The term Deleuze uses here, "sqvoir", generally refers to knowledge in the sense of an institutionalized body of knowledge or a discipline (for example, Foucault's book L'Archéologie du savoir (Paris: Gallimard, 1970)). Deleuze often uses the term "connaissance" to refer to the knowledge produced in the process of learning he describes (see above, p.18), but a more thorough study would be necessary to determine if this usage is systematic.

[25]See above, p.11.

[26]See above, pp.4-5.

[27]See above, pp.12-13.

[28]For example, the discussions of "Chronos" and "Aion", as well as the three syntheses of series, in Logique du sens.series 6,7,10,15,20 and 23, and the three syntheses of capitalist production in Deleuze and Felix Guattari, L'Anti-Oedipe (Paris: Editions de Minuit, 1972 Chapter I.

[29]Lyotard, Heidegger et "les jiufs" (Paris: Galilee, 1988), p.28-29.

[30]Hardt (op. cit.) traces this development with great clarity and sensitivity.

ALISTAIR WELCHMAN

On the Matter of Chaos

At several points in *Mille Plateaux*, Deleuze and Guattari address the theory of hylomorphism as an enemy of the rhizome. Hylomorphism, the designation for the theological doctrine of form and matter derived from Aristotle, appears to be an arcanum of modern scholasticism. Admittedly, *Mille Plateaux* is a book written *against* a huge number of named mistakes; but to attack hylomorphism seems somewhat irrelevant, even for their global-scale attempt. One reason why it makes its presence felt is that it characterises a miscomprehension of the machine which must be eradicated for Deleuze and Guattari's programme to begin. But it also facilitates a carefully mobilized elision between the transcendental thought of representation which is almost constitutive of the theorization of the modern, and a dogmatic, ancient thought of the cosmos. In fact, hylomorphism, as a privileged theorization of the general doctrine of form and matter is an abstract machine (although an illegitimate one) of the utmost range and power. Perhaps it is the abstract machine of all transcendent abstract machines. As a temporary point of attack, it permits not only the strategic evasion of any attempted reduction of the transcendental to a thesis of representation; but also a generality which opens out onto the elemental. One might pick, somewhat at random, the following four lines along which it is effected:

1. The theological: point of origin. This covers not only the theology of Plato and Aristotle, but also the protestantism of Milton and the transcendental (rather than the specifically theological) in Kant. Although the doctrine of hylomorphism is specifically derived from Aristotle; the account of the creation given in Plato's *Timaeus* is essentially hylomorphic in that it

supposes a 'neutral plastic material"[1] and an original model. That the model is *eidos* and not *morphe* marks a dialectic between Plato and Aristotle whose object is the merely interpretation of the status of the formal component. There is, across this, an invariant component which remains; the focal point of the activity of formation itself. The hylomorphic line is transversal, it cuts through the points of inflection indicated by the tradition: Plato and Aristotle; Catholic and Protestant. Even the theological and the modern. Not only Kant as an originating figure of modernity; but also the whole cultural theology of the frontier, the naturalised theology of the westward migration of the Church Militant -- from oriental homeland to occidental (European) heartland to "the American strand"[2] And then Westward still, from New England onwards and jettisoning the christianization of spirit for the civilization of capital all the way.

Recent events in the old wild west demonstrate a certain involution of the frontier which is, perhaps, no longer an extensive line enclosing a hermetic space of formality and reproducing its continual conquest of the unformed. The frontier has become introjected. What has been produced is an internal frontier consequent upon the globalization of capital and the passing of remoteness. The migration is now, not an immobile voyage, but a labour of interior colonisation and conquest; it has to do with the unconscious and not the object as matter to be formed. In all its imperatives: to convert the pagan, to Edenise the wilderness, to invest the periphery, to site the ego, there where the unconscious was; to reclaim the land from the sea, what is invoked is the formal spiritualisation of the uncultured, uncultivated matter. Hylomorphism.

2. The economic or etymological. The *Hyle* means wood or forest, and then (doubtless by synecdoche) matter or fuel. The primary modality of the cultured may therefore be thought as wood-carving; specifically and empirically, as the production of the product. This thought of production embedded in hylomorphism itself necessarily involves the tool or the machine in its broadest, but still technical sense. The line or

phylum of technical production is again perpendicular with respect, for instance, to Marx's delineation of *modes* of production. Its abstraction implies nothing more than the naked sense of production, and knows nothing of modes; still less of modes as property as ownership of the means of production. The matter-machine/tool-product line is effected equally (or rather unequally but nevertheless pervasively proliferated) in the wood-carving as in the computer with its nested sets of input/output registers.

Already the wood-carving is ambiguous between the aesthetic and the technical (or *techne*) -- although this is clearly all anachronistic way of putting it. The product of art as distinct from the product of the artisan is evidently a recent break (a Romantic one traditionally, but in the vocabulary deployed in the Plateau on the *ritournelle*, rather the Classical) [3]. The achievement of a relative autonomy for the production of art over the merely technical is a significant intensification of the thought of production within hylomorphism, and merits being treated as a special case.

3. The re-productive. The alignment of the poles of hylomorphism, form and matter with the distribution of sexual labour (action and passion or patience) needs little elaboration: it is the first "metaphor" to which Plato appeals in the creation -- Idea + prime or elemental matter = things; father-model + mother- receptacle = child-product.[4] The theory of the *homunculus* is not just presented on the ideal plane of the metaphorical, however problematic that may actually be, but is an example of the application of hylomorphism not only in technical production but also in tile sciences of re-production. The homunculus was a miniaturized or diminutive man shorn of as much materiality as was possible in the fleshy world of reproduction -- and therefore the representative of the formal -- who inhabited the eighteenth century spermatozoon. Indeed some claimed actually to have seen it in the sperm cell, with the aid of a microscope. This was an empirical scientific discovery. To the visual and hence negligibly material form, was added the egg as mere *milieu* of utilizable matter or fuel. *Tristram Shandy* is the narration of a *homunculus*.

As late as Freud, the *libido* was in essence a male principle, and the female the object of a mature genital appropriation of the libido within hylomorphic transitivity whose own development could at best be asymptotic to the genital through the exchange of signifiers -- shit - penis - baby - husband and the conditioning factor of money. Freud writes:

"Maleness combines (the factors of) subject, activity and possession
of a penis; femaleness takes over (those of) object and passivity".[5]

Freud is, despite this, to some extent a genealogist. His concern is with the genesis of forms, of subjects and their capacity to take objects. This becomes explicitly theorized in his writings with the rejection of the dualism between the pre-given ego-drives and the libido in the theory of narcissism. But even in this attempt lodges the origin of the subject in the narcissistic investment of the penis as the model of all stable investments. The male is combination or synthesis; the female is mere annexation, taking over of the material residue of the synthetic penis.

4. Language. Today the productive or creative efficacy of linguistic representation is a commonplace. But even in the medieval debate between the nominalism and realism of (linguistic) universals indicates that just the sign- referent relation thought dogmatically as nomenclaturism is imbued with a certain formative capacity with respect to the pre-linguistic datum. Saussure, and the turning point in thought for which lie is presented as being responsible, merely radicalized the *arbitraire du signe* which was already present in Augustine or even Aristotle[5]. Standing on the back of Kant (to put it politely), Saussure's *la langue* is a mysterious and spontaneously active principle whose function is to articulate (in the sense which a lorry rather than necessarily a signifying creature is said to be articulated). This sense of articulation is evidently morphic; and what is articulated is equally hyleic or materially unformed: the undifferentiated mass of pre-phonological white

noise and as well the pre-conceptual mass of white thought.

Upon each of these axes of hylomorphism a mode of activity is elaborated at the formal origin: ultimate agency, spirit; labour; imagination; sperm; infolded or topologically ambiguous spirit. The last is the most elusive. Its function is to support a second naturalization or immanization of the transcendental. This is a derivative move because the transcendental itself is already an immanization of the theological in the movement from revelation to reason; from external to internal law. This second derivative of the atheological is determined (at its induction with Saussure) to make the transcendental non-transcendent; that is empirical. Thus *la langue* is at once a product or output of the human *parole* machine and condition of what is now a seamlessly linguistic experience -- an experience whose interior and exterior are no longer topologically distinct. *La langue* is still spiritual and formal; and its (quasi-transcendental) object still informal and material. *La langue* is "Spirit *(l'esprit)* (which) breathes itself into a given matter and vivifies it"[7]. And this matter (equally the object of linguistics before Saussure's critique and the bizone of white-noise white- thought) is a confused mass of heterogenous things without ties between each other ... an amorphous and indistinct mass of thought .. chaotic by its nature ... nebulous ... plastic matter. [8]

But this spiritual form, whose exteriority to the subject is attested by its inevitable appearance as bequest, is at the same time produced by the unclassifiable empiricity of the individual's speech *(parole)* as it is embedded in history. The origin of language is thus an intrinsically insoluble problem: "Not even a question to be posed", Saussure writes[9]. With lines of transcendental and material (historical, chronological) causation running in opposite directions language must appear, at its inception, as something with a history. It appears always in its middle -- as a mezzanine?

This is a problem which Deleuze and Guattari confront as that of the State; the Urstaat. And it is not surprising. Even Saussure notes the tendency of language toward the production of a dominant and imperial State language (which he denotes, quaintly, by the euphemism "literary language" *10*; indeed it is only at the point of formation of a majoritarian dialect that even blurred lines can be drawn around the object of linguistics. It is the same with the State as it is with language because the two are fundamentally the same. Deleuze and Guattari write this about the state:

The more discoveries archaeologists make, the more empires they uncover. ... (The State) always appears as pre-accomplished and self-presupposing ... That is why theses on the origin of the State are always tautological.[11]

The absence of a ground or reason on which the state might stand, marks, for Deleuze and Guattari, not an inexplicable intrusion into social evolution (as with Pierre Clastres); but the fact that the state always exists with an outside which is not another state -- interaction with which is not reducible to "foreign policy"[12]; an absolute and not a relative exteriority. They lay their emphasis,as it were, on the other side of the piece of paper. Although Deleuze and Guattari speculate that "it is hard to imagine primitive societies that would not have been in contact with imperial states" *13* this is clearly not a theory predicated upon either efficient or formal causality. Nor could it be. The capacity of segmented non-state societies to attempt actively to prevent the development of the state does not depend on actual interaction with a pre-given state.

It is rather the state-form or Urstaat which is prevented, and therefore at the same time anticipated by the activity of the non-state. These mechanisms of anticipation-prevention demand a different mode of activity both from the efficient arid from the formal. This mode is distinguished from efficient causation by inversion of sense; that is, it operates in the opposite direction. On its own, however, this inversion would just result in a teleological, evolutionary or formal causality. Thus it is distinguished from this by a second inversion. Through this inversion it operates by involution rather than evolution. And this in turn has to be distinguished from a simple reversal which would be regression; just as the first inversion is not final. There is thus a causality which is contra-final, but futural; and contra-evolutionary but not regressive.

The state is not merely an example. It is the state, or the Royal against which Deleuze, more than anything, tries to think, to write. And its relation to structural linguistics and anthropology, the transcendent signifier, though qualified in *Mille Plateaux* tends toward identity in *The Anti-Oedipus*. This clearly bears a certain weight within the intellectual *milieu* in which he and Guattari were writing. Nevertheless, the thought of activity that is elaborated in the mechanics of the anticipation-prevention of the state-form by its absolute outside, is fundamental both to the rejection of hylomorphism, and to the relation which replaces it, ultimately of that of the body without organs to the strata. Consistency of vocabulary would name this mode of activity hylozoism: "the life proper to matter ... dissociated by the hylomorphic model", they write in the Treatise on Nomadology. [14] The preferred term is in fact, however, pan-metallism in the sense in which metallurgy might be provisionally contrasted to wood- carving.[15] The contrast is only provisional because, as Deleuze and Guattari demonstrate, even wood-carving does not conform adequately to the model of hylomorphism. Ultimately neither does hylomorphism.

The position then is this. Hylomorphism with its four (or five) poles of instantiation, invests all productive activity on the side of the formal and hence in the privileged representatives of the despot, the father, the labourer, the special case of the labourer as genius, and finally, God. It does not matter in the least at which end God stands: whether as efficient or final cause, Use productive role is indistinguishable. This model is rejected by Deleuze and Guattari in favour of u type of activity that is not formal, but material; a material causality that, unlike Aristotle's, merits being a causality.

It is this that Saussure and the linguistics which follows him still, were unable to think. The mere juxtaposition, aggregation, of

143

the two directions of production: formal production in the evident transcendental efficacy of language, and the empirical production of chronological history, results in a blank paradox the only solution to which is the eradication of history from the construction of the object of investigation. He writes in the *Cours*: "The intervention of history can only falsify his (the linguist's) judgement"[16]. In fact the consequences are worse than this. He is only able to invoke history at all through a certain elision of the relation to transcendental thought. Saussurian linguistics is actually a simple extension of Kantian idealism, determining the condition of representation in the condition of linguistic representation, homogeneously conceived. But Saussure, when the occasion demands, ignores this and presents his work as a *transportation* of the critical *technique* to an entirely separate field of enquiry, language. He is thus able to evade the issue of time or history by appealing to an illegitimate empiricity. He completely forgets the transcendental constitution of representative experience by the novel, but unfortunate, operator which he introduces. There is, therefore, all almost entirely negligible attraction in Saussure's writing over that of, say Levi-Strauss inspired more overtly by Jakobson [17] in that this theoretical naivety at least presents time as a problem, as something which is significant enough to merit active disregard and positive exclusion.

The absence of any thought of causality akin to that Deleuze and Guattari develop, promotes an obvious objection to hylozoism. *Mille Plateaux* records the tradition's comment on the removal of the formative power of the privileged agents of hylomorphic production:

Chaos ... How could unformed matter ... be anything but chaos?[18]

There is a certain incongruity about this objection to the subtraction of form. On the one hand, it is a direct correlate of the appropriation of production by the formal that matter is thought as utterly inert and dead; and therefore, one would have supposed, hardly a threat. But on the other, the result of the operation of subtraction is thought of as an unleashing precisely of uncontrollable force -- chaos. This is the argument of a state: 'The IRA don't represent anyone -- especially not a state -- and are therefore not the object of foreign, or rven of domestic, policy, are utterly unimportant; and so we must institute the Prevention of Terrorism Act to control them, and bring in the army and then the sccret services to annihilate them.'

From classical times, the notion of prime matter has sat ill at ease and two-faced between these two limits: the amorphous mass of Anaxagoras and the evidently unClauswitzian war of the elements in Ovid's chaos (Ovid actually uses both models on the very first page of the Metamorphoses)[19]. In both cases form is demanded; but the demand is in a rather different voice. In the first case, as in Milton's theology, form is demanded through the resources of a puritanical duty of philological assertion: from the transitivity of the verb 'to create' it follows that there must be a form which could order the material.[20] In the other, as in Milton's poetry, form is demanded in the voice of an absolute imperative: matter-chaos, whose depiction in *Paradise Lost* is an extreme intensification of Ovid's war, is what must be ordered. God must order it; or order that it be ordered: subdue, pacify, circumscribe, order the cataclysmically threatening, kill it. This activity of formation is not so much hylomorphism as all act of attempted hylecide.

The immanence of the strata to the body without organs entails the impossibility of idealism; there is always a line of flight produced, even, especially even, in, the state. Hylomorphism is the most abstract intervention of the failure of idealism. It is always going wrong. Dead matter sprays out from it, bizarre and unwarranted, in every direction and threatens the universal infestation of its pallid vivacity; threatens God with the only consciousness proper to him, that of his own redundancy. Take Milton again; a subtle example perhaps. The wilderness has a traditional spiritual-theological function in *Paradise Regained* (a theological poem). It is a territorial zone of ascetic conquest, of cathartic resistance, of refuge, of delayed discharge. It is concomitant in many respects with the representation of the New World by the Puritan settlers. But the wilderness as adjective, wild, already disruptive of any spatial topology, wanders erratically across the text of *Paradise Lost* making unimplored and unsanctioned connections across the whole plane of spaces, persons and activities. From its primary invocation in matter as chaos which is "Outrageous as a sea, dark, wasteful, wild" [21], it moves unsurprisingly through hell [22]; and the somewhat surprisingly into heaven. This is the more surprising in that it is not only an understandable response to Satan's initiatives [23], but is also the character of the angelic troops' dance [24]. Thence it proceeds inwards, to the vegetation of the prelapsarian Eden [25]; traversing the persons of the fallen pair; [26] the unfallen Eve [27] the serpent [28]; in still further to the internal geography of the faculty of imagination in the production of dreams [29]; and finally emerging in substantive and territorial form again at the end of the epic as "the world's wilderness" [30] ready for co-option into the progress of Bunyan's pilgrim.

The wild activity of chaos is obviously not inert; but more importantly - it does not conform to the model in being entirely without form. Perhaps a mutation of vocabulary would be preferable -- it has mobile traits of relative formality. The embattled elements, though strategically inept, that is to say, ultimately goalless are not without immediate tactical mobility they move in temporarily assembled and disassembled "clans" or "factions"- they "swarm" in statistical aggregates or populations" [31], and produce only temporarily stable wave formations -- always "from the bottom upturned" [32] and never from the top, even if it is the wind which is the involuntary agent of the transformations. This is effective presence of what in the creation passage is just the "Matter unformed and void" [33]? Even unfallen nature, product of chaos under the conditions of transcendent violation, and hence chastened to some degree, retains, as the descendent of base matter, a certain autonomous formatogenic capacity: she

Wanton'd as in her prime, and *played* at will
Her virgin fancies pouring forth more sweet,

Wild above rule or art. [34]

This serves in fact as a definition of the wild: productive power in thrall neither to formal abstraction, nor to exteriority of the rule nor to the intentional and conscious idea of the product of art. Hylozoism is wild matter, wanton synthesis and formal redundancy.[35]

A second example following from this. Take Kant. This is the official rigour of the critical philosophy in its argumentation on the subject of Hylozoism: "the possibility of a living matter is quite inconceivable". This is expanded upon only in a tautological attempt at explanation: "The very concept of it involves self-contradiction, since lifelessness, *inertia*, constitutes the essential characteristic of matter" [36] Both in the aesthetics and the teleology there is, infamously, a chaotic matter which elides with the dead, suicided, matter; and one which also displays the character of auto-induced partial formation. Aligning with Milton's warring elements of chaos and the excessive, wild paradisiac vegetation are the Kantian sublime ("War itself ... has something sublime about it" [37]) and the furthest extent of the beautiful, the English garden, Milton's model of Eden a century previously, which Kant describes as of "wild and irregular beauty nature subject to no *artificial* rules and lush in its luxuriant variety".[38]

Evidently, the baroque foliage of the critical system itself makes this no mere contradiction; and one would have to take account of many segments of the thought in order to appreciate fully the cryptoformatogenic capacity of matter: not only the arch-hylomorphism of the phenomenon/noumenon distinction, but also the succession of relative and partial codings to which the real is made to submit, from the pre-coding of sensation almost flush with the real to the part-unity of the manifold of intuition through to the theoretically illegitimate unification of the manifold of diverse concepts under reason; all under the increasing dominance of the distinction between reflective and determinant judgement. Even so, there is merit in disregarding this, and thinking rather the relative escape from subjectification performed by Milton's opening onto the cosmos, even onto the chaosmos over Kant's insertion of production into the mechanisms of subjectification. English puritanism versus German; Gerrard Winstanly and the Diggers versus Luther and Calvin -- "our religion" according to Kant.[39]

The primary action of hylomorphism thus has a presupposition. To be entirely rigorous, one. might relate this to Aristotle's distinction between remote and proximate matter. But, in general, the two types of matter, dead and alive, are ordered and distributed into a closed hierarchical series. First, matter must be prepared scientifically, to receive form. Live matter must be assassinated; a process of blanching, the induction of anaemia and iron loss. There is thus a pre-product of this process of pre-formation of matter which is the corpse of chaos. It is this that spirit, bloated with the life-blood of its victim, an impudent and necrophilic vampire, may then impregnate. Matter is justly termed the raw material for a process of production. Marx uses the term precisely to indicated this process of preparation:

If the object of labour has been, so to speak, filtered through previous labour we call it raw material ... Products are therefore not only the results of labour, but also its essential conditions.*40*

This is indeed the structure of all hylomorphic activity: pre-production; preformation; pre-product; and thus Deleuze and Guattari can say of the state that in it:

the mutilation is prior, pre-established ... the state apparatus needs pre-disabled people, pre-existing amputees, the still-born, the congenitally infirm. [41]

The capacity of form to interact with matter, precisely to form it, is predicated upon its prior disablement, and the extraction of its capacity, to be given over to form as what is now its efficacy. Limbo, the home of "all the unaccomplish'd works of nature"[41], is the most truly characteristic act of the redundant God. When the abortionists of unity are invoked at the beginning of *Mille Plateaux* it is not as a subtle degradation of the apologists of total unity who come first; but as their prior condition. The book argues later: "accidents are the result of mutilations that took place long ago in the embryo of our world" [43]

If the usurpation of activity on behalf of the agents of form is the model of production in hylomorphism; then the condition of this appropriation or capture is that of exchange. The subordination of production to exchange is what creates the possibility of the creation. Hylomorphism is never a binary operation, even if it attempts to present itself as such on occasion. There is always a *tertium quid*. And things need not stop there. Plato demonstrates that there need to be at least two mediating factors between the upper and the lower elements. Four-way machine. One could envisage five or more; in fact the necessity of C to make possible the connection between A and B may, upon sophisticated analysis, require D to effect connection between A and C; and then E for B and C. The general algorithm is potentially unlimited in extension; even if this particular structure is banal. Exchange does not just equalize difference; although part of its function is to undifferentiate. But it does this by extracting or integrating differences in intensity, and making off with the excess which can then be appropriated by form and subsequently redistributed in the singular activity of formation as extensive difference or inequality.

Thus in Marx, abstract labour not only makes possible the comparison and exchange of qualitatively or intensively differentiated concrete labour; but also generates the conditions for appropriation of surplus and redistributes inequality -- or even incommensurability -- extensively in the form of poverty between the sets of terms of final exchange under capital: capital and labour; core and periphery. Or in Kant, time as the "common form" between concept and intuition in the schematism provides a homogeneous medium of exchange between the two.

As well as this, however, it also makes possible the extraction of intensive and differential magnitudes as the (already coded) representatives of the real through their difference from pure intuitions voided of the reality of sensation - - at degree zero (Deleuze and Guattari call attention, although in a different context, to this passage from Kant in *The Anti-Oedipus*[44]). This extraction is the site of appropriation of spontaneity by the transcendental subject whose efficacy was always dependent on the real as the source of maximally free spontaneous action tending toward the intransitive. That is, it ensures the subordination of intensity to the axiomatics of the extensive through the ever present possibility of their complete evacuation. A possibility which is actualised, demanded, in the second critique, with an unprecedented and unrequited force.

Exchange and production are factors of capital. There is sense in which, like the state, capital is always there. But its factors operate at varying degrees of intensity both absolutely and relatively. Capital is nominated when one or more of its factors achyieves a threshold or breakthrough level of intensive development. What we are apt to call the rise of capitalism in the seventeenth and eighteenth centuries in Europe marks an exceptional development particularly of the factor of exchange. Smith's pin factory is rather less important to his model than the atomistic conception of the market, and its mechanisms of attempted equilibrium, which he was the first to theorize. His was the age, above all, of the market, of mercantile capital; of the radical devolopment of what Deleuze and Guattari call, though referring to its inception at an earlier stage in history, the apparatus of capture: the exchange-extraction.

The industrial revolution through the course of the nineteenth century, and primarily in Britain, marked the development of the forces of production both absolutely, and perhaps more importantly: relative to exchange. The priority of the market as the site of exchange over the site of production was reversed in the appearance of the factory, the first abstract space of generalized production. This priority has always been problematic; threatening as it does the capacity of the hylomorphic action to perform its initial manoeuvre through the mechanisms of appropriation lodged in the relation of exchange. As in Marx's model: the assumption by capital of the subject position and an automatic and increasingly intransitive productive role in the M-C-M formula is mitigated by its prior origin in the explicitly exchange-oriented formula of C-M-C which points back nostalgically to mercantile capital. The general formula for capital, and at this time predominantly industrial capital, is derived from the market.

This movement is, anachronistically, apparent in Milton. It constitutes his prophesy: his anticipation and simultaneous warding off of the future of industry. God's primary and evidently hylomorphic creation is perturbed by a Satanic production oriented toward an elemental mining operation involving:

Deep underground, materials dark and crude,
Of spirituous and fiery spume...
The originals of nature in their crude
Conception.[45]

An operation which rubs up against a pure war machine of "devilish enginery"[46]. It is the threat of this pure informal production that provokes Milton's hylomorphic God to institute the terrain of Hell over and above the residual ferocity that even an already aborted chaos is able to unleash. Over and above: Satan's bridge is therefore constructed across, over, and on top of, above chaos.[47] This is the presentation of God's success: reinstalling a means of exchange between Hell and earth effecting the capture of a new, although displaced, hylomorphic relation which obliterates chaos as the smooth space of pure transition. The creator is assigned a new function. As Deleuze and Guattari say: "The artist no longer confronts chaos, but hell and the subterranean"[48]. Milton, as commentators from Blake to Empson have suggested, stands just on this threshold between a classical God creator in communion with chaos; and a romantic Satan artist wading between earth and hell. Hell is the secondary symptom, demanding pseudo-repression: of the primary repression of chaos itself. Everyone knows that hell will come to be modelled on the family: this, the psychoanalytical unconscious, is, as The Anti-Oedipus argues, merely the symptom of a prior repression.

There is no concept of exchange in Deleuze and Guattari: "exchange" they write, "is always an appearance"[49]. Of Marx's four terms of analysis of economy in the introduction to the Grundrisse, they use only production, distribution and consumption for their tripartite Kantian schema in The Anti-Oedipus. What replaces exchange is becoming. In Deleuze's contribution to the Dialogues with Claire Parnet, he explicitly contrasts the two:

(In becoming) There is not a term from which one starts off, nor another at which one must arrive. Not any more two terms which exchange themselves ... (Instead) a single and identical becoming, a single bloc of becoming.[50]

Indeed, the whole of The Anti-Oedipus could be read as the account of the single bloc of becoming which encompasses the privileged particle-waves of primary production (connection) and the auto-production of its condition as the production of production or disjunction, which form a becoming bloc in their conjunction. This would be a very abstract reading. Nevertheless, it is through this that the attempt occurs, contra Mauss and his followers, to account for the phenomenon of pre-state or primitive exchange in a way that makes it not just a reproduction of fiscal exchange under capital. The modified marginalism which distinguishes between the limit and the threshold, makes the former part of an anticipation-prevention mechanism whose object is the transition between one assemblage or another; that is a becoming. The becoming, or the substitute for hylomorphism's presupposition of extraction-exchange, is thus the very same thing as informal activity, or the substitute for hylomorphism's production.

At the level of immanence, exchange and production are an identical activity. Nevertheless, the body without organs requires a twofold process of synthesis and analysis to operate at full intensity. It must be produced; and then it must be made to flow, or rather intensities must be made to flow across it. The idea that this can go wrong, that there can be a wedge between the production of the body and the facilitation of its flows, is new to *Mille Plateaux*. That the body may be produced, but ineptly, that there may be deterritorialization unaccompanied by any correlative reterritorialization, and yet that it may yield a permanent unproductive and blank nonfacilitation; this has no place in *The Anti-Oedipus*. The result of this ineffectuation is the empty body, the masochist body, the body without the organization of the organs and without organs. In the concluding plateau they name this possibility chaos.[51]

There thus remains a sense in *Mille Plateaux* through which the deduction of transcendent and redundant formality can still be a threat -- empty body, chaos. Not only this, but the identification of the empty body, the dead body, with a chaotic anti-formation actually reproduces an ancient ambivalence toward matter. The chaos of unformed matter, is that of dead, suicided, empty and null matter. This is nothing but a hylomorphist's wet dream.

In *The Anti-Oedipus* the distinction between on the one hand revolutionary / reactionary investments, and on the other molar / molecular investments was absolute. Perhaps it was not theorized enough; one cannot help suspecting that it served to some extent merely to site the book in a distinctive relation to George Marchais and the French Communist Party, at a time when this was still relevant, if not obligatory. But in *Mille Plateaux* it is effaced, along with the apparently simplistic Kantian vocabulary of legitimacy arid illegitimacy. Directly molecular investments can turn out bad; on the body without organs and not only on the socius. The problem is one of thinking the included disjunction of the legitimate and the illegitimate; of thinking the transcendent such that its relation to the immanent is itself one of immanence. Doubtless, they have been criticised for this; it certainly requires an ease of thought which is attained only with a type of difficulty. And

Mille Plateaux rails often enough about an over simplified dualism between good and bad; bad words for legitimacy and illegitimacy. But this distinction was never simple.

The thought of hylozoism or "technical vitalism" [52] which informs Deleuze and Guattari's critique of hylomorphism is not exactly new. Even the reverse: there are lines always and everywhere. What is new, or at least without parallel today, is that this line is presented not as a flight from something else; as an aberration. Instead, it invests entire texts, or nearly so. The Deleuze and Guattari texts are composed of an approximation to a completed aberrancy.

Notes

1. 50.
2. George Herbert's phrase in *The Church Militant* (1. 236) written during the welling Puritan emigrations from Britain in the first half of the seventeenth century.
3. Cf the discussion of classicism in *A Thousand Plateaus* trans. Brian Massumi (Minneapolis: University of Minnesota Press 1981)) p. 338.
4. Op. cit 50.
5. Freud 'The Infantile Genital Organization (An Intprpolation into the Theory of Sexuality)' in *Pelican Freud Library Vol 7 On Sexuality* p312
6. See Augustine *Confessions* 1.7 arid Aristotle *On Interpretation* 16a. Examples could be multiplied endlessly up to the Saussurian turn.
7. *Cours de Linguistique General* (Paris: Payot 1962) p. 122; a sacred reference to Ezelkiel 37:5.
8. Ibid. pp. 155-6
9. Ibid. p. 105.
10. Ibid. pp. 267ff.
11. Deleuze and Guattari op. cit. pp. 360; 427.
12. Ibid. p. 360.
13. Ibid.
14. Ibid. p. 411.

15. For the comparison between the hylomorphist wood-carving model and the hylozoist abstract machine of metallurgy cf. *ibid.* p. 40A; it is evident that even wood-carving is not actually hylomorphist.

16. p. 117.

17. See Levi-Strauss 'Introduction a l'oeuvre de Marcel Mauss' in *Marcel Mauss Sociologie et Anthropologie* (Paris; PUF 1968) p. L note 1; trans. by Felicity Baker as *Introduction to the Work of Marcel Mauss* (London: Routledge & Kegan Paul 1987) p. 72 note 17.

18. Deleuze and Guattari op. cit. p. 503.

19. l. lff.

20. *Milton Works Vol XV* pp. 15-16.

21. Book vll l. 212.

22. "The dismal situation waste and wild" Book I l. 60.

23. "Wild work in heaven" Book VI l. 698

24. Book VI l. 616.

25. Book V ll. 294-7; cited below with discussion.

26. "naked else and wild", Book IX l. 1117.

27. The vocabulary which surrounds the unfallen Eve and the outgrowth of natural forces in eden is complex: in this respect it is the fetishization of the hair which is instructive. The adjectives used both of tlie unfallen Eve's hair, and the fallen Eve's lust are "wanton' and "dishevelled" or "disorder'd" (Book IV l. 306; Book IX l. 1015; 911). There is in fact a complex of descriptives which connect with the wild(er)ness; of which wanton is the most prominent libidinal representative.

28. The whole of the scene of the Fall is discussed by Satan in the temptation in terms of the wild and wanton nature of the prelapsarian.

29. Book v ll. 95-113.

30. Book VII l. 313.

31. Book II ll. 890-920.

32. Book VII 1. 213.

33. Book VII l. 233.

34. Book V ll. 294-7.

35. Milton is a subtle example. The relation of Milton to Deleuze's destruction of hylolnorphism might be provocatively enlarged. His near heretical Socianaranism on the issue of the relative

priority of matter and God is evaded by the introduction of a certain Spinozism in his thought of God. The transitive nature of creation as such implies that the creation have material. This material cannot itself have been created prior to the creation on pain of infinite regress (although in fact Milton is content, doctrinally, to enlarge upon a number of possible regressive stages). The solution which he is finally forced to adopt is to make matter God's substance. Ultimately this is to say that God is that in which everything inheres (cf. Works XV pl. 18-19). And this is a Spinozist thought. The unspinozist and hylomorphic theory of production-creation which is necessarily grafted onto this might be fruitfully compared with the way Deleuze and Guattari graft a certain thought of production -- ultimately Kantian as The Anti-Oedipus makes clear -- onto a body without organs which is increasingly, from The Anti-Oedipus to Mille Plateaux, thought in Spinozist terms.

36. Critique of Judgement § 73

37. Ibid. § 28.

38. Ibid. § 22

.39. Critique of Pure Reason A817/B845.

40. Marx Capital VoJ 1 trans. Ben Fowkes (London: Penguin 1976) p. 284.

41. Op. cit. p. 426.

42. Milton Paradise Lost Book III l. 455.

43. p. 426.

44. The relevant passages are in the first critique: the Schematism (A137-47/B176-87) and the Anticipations of Perception (A166-76/B207-18). Deleuze and Guattari cite the latter in The Anti-Oedipus trans. Hurley, Seem and Lane (London: Athlone 1983) p 19.

45. Book VI ll. 478-9; 511-12.

46. Ibid. l. 553.

47. Paradise Lost Book X. The construction of the bridge is the most forceful example of a set of creative acts depicted in Paradise Lost which mark a prophetic romanticism in their essentially irresponsible nature. The subject of the act (Satan in this case) is not the agent of the act (Sin and Death). Perhaps the most prominent instances of this are the appeals to the muses; and hence the creation of the art-work itself. The irresponsible creation of art is a first phase of the development of the thought of active matter.

48. *Op. cit. p. 339.*
49. *Ibid. p. 439.*
50. *Dialogues (Paris: Flammarion 1977) pp. 8-9.*
51. *p. 503.*
52. *Op. cit. p. 407.*

JACK FULLER

Distillations - A premonitory reading of Deleuze

The enticement of incoherency overpowered by the necessarily superior enticement of a new coherency
- Rene Girand [1]

Reading is situated beyond or before comprehension
- Maurice Blanchot [2]

Since this voice speaks to them in private through what is properly their idiomatic feeling, their desire or their pleasure, they make it say what they want. On the other hand, you do not make the voice of reason say just anything.
- Jacques Derrida [3]

(-Always late. And soon too much. I can imagine a temporal structure whose elements are perhaps laughable. It is necessary to parody, to imagine the machine, to make or build its products. without coming too close, but already having come closer than was needed (for example to further understanding), closer than one person might want, close enough to think that one was capable, even in blindness and error, of enhancing the writing the discourse the speaking of the other one. This "other one" isn't some other isolated on the outside or beyond a door that a reading causes to appear and then open - this other is perhaps Rilke's self-as-other, or the **subject in otherhood.**

Close enough to affirm through a distant relation, whose detachment exaggerates a temporal scheme it is not too easy to leave intact and unanalysed. Unanalysed I admit it remains.

As a distillation of what a premonitory reading events, or rather enhances, what follows is, as it is defined for us, "a previous notification" which possesses - and this is what I felt

159

like following, because it never seems to want saying (in the two senses: never wanting to be said and never not, never lacking its saying- priority in "order of importance." One is led to prefer this "superior" instigation, for reasons we may imagine and theorize but which won't detain us here: one is led into a rapport with its very firstness, as it were. This instant, this "immediacy" as Blanchot will call it, I wanted to let stand-or sway as the case may be: before, in fact, any "case" as such may be made or appear to have been forming (- all by itself?). The question will arise, how are we to think this "before"?

Here we are in the presence of some thing that impends: some thing as yet "off" which is imminent and calls to our reading, or else is our reading, in that reading's outset, in its very embarcation.
What follows comes forth in drops, by distillation. I am attesting too to the wish or the hope, the prayer to be poisoned through medicine (the medicinal action of a discourse which locates the subject).)

My comments - they are nothing more, nothing propositional - will concern a dramatized tone, one that is as much mine as it is his and his and possessed accordingly, as it is theirs. (Moreover who are "they"? "Deleuze," "Guattari"-Both them and all that befalls their names, or befalls them in their names, fired back at they-in-themselves as legitimate alter egos.)
I will not attempt a staging of Deleuze's work (or presume some context proper to its disparate workings), the work of many years, either in a dramaturgical or a topographic sense. I will not situate what as yet occupies a space I would like to call *weak* or *failing*, and remains for all of this time (the time I am going to talk about first) *in waiting*.
We begin-first part (but it is a whole as anyone can see) - in the delirium of reading, in its indecision or, to be a bit more accurate, its freedom from decision, a freedom nevertheless conceding to a certain Necessity which is capitalized each time. I refer in passing to "the light, innocent yes of reading," as Maurice Blanchot has it: the "utterly happy and transparent consent (which is) the essence of reading." "Reading is the easiest thing. It is effortless liberty, a pure yes that blossoms

in immediacy."[4]

Inquiry proper, so to speak, will have begun. But only just, only in the deformity of nascent, fugitive, impossible reckonings: reckonings we cannot (p)reserve til a correct moment, an impossible coming.

Second whole part, nothing more than a set, a series of questions awaiting analysis, I call an "analytic post-script" but which far from being a post mortem begins before the first page of the first part. (As usual? I would add. Isn't this quite usual? You know: the last first... *(after is thought before)*, etc?) Situated in this mediating commentary, or approach, is a certain time sequence already remarked as troubling.

(I) VIRTUALITY, IDIOCY, PREMONITION

§ *Some writing bursts upon us.*

This moves me: Not wanting to disavow the seductive allure of an other's text-not-yet-mine, wanting, rather, to substantiate and clear a space for the pleasure, certainly, but more than this the indefensible strangeness of a text: *a reader may be predisposed merely to haunt.* (In the same way Francis Ponge has demonstrated we can haunt a painting.)

The not-yet-ness of this text, therefore, its elliptical charm (we can speak of the charm, and the grace, even the spells of a text), is what infuses a not-myself which is, despite appearances, proper to me. (It will have seemed that "I" was always me.) By way of the text's becoming, something essential to the occasion(s) of reading (an encounter which is always an occasion of appropriation, but whose initial momentum may reside precisely in what, to use Derrida's/Lacoue-Labarthe's term, desists) recedes into a night Blanchot is so often led to recall.

What is a book no one reads? Something that is not yet written. It would seem, then, that to read is not to write the book again, but to allow the book to be: written-this time all by itself, without the intermediary of the writer, without anyone's writing it. The reader does not add himself to the book, but tends primarily to relieve it of an author. And all the alacrity in his approach (in this shadow which passes so vainly over the pages and leaves them intact) everything that lends reading its superfluous appearance, including even paltry attention and lack of grave interest: all the reader's infinite lightness, then, affirms the new lightness of the book, which has become a book without an author. Now it is a book relieved of the seriousness, the effort, the heavy anguish, the weight of a whole life that was spilled out into it. It has become a book minus the sometimes terrible, the always formidable experience the reader effaces and, with providential unconcern, considers as nothing.[5]

§ *I anticipate a poisoning to come.*

To haunt the text of another? The haunting will always remain with-in the sense of extending or preconditioning - the otherness of his and her words, citing and reciting. Normally one escapes one's haunting. Only the mad imagination (artist-visionary, sinner-supplicant) haunts its own haunting: it remains, restive and inert, before what it is said to abort: interpretation, construality, sense, building. Knowing that we are prone to parasitism, one enters certain texts with this mixture of trepidation, revulsion and exhilaration.

(-The purity of the other's writing, frozen in alterity, chosen to be forgotten, activates a phantasmic visage: his text in its *beforeness* -)

To write while acquiring for one's own invisibility the other text's very RELUCTANCE; to accumulate material from the crumbs of its resisting No; to accord to the not-yet a positive role (though nothing so much as takes (its) place: where "place" indeed is not placed or on site) . . . These movements, these receptive caresses (which add up to a killing of sorts) serve no intention but spring, if we can say that, from a certain abundance of the *pre* [6] An abundance, a surplus of a kind not to be garnered.

What can we say about this non-presentable or barely present "reading", if we insist on calling by this name what is happening? May we venture the view that even in its lack or imprecision it goes some way to shaping what constitutes a proper integration? The idiotic reading (reading from, of and into one's pure(?) idiom, into what at once both suppresses and necessitates translation), this "formless"(?) reading, partial, enthusiastic [7] will perhaps lead more or less directly to patterns of acceptation and adaptation of what we can only describe as the text en route. The text on its way, in transit, becoming, arriving, receiving its determination, not least its gender.[8]

Jacques Derrida, when he is writing of a necessarily unrehearsed opening-up and onto *his* Roland Barthes: "I read the first and last Barthes, with the welcomed naivety of a desire." And later in the same piece: "I was looking for the freshness of a reading... His texts are familiar to me, but I don't know them-this is my certainty-and this is true of all writing that matters to me." All reading, with its trans-actions, translations, transferences and depositions etc., always, at a certain point, now soon now later (and perhaps at every instant), betrays the premonitory, the "fresh" sense through which, at a beginning of sorts, in the fear and lapse of the unbegun conquest, one looks alongside Barthes "for what comes *to him* and suits him, what agrees with him and fits him like a garment... (conforming) itself to the inimitable *habitus* of a unique body."[9] Certain filaments - formed by an intersecting and cacophanous variety of lines of difference, tension, accord, agglutin(iz)ation - the filaments of a nascent reading, are determined through, as they characterize, the proper. Across the spinal edge of a premonitory death, one may isolate every reading, even when the subject lives: in that certain text by Jacques Derrida on the figure and the text and the life of one Roland Barthes, a certain Barthes, one whom the reader gets only so close to before he (if "he" is and is there) disappears again, we could rename this a Text Which Is Not One. This text in fact *dis* owns its object...

The writing produced in Deleuze will have operated on the edge of a certain thought *un* (a gesture which while it is in play attempts to inscribe the naivety of an "undoing"~an unframeable doubleness, no, more: a multiplicity stretching to absurdity the wait for a hoped-for *sur* face, a shelf of paper allowing and incurring yet other, yet more fantasy: that of pure, motioning energy feeding the subject (inverse retention). The multiplicity [10] that is evoked achieves, or aims towards, untenably, a great scattering in the eyes of the One. It plays on the crumbling edifice of the "true," the "idea," "telos," "tyranny," "narrative," "force," "negation," etc. It forms a *non-representational map.*

In this writing the question at times comes down to us as an apparent freedom to opt for a restricted economy (on the one hand) or for a general economy (on the other), the latter marked by excess, expenditure and insufficiency, by motility, "flux," fluidity, in short by what stands, verily, as that which was occluded and repressed: a "feminine" economy, a "chaos" perhaps, at any rate a (new(?)) well-spring which can act as a kernel, like the psychic nucleus presupposed by psychoanalysis and therapeutics. This otherly and external thing, a something "invisible" and left absolutely (on the) "outside," Derrida rightly shows erecting itself - and this is the point - as a tomb(stone):

Of the remain(s), after all, there are, always, overlapping each other, two functions. The first assures, grounds, assimilates, interiorizes, idealizes, relieves the fall into the monument. There the fall maintains, embalms and mummifies itself, monumemorizes and names itself-falls (to the tomb(stone)). Therefore, but as a fall, *it erects itself* there. [11]

It is the overlap binding the two which we are thinking. In Sollers' "interstice." Between: *"as if__"*

Well, where is the one and (not) the other? Where is the voice of reason which Kant spews and espouses and generates (above all generates, without gender-but, alas for magisterial aloofness, always always gender[12]) in distinction from and over and above the "oracular," the idiomatic voices (always multiple, yet united: united in that sumptuous babble which whispers in the ear of the initiated), the climactic imminent deliverance of the "mystagogues" (plural - and why plural, why a band? - how to trace that?).[13]

Where is the true voice which the feminine set in motion in prisons, in that text of Genet explored and rummaged on the right side of Derrida's book? Where is the woman - Truth in texts which powerfully and alluringly establish her voice, its flows, its slipperiness? Where does this text, if it is presentable, make itself heard?

This feminine is the Other of a masculine coming to save it. I can't decide who will have saved whom in that equation; is it him, his masculine, or her feminine? and what comes next: Yes. At the very worst (which is to say without our having much considered the details betrayed by genre theories, gender theory, etc.): a mixing of the two -- perfect solution - bisexual utopia. Freedom, it seems, to range from one to the other or to attempt a mingling. Which liberates us. A reconstruction, a synthesis rather of two hitherto opposed economies.

In the encounter it should never be a case of reducing a text, as text, to the many incapacities detected within its enforced boundaries, where and whenever we make them appear: a text operates upon us by way of an immense generosity one can only affirm. And the Deleuzian text, even where it falls victim to now this and now that politics, headings, strategy, etc, is above all a text which it would prove easy to do without, or to deny, or reject as indecent or insupportable (this means untranslatable) or *wild theory*, all of which lose sight of the difficult issues put in play by such writing.

In the cascade of reductions and de- (and then re-) infinitizations, the movement is the thing for Gilles Deleuze: movement from molar to enemy [14] sweeps the reader along rails that derail, lines that snap frames. Every supra thing inside and constituting (narrating, dramatizing resistances) the text-" state appuratuses," "signs," "ideologies," "matter," and the like-appears in a dual dance with agents of disolution each one incorporates, ejects, reincorporates....Everywhere it would appear - and this os first oof all a feeling on opening *Mille Plateaux* - a certain legality (generic constraints) boxes us in. The text of Foucault has been likened to inscriptions upon a wall whose edges draw in, like the zoo-cage motif in Francis Bacon's papal anti-portraits... Concerning the purity of dis-course, which always seems self-evident in the writing of Michel Foucault - that is to say: the standing-free of categories and concepts, their *monadization,* if you like, their activation (be-cause, set or whipped into play they perform a limitational function-they put a (temporary) end to the agitations racking and delivering-forth the body - it provokes and positions bifur-cations within the text which are phrased as either-or choices. [15] And the subject is, as in a grammar, enclosed in circumscrip-tion.

In his "Fluidentity", [16] Peter M. Canning writes:

Capitalism and Schizophrenia is a writing on the body of capital. An intensely complicated matter, an entire economy of libido, work-energy is involved, implying an unconscious "geology"..... Layer upon layer of moral systems to be ex-plored carefully, with archeo-philological finesse. For each stratum is a "judgement of god" binding organ-energy to certain destinations, forecluding others, clearing pathways or blocking them, demanding the password (code), locking and unlocking passages . . . to have done with the judgement of god. To ask to be shown the desert, to form a body outside the gates of paradise (where priests never dare) - is it mad-ness?

Now it is precisely this desire for the desert which nevertheless, or perhaps essentially, with a necessary license, "forecludes," as Canning says, "certain destinations," which we will have to read and negotiate. Not least because of the desiring-machine's ineluctable *selectivity*.
But we should notice what I think Canning correclly identifies in Deleuze and Guattari's text: that it is a "geology" of a sort - a post-Foucauldian archeology. This "entire economy of the libido" runs the risk of chancing entirely and of losing all, because it proceeds by foreclusions, as Canning points out, avoids "certain destinations," locks certain "passages," gen-erally an archically disrupting its own unity, a unity it pastiches while failing.
It is in its formation of and formulations around "a body" that Deleuze's writing passes for a cartography, a redoubling of the already hysterical drive to regulate and demarcate through isolation. We need to read our reading-something I think Deleuze neglects or fails to apply with a balancing rigour.
As for "(asking) to be shown the desert," this will no doubt be analysed-and ignored, in the same blow, in accordance with

a law of reading (I mean the law which induces a stupor when we crash against thematism, the applications of this or that archetectonic interpretive scheme-with what will always seem a too-reductive psychoanalytic critique: because perhaps the truth, such as we would find it, of the writing of one Gilles Deleuze lies elsewhere, needing an obscurity such as Blanchot's to guard it within us. Some writing, as well as bursting upon us, needs to remain, with a necessary discretion, as *gesture* ... I am thinking of a certain weakness that Helene Cixous inscribes: it performs an accompaniment whose murmur escapes and re- covers itself inside the veiling noise of "communication."

It remains for us, as readers both faithful to and acquisitive of the text of Deleuze, to attempt to think this reactive schema within a social space unendingly reified and eschatologically prescribed. What remains to be thought of the oppositions of *active* and *passive*, of *movement* and *stasis*, of *irruption* and *retention*? Without according undue weight to the theoretics of gender, the gender/genre of a text (between it, him, me, you), how necessary is it that we negotiate a discursive space around (that is, in a *circum* scription) the apparent insecurities of this writing? And does it matter, that we defer a reading, on account of which, as it happens, everyone pays. And: *for what?* Clarity is always called upon in the service of someone, some group, some imagined community.

Not the first feminist criticism, [17] Alice Jardine writes: "When enacted, when performed, (the promises offered by Deleuze and Guattari's theory) are to be kept only between bodies gendered male. There is no room for women's bodies and their other desires in these creatively limited, mono-sexual, brotherly machines."[18]

This is certainly the most extravagant and marked "foreclusion" the schizoid text operated by Deleuze and his friend effects. And in certain respects its scandal, such as it is - and It "Is" where we or one finds it as such--could be analysed in terms of negations and relinquishments: I mean that it is suspect, as we say, politically and perhaps ethically, in so far as it performs an exclusion, and in as much as exclusion, under the (perhaps too-facilitating) rubric of enfranchisements and the watchful eyes of liberty and equality-giving of voices to, representations of, they who are "underdeveloped" and invisible - is a criminal, a violent act. We would perhaps miss too much of the point of a text - such as it is when we find it-if we were to invalidate it with respect to an agenda or a set of socio-political or metaphysical tenets. Even where these are noble, honourable, just, and so on.

(II) ANALYTICAL POST-SCRIPT *(Simply a question)*

- Question. About the impetus towards and identification with what I referred to as the "purity of discourse," the attention or attentiveness to the letter and the letters of the archive (by way of varying operations upon and through definitive words, word-universes), we ask: to what degree does a plurivocity such as Deleuze's, recapitulate - through a *set*, a *series* of isolable objects, moments, stages, more or less refined *instances* - and reinstate this drive in its very nudity as it were? In supplying, via pastiched scientistic analyses, an entire topography of otherwise solicitous and irrecoverable *phenomena-in-motility*, by enumerating surfaces, or forces, or the mere crumbs of a fragmented unity, through a process of extraction and dis articulation, are we not encountering here an echo restituting the subject and the object in an ancient coupling? Perhaps we can say that here the archive is *refurbished.* In Deleuze's text there is an irrefutable appetite for identification.

- Question. Is there an ideology of revenge-on-consciousness? In conformity with laws of substantiation, the suppressed is made to appear again and again. Again and again a pantomime revenge is exercised upon a increasingly frail and insupportable edifice.

- Question. In Deleuze's text, is there a tyranny of the idiom? An eternally authoritative feminine? Does the text liberate "desire"? Can this be targettable, and what would be "desire?"

- From what harbours within itself a secret, like a desire or an infinite shuddering, to the loss which usurps it for the minor, the restricted "power," as if it could be harnessed as a use-value or made to conform to a present, hoarding, saving practice, between these two is where the gift, too, operates. It can never come down. Our question: with regard to the gift (cf. Cixous, Derrida, Celan), to what degree is its hesitation, its twilight "efficacy," killed-off by a text whose desire it is to present desire? And right in the face of fathers, straight into the faces of clinic-nurses and welfare-police? To what extent is the "essential reserve" (Derrida) of the text reneged-upon by the initiation or *initialization* of a delirious cartography of thousands of plateaux, each one a shifting ice flow? To what end, finally (impossible question, impossibly crude), does such a diagrammatics lead, and with what consequences?

Giving voice to the idiom, adding it to the scales, representing intensities and flows [18] -this is what Kant/Derrida [19] make the "mystagogues" intimate: "(T)hey say they are in immediate and intimate relation with the mystery. And they wish to attract, seduce, lead toward the mystery and by the mystery." This immediate, this energetic voice (Nietzsche laughs at this, and thereafter Bataille), feminized *so strangely*, so *strange* in its otherly femininity (alien to women is it? and what is "woman" in this?), this text of the newly-voiced man conducts itself through what Derrida has called "the hermeneutic or hermetic seduction." [20] It raises the tone, says Derrida, "dominated by the oracular voice that covers the voice of reason... (causing) it to derail or become delirious." The inner is *ex* POSED, and put to play. Yet is this vertiginous play (traced and retraced, marked and unmarked, highlighted and unanchored) of the delirious text safe from a grave, a gravelly, laconic disposition? (I mean to read that word in all its senses.) That's to say: is something - something too close for a "deep" empiricism to ignore or neglect effecting-called up only to be buried, funeralized, obsequiously registered?

And then is Order not thrown over to "chaos" at such times, only: *on behalf of* order? As the recommencement of a restituting power? On the side of making-appear-and not just anyhow, but shaped, contoured, outlined in accordance with a general ruling, with naming, with titling imaginary spaces, ad other arrestments of motion?

-The Deleuzian text is one written in the shadow of a Real, a text which opposes a colossus, a reified unity it never fails to reinscribe. We are in a combat zone perpetually refreshed through countless embarcations and pseudo-insurgences.

-A giving-way (which is a granting of place perhaps), an over flowing, a explosive, ransacking flight toward unformable horizons, it is this "leap toward the imminence of a vision without concept," a liberating "poetico-metaphorical over-abundance,"[21] which comes from feelings. And feeling, we are all certain of this (with a certitude as yet only inadequately or even casually analysed), is a Paramount Value. Feeling, as the exemplary *emphatic*-what shows itself with a fully-weighted privilege (both Holderlin and Keats know about this-is precisely what needs to be thought. (But no more about that here.)

-Law of a machine: *as a machine* (which is to say in its parts) precisely to unburden and burst its unity, or rather unities, for they supersede, modify and substitute for one another as soon as an assemblage has exhausted its capacity to cohere and technify.

To burst like a machine is not to return or relapse into excitation, motility, "flow," but rather to reply with its inner feeling (Bataille's "supreme giving-way") to the supremacy of the concept.

-In Deleuze's system - yes it perhaps raises itself up as one - imminent collapse is instituted: How can "saving" be possible? On the very backbone of the possible/impossible divide, is an unbearable stress....

-Here comes everybody in an ethereal archeology, energetics of the horizonless concept.

-The Deleuzian text: isn't it a talking of everything and an everything taking? In Deleuze there may be much over which Heidegger, for example, would pass in silence. Blanchot:

Hence the strange liberty of which reading - literary reading - gives us the prime example: a movement which is free in so far as it does not submit to, does not brace itself upon anything already present.

(For:)

There is in reading, at least at reading's point of departure, something vertiginous that resembles the movement by which, going against reason, we want to open onto life eyes already close This movement is linked to desire which, like inspiration, is a leap, a infinite leap: I want to read what is, however, not written. [22]

This is perhaps how we must read the gift of Deleuze's writing. As if it were a thought stubbornly outside, feverishly nocturnal.

- To be continued

NOTES

1.   Girand on Deleuze and Guattari's writing, in: "To Double Business Bound", *John Hopkins University Press, 1978, p. 118.*
2.   *Maurice Blanchot,* The Space of Literature, *University of Nebraska Press, 1982, p. 196. All future Blanchot citations are from this book. The chapter is entitled "Reading."*
3.   *Jacques Derrida,* Glas, *University of Nebraska Press, 1986, p. 11.*
4.   *(Op. cit) ibid*
5.   *(Op cit.) p. 193.*
6.   *For a play in poetry and prose on the prevalence of the prefix "pre" (its privileges and referrals to an origin, etc.), see Francis Ponge,* The Making of the Pre, *University of Misssouri Press, 1979.*
7.   *"Reading," writes Blanchot, "does not produce anything, does not add anything. It lets be what is. It is freedom: not the freedom that produces being or grasps it but freedom that welcomes, consents, says yes, can say only yes, and, in the space opened by this yes, lets the work's overwhelming*

decisiveness affirm itself, lets be its affirmation that it is - and nothing more." p. 194.

8.   *This is precisely what the Deleuzian text is mobilized to vanquish: any eschatological reduction or even the very (anthropological) notion of settlement(s). With regard to what I attempt to cite here I recommend Derrida's varied remarks on the issue of gender determination and determinability. See for instance "Women in the Beehive: A Seminar with Jacques Derrida"* in Men in Feminism, *Alice Jardine and Paul Smith, Eds.,* Methuen, London, 1987 *and* The Ear of the Other: Otobiography, Tranference. Translation: Texts and Discussions with Jacques Derrida, *Christie V. McDonald, Ed., University of Nebraska Press, 1988.*

9.   *"The Deaths of Roland Barthes,"* in Philosophy and Non-Philosophy Since Merleau-Ponty, *H·gh J. Silverman, Ed.,* Routledge, London, 1988: *respectively, p. 262,264 ad 265.*

10.   *Multiplicity derives its fullest (its most constipated, pretend-explosive) power from a One-not-one.*

11.   *Glas, (op. cit) p. 1. (Emphasis added.) He goes on: "The other - lets the remain(s) fall. Running the risk of coming down to the same." The opposition of repressed to coherent, of madness to normalcy, affects what comes to be known (and, this is Derrida's point, encrypted thereupon) as the "libertarian," the emancipatory.*

12.   *Box for Foucault? Boxing-in limit which some texts refer the reader to perpetually. Without "meaning to," as a kind of side-effect, an unintentional, undesired echo.*

13.   *I am relating the analysis put forward by Jacques Derrida in "Of An Apocalyptic Tone Recently Adopted in Philosophy,"* (Oxford Literary Review, Vol.6, no:2, 1984). *An analysis of extraordinary suppleness, which never for a moment settles matters but rather establishes, along the ridge of the proper and philosophy's relation to the voice (to questions of equivocation/ unequivocation), the* unsettling.

14.   *I maintain that the particles and droplets, winds and atoms of this text are the "enemy" to the molar.*

15.   *In these dualities, pairings, couplings etc. the logic of the text demands that we privilege a term over its partner/opposite/ remedy. The two are involved with each other, expose and limit each other. They are infinitely two. They integrate, certainly.*

And in so doing they extend, beyond two, a still essential parallellism. Irretrievably contained in the endless play-off between the two terms, between the two-ness of term(ednes)s, whatever they may be, however they are modified in the direction of a plurality and therefore away from the dialectic, the spirit of the text is at once utterly free to choose and yet contractually bound to the springing effect (jouissance in a jar) of that liberty. It is an always suited liberty. It suits itself. It longs to be, and its longing is erotic: Reason has reached apparent dissolution of itself.

16.   SubStance *44/45, (Deleuze edition) 1984, p.35ff*

17.   *Julia Kristeva has mentioned, alludingly, ˝current attempts to put an end to human subjecthood (to the extent that it involves subjection to meaning)... proposing to replace it with spaces (Borromean Knots, morphology of catastrophes), (where) the speaker would be merely a phenomenal actualization,˝* Desire in Language, *Blackwell, Oxford, 1984, p. 280.*

18.   *˝Woman in Limbo,˝* Substance *44/45,1984, p. 59.*

19.   *Jacques Derrida, ˝Of an apocalyptic tone... ˝(op. cit.), p. 11.*

20.   *Ibid*

21.   *Op. cit., p. 12.*

22.   *Op. cit., p. 195.*

Dedicated to Fraser Goodall

BRIAN MASSUMI

Everywhere you want to be: Introduction to Fear

They Take a Licking, But They Keep on Ticking

Lynn Hill, the world's top female rock climber, fell 85 feet and landed on her tailbone after she failed to secure the knot in her safety harness. A twenty-foot fall can be fatal. Her worst injuries were a dislocated elbow and a "sore butt." Lynn is wearing a dress watch from the Timex women's fashion collection. It has a very secure buckle. It costs about $45.

Pilot Hank Dempsey fell out of an airplane at 2,500 feet when a rattling door he was checking suddenly opened. He hung onto stairs outside the plane and was inches from the runway when his co-pilot landed twenty minutes later. Hank is wearing our flight watch, the Timex Zulu Time. It has three time zones, and costs about $60.

Helen Thayer, age 52, skied to the magnetic North Pole with her dog. She pulled a 160-pound sled for 27 days and 345 miles, surviving seven polar bear confrontations, three blizzards, near starvation, and several days of blindness. Helen is wearing a very civilized watch from the Timex women's fashion collection. It costs about $40.

The most remarkable people in this world don't appear on movie screens or in sports arenas or on television tubes. They drive cabs and work in offices and operate machinery. They're just ordinary people like us who happened to have experienced something extraordinary. And survived.

Name That Fear

"We" are all survivors. "People like us." "We" have all fallen. Perhaps not from a cliff or a plane, but at least down the stairs. That can be fatal, too. We "ordinary people" confront our polar bears in the neighbour's pit bull. Our North Pole is the nearest mall. With "parking-lot crime" at "epidemic" proportions "we" might just as well make a polar expedition as hazard a run from the car to the store after sundown. "We" have all heard about the cabbie shot for small change. Even the office is a danger zone, with stress ailments a leading white collar killer. And don't the papers say that work-related accidents are on the rise? "Ordinary people like us" all experience something extraordinary at one time or another. Some, intact, do not survive. Did I say some?

BERLIN DISCO MOGADISHU MUNICH OLYMPICS
ACHILLE LAURO MCDONALD'S

In the long run, we are all dead. - John Maynard Keynes

On December 6, 1989 a lone gunman entered the University of Montreal engineering faculty. He walked into a classroom and ordered the women to one side and the men to the other. Then, screaming epithets at 'feminists," he sprayed the women with bullets. Fourteen women died in that volley and the shooting spree that followed.

The shock was palpable throughout the city. Nerves were raw. Emotions flared. There was a sense of collective mourning that seemed to leave no one untouched.

The press was quick on the uptake. Within minutes, "man"-in-the-street interviews were registering the reactions of "ordinary" people. Disbelief. "Things like that happen all the time in the United States, but never in Canada. We're just not used to it here." Incomprehension. "He was a madman." Empathy. "It could have been my daughter in there." One of the women was the daughter of the city police director of public relations, who arrived on the scene just in time to see her body carried to the ambulance. Tears.

The press loved it. In particular, the madman theory. Within minutes, TV reporters were busy piecing together a portrait of the killer. Mug-shot style photographs appeared in all the papers the next morning. A slight problem arose. The landlord, family, roommate and acquaintances, all emphasized how embarrassingly ordinary the "madman" was. A bit odd, a bit shy, never dated, but nothing anyone could remember in his past or manner prefigured the extraordinary act he would commit. For most commentators, that made the story all the more extraordinary. "It could have been my son." Who knows what lurks in the hearts of men?

The few feminists given a chance to speak in the media questioned the way in which the press had turned the event into a fifties horror flic starring the nice post-adolescent male with girl trouble mysteriously metamorphosing into a monster. What was remarkable from their point of view was not that the ordinary could conceal the extraordinary, but that the extraordinary had become the ordinary. There is only a difference of degree, they argued, between the spectacular deaths of the women at the Ecole Polytechnique and the less newsworthy deaths and injuries suffered by the thousands of women who we mentally and physically abused each year by men. There is a difference of degree, not of nature, between the terror provoked by a mass-media anti-feminist massacre and the everyday fear that has become as pervasive a part of women's lives in North America as the polluted air they breathe. Over the next twelve months, Montreal recorded the steepest rise in its history in the incidence of rape, battering, and murder by male partners.

The anniversary observances were for the most part a solemn affair. The women of the Polytechnique were now in august company. Their day of mourning fell two weeks after the seventeenth anniversary of the assassination of John F. Kennedy, one week after John Lennon's tenth, and a little more than a month before the twelfth anniversary of Martin Luther King's assassination. Now images of blood-spattered school desks joined Kennedy's famous flying skull-and-scalp fragments and the pathos of the Memphis balcony scene in framing the Christmas shopping season. Some observances were disrupted by feminist activists enraged by the way in which the media's canonization of the fourteen women had erased the specificity of their deaths and women's grief, and the social issues they raised. But it was too late. They were martyrs now. The Montreal massacre had entered the annals of media history. It was an event to be remembered. Vaguely. Blurted into the series. Like the others, all that would remain of it, in its annual re-screening, would be an aftertaste of fear and a dim foreboding of future events of the same kind. "Like the others ... of the same kind." The media event is the generic event. Broadcast as the advent of the event without qualities.

LOCKERBIE CANARY ISLANDS KAL 007

He who falls, was. - train suffer, Rio de Janeiro

Timex wearers Lynn Hill, Hank Dempsey, and Helen Thayer are extraordinary people, not because they have qualities that place them a notch above the rest of us in the chain of being, but because of something that happened to them. An event. They experienced danger, and lived to tell the story (and buy a watch). What is remarkable about them is something that befell them or in the first two cases, something they fell from. Their noteworthiness is external to them. It is not of them, but comes to them, by chance. Their personal value is a contingency, their distinguishing quality of the nature of the accident (in the case of Helen the musher, the accident avoided, in spite of her heroic self-exposure to danger).

The identity of these model consumers is defined by an external event. The event is the accident, or its avoidance. The exact nature of the accident, even whether it happened, is not terribly important. What is important is a general condition, that of being on uncertain ground. Taking the cue from Lynn and Hank's overdetermination of the experience, falling can be taken as the exemplary accident or event founding the consumers' identity. It would be more precise to say that their generic identity-their belonging to the class of remarkable peoples defined by the condition of groundlessness. Their *specific* identity is defined by a commodity and a price tag: what individuates Lynn is her fancy ("a men's dress") watch with a secure buckle ($45); Hank has a most masculine "Zulu" timepiece (he's a top earner in an exciting profession requiring multiple time zones); plain Helen has a merely "civilized" watch weighing in at a rock- bottom $40 (evidently a home-body when she's not out staring down polar bears).

Timex philosophy (axiom 1): identity is an act of purchase predicated on a condition of groundlessness.

BUDDY HOLLY OTIS REDDING JAMES DEAN JANE MANSFIELDLYNYRD SKYNYRD

Who among us has not fallen? If you haven't yet, you will- "in the end, we are all dead." The most remarkable people in this world don't appear on movie screens. They're ordinary stiffs "like us.""We" are all Lynns or Hanks or Helens. "We" are all Otis Redding and Jane Mansfield. "We" are all subsets of the class of remarkable people. "We" are Timex philosophers.

The commodity endows us with identifiable qualities. It registers our gender, social status, and character traits: buckled up and prudent but still stylish; multi-time zoned jet setter; homebodyish, with an adventurous streak. The commodity stands (in) for our existence. The ground(lessness) it stands on is the accident in its most general expression the accident-form, exemplified as downfall, the unqualified or generic founding even! Our generic identity (our subject-form, or humanity) is the generic event (the accident-form); our specific Identity (the content of which is our "individuality" or "self") is the sum total of our purchases (axiom 2). In other words, contingency is the form of identity, and identity is determined (given content) through the serial commission of the act of groundless consumption. We buy and buy, until we die. We are in free-fall, held aloft by the thinnest of credit cards. "Shop till you drop" is our motto. We know we alive or at least in a state of credit-suspended animation as long as we are shopping. "I buy therefore I am" (axiom 3). The commodity encounter not only specifies but actualizes the subject of the purchase. The subject of capitalism cannot be said to exist outside the commodity relation.

In the Vogue magazine issue in which this Timex ad is found (December 1990) there are what would seem to be an unnatural number of watch ads (fifteen). Almost all revolve around the accident or tradition. Tag Heuer warns a ski racer not to "crack under pressure." Movado exhorts us to "share the heritage," while Noblia asks that we buy an expensive watch "for our great-great- grandson". Accident and tradition as two dimensions of time are not contradictory. Fendi tells why. This mountain goat of a "timepiece" is perched on top of a craggy peak. The sky above is an ethereally white, and somewhat out-of-focus, statue of a Greek goddess. If we don't fall during our ascent up the mountain we not only become a watch owner but share in and reflect the subtle glow of cultural tradition personified (generic culture). The continuity of time hovers above the summit of the accident avoided. The seemingly smooth horizontal timeline of tradition is in fact discontinuous: the flash of a peak experience separated from others of its kind by deep ravines. To reach the next cultural high we have to descend again, then climb the neighboring summit. The mountains, of course, are price-tags. The peaks are purchases. Diachrony is an aura or optical effect emanating punctually from the purchase, as accident (avoided). The apparent continuity is the result of commodity afterimages blurring together to fill the intervals between purchases. The filler material is use-time, the time of consumption: the buyer coasts on credit to the next purchase by wearing or otherwise consuming the commodity, in combination with other commodities. Consumption is not the end, but the means. The defining experience is the peak experience. Time of consumption is a secondary extension of the prime time: buying time, the time of consummation. It is a lag-time, climbing time, during which the lingering afterglows of past ascents form interference patterns dopplering into a personal "presence" (seemingly continuous aural spectrum). The consumers identity is a mix-and-match body-specific tradition self-applied through serial purchasing. A supplemental optical effect filling the void of the accident.

The commodity is the hinge between two temporalities, or two time-forms: the primal accident-(avoidance)-form constituting the consumers generic identity or humanity; and its derivative, the personal cultural purchase tradition constituting the consumers specific identity or self. Specific identity is duplicitous, having as it does two modes, consummation and consumption, whose difference it blurs into an atmosphere of self-sameness. Generic identity, or the capitalist subject-form, is not a "synchrony" in answer to this diachrony-effect. It is neither a simultaneity nor a synthesis of successive moments. It is the complete interpenetration of two mutually exclusive tenses. The founding event is at once instantaneous and eternal. It has always already happened ("the world's top female rock climber fell"), yet persists as a possibility (don't fall, "don't crack under pressure"). The accident as advent and threat: the pure past of the sudden and uncontrollable contingency, and the uncertain future of its recurrence. Future-past. The hinge commodity, in its double modality of consummation\consumption, fills the hyphenated gap between past and future, holding the place of the present (Lynn is weaning a dress watch... it has a secure buckle... it costs ...). Buying is (our present presence). The commodity is a time-buckle, and the time-buckle is a safety belt. The consumer "good" reassures us that we are, and, traditionally, will continue to be, unfallen from our groundless peak. Buying is prevention. It insures against death.

The inevitable. We all know our time will come. But if we follow the existential imperative of capitalism - don't crack under pressure (pick the right watch, we don't have to worry about never having been. Even if we take a licking, our consumer heritage will keep on ticking. We will live on in the sparkle of our great great grandchildren's fashion accessories. Our purchasing present may vanish, but our future past will never end. We will glow on, dimly, the afterimage of the afterimage of our former ravine river presence, now stabilized into an objectified memory. We will not be forgotten (unless it is we who forget-to write a will). The future perfect-or to translate the more suggestive French term, the "future anterior" is the fundamental tense of the time-form constitutive of the consuming subject ("will have...": also readable as an imperative, the existential imperative of capitalism in its most condensed expression). "Will have bought = will have been": the equation for capitalist salvation.

What, in the Real, Takes the Place of the Possible?

"If this isn't terror, it is difficult to know what terror is," Begin said, referring to Arafat's renunciation of terror...-   Montreal Gazette, 27 March 1989

The assassination of John F. Kennedy marks a divide in American culture. It was the end of "Camelot." No longer was it possible for Americans to have a sense of oneness stretching back in time to a golden age waiting just over the next horizon for the long expected return of the citizens of progress. The far past of the founding age and the imminent future of its utopic repetition were telescoped into the instant, in the view-finder of a high-powered rifle. It was the end of mythic cultural time as the dominant temporal scheme of American society. Diachrony would never be the same.

In the immediate wake of that too-sudden event, it was still possible to believe. What many believed was conspiracy. Oswald was KGB. He was an aberration, an agent of subversion who slipped in through the cracks. The enemy, in that age of brutal "innocence," was still primarily on the outside, beyond the borders of the nation-state. The spectre of the subversive, however, had brought it closer and closer to home. The borders were as much ideological as geographical. The black lists were a constant reminder that even a red-blooded American could turn-Red all over. The Cold War was a war on two fronts. As Vietnam was soon to suggest, if the war was to be lost, it would be lost on the home front. The defeat would not be of one ideology over another. It was to be of ideology itself. The winner was not the rifleman. If there was a winner, it was the bullet. The senseless, instantaneous impact of the "will have been."

Cracks began to open all around. There was no longer any safe ground. The shot could come from any direction, at any time, in any form. Oswald's direct inheritor was not James Earl Ray, Martin Luther King's assassin. It was the gunmen in the Texas Tower, who shot passers-by at random for no reason comprehensible to the "ordinary American." The incomprehension spread. Why Watts? A rift opened between the races. What is becoming of our children? The "generation gap" threatened to undermine any possibility of cultural tradition based on shared values passed from progenitors to off-spring. Gender became a battle-field in the "war between the sexes." About that time, planes started raining from the skies. It was bad enough that Ralph Nader had already soured the romance with the car, turned killer. Even pleasure no longer felt the same. Smoking was the insidious onset of a fatal ailment. Food became a foretaste of heart disease. The body itself was subversive of the "self": in the "youth culture," the very existence of the flesh was the onset of decline, which could be slower or faster depending on the beauty products or exercise accoutrements one bought, but was ever-present in its inevitability. Industrialization, once the harbinger of progress, threatened the world with environmental collapse. Terrorists, feminists, flower children, black power militants, people who don't buckle up, guilty smokers, eaters, polluters, closet exercise resisters... Everywhere, imminent disaster.

THREE MILE ISLAND CHERNOBYL SEVESO ALASKA
BHOPAL LOVE CANAL

"We" live there. It is our culture: the perpetual imminence of the accident. Better, the immanence of the accident. Today, conspiracy theories for both JFK and King favour a domestic culprit, the CIA. "We have met the enemy and he is us" (Pogo). The enemy is no longer outside. Increasingly, the enemy is no longer even clearly identifiable as such. Ever-present dangers blend together, barely distinguishable in their sheer numbers. Or, in their proximity to pleasure and intertwining with the necessary functions of body, self, family, economy, they blur into the friendly side of life. The Cold War in foreign policy has mutated into a state of generalized deterrence against an enemy without qualities. An unspecified enemy threatens to rise up at any time at any point in social or geographical space. From the welfare state to the warfare state: a permanent state of emergency against a multifarious threat as much in us as outside.

BLACK PLAGUE SYPHILIS TUBERCULOSIS INFLUENZA CANCER AIDS

Society's prospectivity has shifted modes. What society looks toward is no longer a return to the promised land but a general disaster that is already upon us, woven into the fabric of day-to-day life. The content of the disaster is unimportant. Its particulars are annulled by its plurality of possible agents and times: here and to come. What registers is its magnitude. In its most compelling and characteristic incarnations, the now unspecified enemy is infinite. Infinitely small or infinitely large: viral or environmental. The Communist as the quintessential enemy has been superseded by the double figure of AIDS and global warming. These faceless, unseen and unseeable enemies, operate on an inhuman scale. The enemy is not simply indefinite (masked, or at a hidden location). In the infinity of its here-and-to come, it is elsewhere, by nature. It is humanly ungraspable. It exists in a different dimension of space from the human "here," and in a different dimension of time: neither "now" of progress, nor the cultural past as we traditionally knew it, nor a utopian future in which we will know that past again. Elsewhere and elsewhen. Beyond the pale of our accustomed causal laws and classification grids. The theory that HIV is the direct "cause" of AIDS is increasingly under attack. More recent speculations suggest multiple factors and emphasize variability of symptoms. AIDS, like global warming, is a syndrome: a complex of effects coming from no single, isolatable place, without a linear history, and exhibiting no invariant characteristics.

The pertinent enemy questionn is not Who?, Where?, When?, or even What? The enemy is a Whatnot?- an unspecifiable may-come to pass, in an other dimension. In a word, the enemy is the virtual.

Discovery Countdown So Smooth It's Scary - Headline, Montreal Gazette

Challenger was scary. Decisively so. But the faultless Discovery lift off? Nothing happened! Precisely the point.

Not only have the specific qualifies of the threat been superseded by the strange perpetuity of its elsewhen and the elsewhereness of its ubiquity; whether or not the event even happens is in a strange way a matter of indifference. The accident and its avoidance have come to be interchangeable. It makes little difference if the rocket goes up or comes crashing down. Not throwing a bomb will get the Palestinian nowhere. The event is by definition "scary," just as the political opponent is by definition a "terrorist".

"Scary" does not denote an emotion any more than "terrorist" denotes an ideological position or moral value. The words are not predicates expressing a property of the substantive to which they apply. What they express is a mode, the same mode: The imm(a)(i)nence of the accident The future anterior with its anteriority bracketed: "will (have (fallen))." *Fear is not fundamentally an emotion. It is the objectivity of the subjective under late Capitalism.* It is the mode of being of every image and commodity and of the groundless self-effects their circulation generates. The terms "objectivity" and "being" are used advisedly. "Condition of possibility" would be better. Fear is the translation into "human" terms and onto the "human" scale of the double infinity of the figure of the possible. It is the most economical expression of the accident-form as subject-form of capital: being as being-virtual, virtuality reduced to the possibility of disaster, disaster commodified, commodification as spectral continuity in the place of threat. When we buy, we are putting off fear and falling. Filling the gap with presence-effects. When we consume, we are consuming our own possibility. In possessing, we are possessed, by marketable forces beyond our control. In complicity with capital, a body becomes its own worst enemy.

Killer Said Mickey Mouse Took Over Husband's Body
- *Headline, Montreal Gazette, 24 Fedruary 1979*

Fear is the direct perception of the contemporary condition of possibility of being woman. If "HIV" is the presence in discourse of the ungrabbable multicausal matrix of the syndrome called AIDS (its sign), fear is the inherence in the body of the ungraspable multicausal matrix of the syndrome recognizable as late capitalist human existence (its affect).

Dress Rehearsal for an Even Darker Future

Was Discovery scary because Challenger was a premonition of (desire for?) an even worse accident the possibility of which the next launch reminded us? Was it scary because we saw in Challenger our future-past the eternal return of disaster?

Or on the contrary, was the none event of Discovery the "darker future" for which the Challenger crash was a "dress rehearsal"? A future that was to be the TV present of image-consumers attracted to satellite-beamed lift-off like flies to a live media corpse.

Which is more frightening: the future-past of the event or the present of consumption? The accident or its avoidance?

1789 1848 1871 1917 1936 1968 1977 1987 1929

The tradition of the oppressed teaches us that the "state of emergency" in which we live is not the exception but the rule. We must attain to a conception of history that is in keeping with this insight. - Walter Benjamin , Illuminations (257)

John Maynard Keynes believed in equilibrium. His economic philosophy was marked by two events: 1917 and 1929. Two crises, one striking capitalism from the enemy outside, the other a self-propelled "crash." The Keynesian wager was to exorcise both threats worker revolution and industrial overproduction—by internalizing them into the ordinary, everyday functioning of capital. Social equilibrium was to be attained by integrating the working class, giving it a measure of decision-making power through collective bargaining and legal strikes: the recognition and institutionalization of the union movement. Economic equilibrium was to be accomplished by increasing demand to meet supply, through Fordism (the principle that workers should earn enough to buy the products made with their labour) and welfare (enabling even the unemployed to participate in the economy as buyers). In return for this universalization of the right to consume, the workers would agree to safeguard management profits by increasing their productivity apace with their wages. Capitalism with a human face: everybody happy, busily banking or consuming away.

The internalization of the two catastrophic limits of capitalism worked, after a fashion. Yet equilibrium proved elusive. Part of the problem was that the integration of the working class involved translating what were fundamentally qualitative demands (worker control over the labour process and collective ownership of the means of production) into quantitative ones (raises and benefits; Alliez and Feher, 320). The success of this strategy meant that unfulfilled qualitative expectations were automatically expressed as escalating quantitative demands which soon outstripped increases in productivity. The response from management to this new threat to profit was to regain productive momentum through automation. But to do so was to fall into a classic trap of capitalist economics described by Marx as the law of the tendential fall of the rate of profit (the higher the proportion of fixed capital, or equipment, to variable capital, or "living" labor, the lower the profit rate over the long run). A complicating factor was that several decades of accelerating production and increased consumer spending had already come close to saturating domestic markets.

By the late 1960s, another crisis point was being reached. Not only was management losing all patience with the now chronic profit problems flowing from the Keynesian social contract, but workers and consumers, glutted with commodities, were becoming less willing to content themselves with quantitative expectations. Demands were being retranslated into 'quality of life' issues that were in some respects more radical than the classical communist concerns with workplace control and ownership of the means of production: the very concept of productivity, the industrial model of production, and even the institution of work itself were called into question in the sudden wave of revolt that spread across the globe in 1968 -1969, continuing into the 1970s and in some countries (most notably, Italy) almost to the end of that decade.

According to Antonio Negri (1988), the 1970s and 1980s saw a radical reorganization of capitalism. The self-proclaimed 'humanism' of the integrative strategy of the Keynesian era was abandoned for often unapologetically ruthless strategies of displacement, fluidification, and intensification that once again averted both social revolution and selfgenerated collapse.

Displacement: Large segments of industrial production were exported to the "Third World," where growing (if still minute in terms of percentage of population) middle classes provided much-needed market outlets for consumer durables. A coinciding move realigned the economies of the "centre," shifting their emphasis from durables to intangibles: information, communication, services (the 'tertiary sector'). This move into new and largely ununionized domains undermined the power base of the institutionalized labour movement, freeing capital from onerous collectively-bargained contracts and constraining government regulation. The new jobs created were overwhelmingly part-time, or if full-time 'unguaranteed' (unprotected by seniority systems, affirmative action agreements, etc.). Employment for growing numbers of people became precarious, regardless of class. Many professionals (especially baby boomers newly arrived on the job market, and older professionals less able to adapt to the new technologies and super-competitive atmosphere) lived in few of falling into the middle class, which was itself on a precipice overlooking the "permanent underclass" created by the partial dismantling of the welfare state. For the underclass, it was not only employment that had become precarious, but life itself, as infant mortality and murder rates soared and life expectancy declined. The abandonment to conditions of extreme hardship of the predominantly nonwhite urban poor constituted a final displacement: the "Third World" transposed into the heart of the "First World."

Fluidification: These displacement strategies had the combined effect of increasing the fluidity both of the work force and of capital. The employed were more easily dismissed, retrained, or transferred; the un- and underemployed provided a pool of potential labour that could be dipped into as needed. Investments could more easily be shuffled from region to region or sector to sector. The commodification of information and services meant that it was not only new products that were entering circulation; the means of producing new products themselves became products (computer programs, design systems, management consulting, etc.). Product "turnover" was now concerned as much with moving from one product to the next as with moving units of the same product. This was the economy's way of responding to the retranslation of social demands into qualitative terms. Qualitatively new products would be created almost instantaneously to fill any perceived need or desire. A new glut: of the qualitatively new. Response: market the qualitativeness of the qualitatively new - sell 'image.' What was marketed was less and less a product designed to fulfill a need or desire than an image signifying fulfillment and the power to fulfill. The adjective of the eighties was 'power' (as in "power lunch"). Use-value was overshadowed by fulfillment effect, or image-value. Images, the most intangible of intangible products, circulate faster than uses. Turnover time was reduced to almost nothing. New products could be marketed as fast as styles could be created or recycled.

Intensification: With the advent of the power lunch, eating became a productive activity. What was formerly in the realm of 'reproduction' entered the sphere of production. The distinction between 'unproductive' and 'productive' labour has become entirely obsolete. "Culture," for example, is a source of capital. Even those in the 'underclass' are 'productive workers' to the extent that they invent new styles that are commodified with lightning speed for 'cross-over' audiences. Education has become more and more explicitly a matter of professional training, though often of a nonspecific kind. If 'liberal' education is back in vogue, it is likely because versatility of thought and character have become necessary survival skills in the super-fluid work/consumer world, rather than for any inherent value it may have. 'Leisure' has disappeared. With the advent of people-meters, switching on the TV has become tantamount to punching a time card for a marketing company. Keeping up with the 'avant-garde' music scene is often a question of image-building to enhance one's personal saleability or, for the growing number of workers in the 'culture industry,' direct market research. Time spent off the job is dedicated to 'self-improvement,' most often oriented toward increasing one's competitiveness in getting or keeping a job, or improving one's health to live long enough for a raise. It is just as well that image-value has replaced use-value - no one has time anymore to enjoy the fruits of their labor. A state-of-the-art stereo system is more a promise of consumption than its realization. People who have managed to stay employed work harder and harder to buy more and more impressive gadgets they no longer have the time to use. What buyers buy are images and services directly implicated in production, or consumer durables that no longer represent anything but the continually deferred promise of enjoyment. The commodity has become a time-form struck with futurity, in one of two ways: as time stored (in an object of perpetually future use) or as time saved (a productivity enhancer optimizing future activity; Alliez and Feher, 351). The two futurities join in a buckle: increase productivity in order to save time and thus earn more in order to buy more objects with which to store the time saved by being more productive in order to buy more objects...

Time is everything, man is nothing; he is at most the empty carcass of time. - Karl Marx

Image-building, self-improvement: what we buy is our selves. Time saved equals time stored: in buying ourselves we are buying time. Once again, the subject of capital appears as a time-form: a future (fulfillment) forever deterred (signified) buckling back with accelerating velocity into an 'having been' (productive). This is the same absenting of the present by the future-past as established by Timex philosophy. Here, the formula of the future-past has been arrived at from the angle of work (the wage relation) rather than that of consumption (the commodity relation). When reproduction becomes productive, the commodity relation and the wage relation converge. They become formally identical and factually inseparable. If the commodity is a hinge between the future and the past, the subject-form with whose empty present it coincides is a hinge between the two axes of the capitalist relation. The subject of capital is produced at the point of intersection of the wage relation and the commodity relation. It is that intersection, the point at which lived space is temporalized and temporality capitalized. 'Capitalization' means 'potential profit.' All of existence is now subsumed by the capitalist relation. Being has become surplus-value: the capitalist expression of the virtual.

The growth in the information, image, and service markets constitute a second axis of capital expansion. Answering to the extensive expansion of industrial production and consumption to the "Third World' is an intensive expansion of the capitalist relation at the "centre," where it becomes coextensive with life. And death. Producing oneself through consumption has its dangers, particularly when the consumption is of cultural images, so free-flowing and seductive. Dangerous it is, but not abnormal.

Roseann Greco, 52, of West Islip, was charged with second-degree murder for killing her husband, Felix, in their driveway in 1985. She insisted at the time that the cartoon character had taken over her husband's body. Roseann Greco was found mentally competent to stand trial.

ROADRUNNER COYOTE MICKEY MOUSE FLINTSTONES
SIMPSONSTEENAGE MUTANT NINJA TURTLES

It is simplifying things to say that capitalism has internalized its two catastrophic limits. At first glance, the formulation is incomplete, because capitalism has internalized other limits as well: its extensive expansion has internalized the boundary between the 'First' and 'Third' worlds; its intensive expansion has internalized the boundaries between the reproductive and productive, commodity circulation and production, consumption and production, leisure and work, even life and death, for example when what is sold is 'health' or when death thumbs a ride on a consumed image turned all-consuming (Mickey). But ultimately, it is the notion of 'internalization' that proves inadequate. For if the capitalist relation has colonized all of geographical and social space, it has no inside into which to integrate things. It has become an unbounded spawn other words, a space coextensive with its own inside and outside. It has become a field of immanence (or exteriority). It has not 'internalized,' in the sense of 'integrating'; it has displaced and intensified, coaching mutually exclusive forms into uneasy coexistence. The 'Third World' meets the 'First World' in the South Bronx. The future meets the past in a Timex watch. No dialectical synthesis has been reached. Capitalism has not after all internalized, or overcome in any way, its two catastrophic limits, social revolution and collapse on the heels of overproduction.

Social revolution has already come, and keeps coming, in the form of accelerated systemic change and, for some in society, as the possibility of breaking free from disciplinary and normative institutions and inventing a self as if from scratch. But that self is invented in and through the commodity. Social revolution comes, but its coming is pre-capitalized. It coincides absolutely with its own 'appropriation' (self-turnover). Extreme change accompanied by utter conservatism: a possible definition of 'postmodernism.' (If 'postmodernism' is so 'radical,' why do people go on behaving as if nothing happened? Why are men still men, and whites still racist? Explain the resurgence of the traditional wedding. Explain baby boomers making a baby boomlet and returning with their spawn to church. Everything happened, but nothing seems to have changed.)

The overproduction/depression cycle, for its part, has been compacted into the perpetual menace of 'stagflation' (the inflation associated with oversupply together with the economic stagnation characteristic of depression), relieved only by interludes of dangerously rapid deflation. Precariousness is by no means limited to employment. Capital has been as fluidified as labour. Corporations die and are born with lightning speed. In the eighties, fortunes were made with corporate takeovers and dismantlings, and through trading in debt (junk bonds). Unprofitability was made profitable. The inability to compete fueled competition. The effects of the tendency of the rate of profit to fall could be avoided by the adroit money manager through the simple mechanism of continually turning over capital rather than commodities. The crisis of production has been made productive by inventing ways in which the circulaton of capital can create surplus-value. No longer is Keynes's goal of 'protecting the present from the future' of catastrophe the guiding principle of economics (Negri, 1988:25). The trick is instead to figure out 'how to make money off the crisis.' The classical problem of the capitalist cycle, or the inevitability of periodic economic collapse, has been solved - by eternalizing crisis without sacrificing profits. The future-past of the catastrophe has become the dizzying ever-presence of crisis. Capitalism has spun into free-fall, held aloft by the thinnest of Savings and Loans. In the crash of '29, capitalists jumped from high ledges. In the crash of '87, they didn't, because the notion that equilibrium was attainable or even desirable had already gone out the window. Being on the brink is now as 'normal' in money matters as the courts appear to think being unbalanced is in subjectivity. Just as insanity is no longer necessarily incompatible with being judged mentally competent to stand trial, insolvency is no longer necessarily incompatible with being judged financially competent to turn a profit.

NEIL BUSH

The policeman isn't there to create disorder, the policeman is there to preserve disorder.
-Former Mayor Richard J. Daley of Chicago

There is an identity between the destitute train surfer in Rio de Janeiro and the Wall Street financier. Both we defined by the statement, "he who falls, was." For both, the subject-form is the accident-form. There is an identity between them to the extent that the capitalist relation has expanded its reach to every coordinate of socio-geographical space-time. Their identities are joined in the ecumenism of the capitalist economy that subsumes them both, along with everyone and every thing on earth and in orbit.

Yet there is at the same time an undeniable difference between them. Capitalists put their money on the line; train surfers, their bodies. Capitalists may indirectly risk their lives to stress-related ailments, but their immediate threat is no worse than bankruptcy. Although the subjectivity of the capitalist and of the member of the underclass are both determined by the intersection of the wage relation and the commodity relation, they are determined by them in radically divergent ways: the former by what kind of access he/she has to them, the latter by her/his exclusion from them. Those excluded from the capitalist relation incarnate its form directly in their bodies: they fall, they were. They are not remembered. Since they do not have access to capitalized presence-effects, they cannot fill the gap. They directly embody the ungraspability of the capitalist present: disaster. North American ghetto dwellers are in a similar position that is different again: they have access to the commodity relation, and can therefore create presence-effects with gold and gait, but since the wage relation is closed to them they must commodify themselves in ways that are just as apt to earn them an early death as clinging to the tops of trains (drugdealing and other criminalized forms of unsalaried capitalist endeavor).

The capitalist relation produces a subjective sameness, but not without creating differences. It does not unify without dividing. This statement, and the many like it in the preceding pages, is not a dialectical contradiction begging for synthesis. Neither is it a paralogism or logical paradox. It is a *real coincidence*. It was argued above that the limits of capitalism have become immanent to it. This does not mean that boundaries have simply broken down. They have been made to coincide really, in *virtuality*): every boundary is really, *potentially* present at every space-time coordinate. No particular boundary is *necessarily* in effect at a given time. Nothing in principle prevents a black from the South Bronx from getting a job, or even becoming a big-time capitalist (a few rappers have done it). The accident-form that is the subject-form is the form of the virtual, pure potential: in principle, it has no limits. In practice, it does. *Boundaries are effectively set in the move-ment from "principle" to "practice," in other words in the actualization of the subject-form.*

Another way of putting it is that the generic identity of the subject of capital is a global form of infinite possibility, but that it cannot come into existence without alienating its form inde-terminate content, in specific identities whose presence-effects are necessarily limited and divergent. A specific identity is defined by whether or not a given body is allowed access to the wage relation and the commodity relation, and if so in what way (how will it be self-consuming? what kind of pres-ence-effects will it produce? what peaks will it climb?). There is an entire technology dedicated to determining the divergent limits of specific identity based on age, gender, sexual prefer-ence, race, geography, or any number of such socially-valor-ized distinctions. Foucault's "disciplinary" institutions and "biopower" and Baudrillard's "testing" procedures (market-ing feedback loops between production and consumption that make the relationship between the product and the needs or desires it supposedly fills a pomo update of the chicken and the egg riddle) are examples of just such appara-tuses for the actualization of the subject-form of capital. There is no contradiction between the different kinds of apparatuses of actualization. They coexist quite comfortably. There is a kind of nonexclusive triage of bodies. Bodies are selected, on the basis of certain socially-valorized distinctions, for priority access to a certain kind of apparatus. African-American men, for example, are favoured for prison and the army on the basis of their skin colour. Women of all races are favoured for biopower on the basis of gender: the medicalization of child-birth and social engineering of the child-rearing responsibili-ties women still disproportionately bear. Priority access to one apparatus of actualization does not necessarily exclude a body's selection by another. The same body can, inevitably is, selected for different apparatuses successively and simultane-ously. Prison follows school follows family. Each of these disci-plinary institutions is penetrated by varying modes of biopower and testing. A black woman's bodily functions are medicalized and at the same time prioritized for disciplinary institutions. Generic identity is the coincidence of functions that may in practice prove mutually exclusive (capitalist and worker, pro-ducer and consumer, criminal and banker) - but then again may not. Specific identity involves a separation of functions in their passage into practice, sometimes but not necessarily with a view to exclusivity, often for mixing and matching. The result is a complex weave of shifting social boundaries. The bounda-ries are not barriers; they are not impermeable. They are more like filters than walls. A black from the South Bronx may be-come a big-time capitalist. But the chances are slim. Bound-ary-setting or the separation/combination of social functions through a triage of bodies based on valorized distinctions works less by simple exclusion than by probability.

The apparatuses of actualization governing this process are power mechanisms. Power is not a form. It is not abstract. It is the movement of form into the content outside of which it is a void of potential function, of the abstract into the particular it cannot be or do without. It is the translation of generic identity into the specific identities outside whose actualization it does not exist, of humanity into the selves comprising it. Not a form, but a mechanism of formation; not a being, but a coming to being; a becoming. Neither generic nor specific. Power is as ever-present as the subject-form and as infinitely variable as its selves. It is neither one nor the other, and nevertheless not indeterminate. It has definable modes, like the three just mentioned, which are distinguished by the kinds of functions they separate out for actualization in a given body (by the kind of socially recognizable content they give a life). Power mechanisms can also be defined, perhaps more fundamentally, by the temporal mode in which they operate. They may seize upon the futurity of the future-past, in which case they can be characterized as strategies of surveillance: on the look-out for the event. Or they may seize upon its dimension of anteriority, in which case they are *statistical* and *probabilistic*: analyze and quantify the event as it happened. The past tense in the Timex ad went along with a fixation on numbers: 85-foot fall, 2,500-foot altitude, inches from the runway, 25 minute flight before landing, aged 52,160-pound sled, 27 days and 345 miles, three blizzards... Mechanisms of surveillance and of statistical probabilization buckle into prediction. A power word for prediction is deterrence. Deterrence is the perpetual co-functioning of the past and future of power: the empty present of watching and weighing with an eye to avert. It is the avoidance of the accident on the basis of its past occurrence. It is power turned toward the event: in other words, as it approaches the subject-form, the virtual.

Power under late capitalism is a two-sided coin. One side of it faces the subject-form. On that side, it is deterrence. Deterrence by nature determines nothing (but potential: the potential for the multiform disaster of human existence). On the other side, power is determining. There, discipline, biopower, and testing give disaster a face. They bring specificity to the general condition of possibility of deterrence by applying it to a particular found body. They give a life-form content. A self is selected (produced and consumed). The in-between of the subject- form and the self, of the generic identity and specific identity-the come and go between deterrence and discipline/ biopower/testing, between the virtual and the actual - Is the same intensive and extensive terrain saturated by the capitalist relation. Power is coincident with capital as social selection and probabilistic control (Deleuze 1990). Power is capitalization expressed as a destiny. But in this post equilibrium world of deterrence in which the accident is always about to happen and already has, disorder is the motor of control. And destiny in the final analysis is only the necessity of chance: the inevitability of the event, the evanescence of consumptive production, a life spent, death.

The act of purchase constitutive of the capitalist self seemed, from the view of the commodity relation alone, an unfettered act of consummation/consumption. It now appears to be universally determined as to its form, at the intersection of the commodity relation and the wage relation. The wage relation may impose exclusions, and always dictates a forced translation or accompanies a retranslation of perceived needs and desires. Power mechanisms specify the translation, or give subjective form socially recognizable content, in a basically probabilistic way. What we call "free choice" is a layering of different social determinations on the foundation of a necessary subject-form, the accident-form, which is the form of chance. The syndrome of the self is the product of a functional coincidence between free "play" (free-fall, the absence of solid qualities) and multiple determinations of evanescent content (concretized precariousness; turnover).

The functional coincidence of freedom and determination is an ontological alienation. The subject-form is only at the price of alienating itself in content. "We" cannot realize our unity without in the same stroke being divided. Power under late capitalism is a state of continual warfare against an elusive enemy that is everywhere "we" are. Our "self" determination is deterrence incarnate, the actualization in our bodies and our selves of the immanence of the unspecified capitalist enemy.

If the capitalist economy is indeed a war economy, only able to proceed by an always more advanced and intense colonization of terrestrial space, it must be recognized that this economy implies an administration of the prospective terror which radically modifies this space. In order to make fear reign a space of fear must be created; the earth must therefore be rendered uninhabitable. The appearance of habitats was a defense, a first form of resistance to colonization. Their current

destruction no longer leaves them with more than their function as a refuge, a hiding place. Now, it is not solely by means
of 'flows of stupidity' that the State produces this fear with
regard to space, but by rendering space truly, biologically
uninhabitable.
- Jacques Donzelot, "An Anti-Sociology"

Replace "terrestrial space" with "cultural space," "earth"
with "city," "habitat" with "neighbourhood," and "biologically" with "socially" and we are back at the Montreal
massacre. Capitalist power actualizes itself in a basically uninhabitable space of fear. That much is universal. The particulars
of the uninhabitable landscape of fear in which a given body
nevertheless dwells vary according to the socially valorized
distinctions applied to it by selective mechanisms of power
implanted throughout the social field. Ah urbanized North
American woman dwells in a space of potential rape and
battering. Her movements and emotions are controlled (filtered, channeled) by the immanence of sexual violence to
every coordinate of her socio-geographical space-time. The
universal "we," that empty expression of unity, inhabits the in-
between of the gunman, his victim, and the policeman. "We"
are Marc Lepine, at the same time as "we" are the fourteen
women of the Polytechnique, and the police official whose
daughter has just died. "We" are every subject position.
"We" extraordinary ordinary people are men or women without qualities, joined in fear. "She," however, has regular
qualities, a 'privileged' specific identity, a predictable function: victim. Capitalist power determines being a woman as
the future-past of male violence.

Now, that could be the Montreal massacre. But then again it
could also be Twin Peaks. Hard to tell.

The "flow of stupidity" in contemporary society consists in the
translation of the "she" to the "we," of everywoman to everyone: a
loss of the specifity of the landscape of fear. It is a re-virtualization of
the already-actualized accident, its re-coinciding with its own variations. It is a retranslation, of content back into form. A com-
modity-form, of course: the media image in its perpetual self-

turnover. The mass media, in their "normal" functioning, are specialized organs for the inculcation of stupidity. Stupidity is not a lack, of information or even of intelligence. Like fear, it is an objective condition of subjectivity: a posture. Stupidity is the affect proper to the media, the existential posture built into the technology of the broadcast apparatus and its current mode of social implantation. It is the inherence in the buyingviewing body of the despecification of intellectual content. A viewer is stupefied to the extent she or he fails to counteract that in-built posturing (through humour, cynicism, appropriation, anger, zapping...). Uncountered, the media's serial transmission of frightful images results in a loss of detail in the who? what? when? and where? This blur-treatment is not restricted to women. It is applied to all specific identities, with variations depending on a limited range of particular characteristics that persist in the vocal and visual residue of the broadcast body: often skin colour and gender (but not always: Michael Jackson); sometimes nationality, age, or profession.

The media affect - fear-blur - is the direct collective perception of the contemporary condition of possibility of being human: the capitalized accident-form. It is the direct collective apprehension of capitalism's powers of existence. It is vague by nature. It is nothing as sharp as panic. Not as localized as hysteria. It doesn't have a particular object, so it's not a phobia. But it's not exactly an anxiety either; it is even fuzzier than that. It is low-level fear. A kind of background radiation saturating existence (commodity consummation/consumption). It may be expressed as "panic," or "hysteria," or "phobia," or "anxiety." But these are to low-level fear what 'HIV' is to AIDS. They are the presence in the discourse of the self of the condition of possibility of being the mediatized human victim we all are in different ways: signs of subjectivity in capitalist crisis. The self, like AIDS, is a syndrome, one with a range of emotional cripplings rather than a range of diseases as its symptoms.

JOHN LENNON JFK MARTIN LUTHER KING ANWAR SADAT
INDIRA GHANDI (RONALD REAGAN)

The emotional organization of a given fear-riven self is a particular limited and divergent actualization of the subject-form: the socially meaningful expression of the "individuality" of the specific identity attached by power mechanisms to a found body. Emotions and the character types they define are the specific social content of the few-affect as the contemporary human equation. They are derivatives of that equation: secondary expressions (in the mathematical sense) of capitalist powers of existence. Character is the derivative of a power equation. It is power determined, as presence-effect. Emotional makeup is the face power turns toward the predictably unbalanced, saleably empty content of an individual life (serialized small-scale capitalist crisis). Life's a soap -when it's not a disaster with your name written on it.

JOHN HINCKLEY CHARLES MANSON HILLSIDE STRANGLER
MARKCHAPMAN

Personalized stationery is one of the small but truly necessary luxuries of life. - Ted Bundy, mass murderer

The mass media works to shortcircuit the event. It blurs the event's specific content into an endless series of "like" events. (Stupidity may also be defined as perception and intellection restricted to a recognition reflex; difference subordinated to an a priori similarity-effect.) "Like" events rush past. No sooner does one happen than it is a has-been. The who? what? when? and where? become a what-not? ('anything can happen') and what's next? ('what is this world coming to?'). Retrospective analysis is replaced by a shudder and a shrug, memory quickly elided by expectation. Broadcast is a technology of collective forgetting. It is not that the event is lost. On the contrary, it is accessible for immediate recall: instant replay. Broadcast (in a widened sense, including the mass circulation print media) is the tendential supplanting of individual memory and introspection by collective technologies of storage and screening.

The externalization and objectification of memory and the infinite repeatability of the event distances cause from effect. The event floats in media-suspended animation, an effect without a cause, or with a vague or cliched one. Thus the Montreal massacre becomes an opportunity to explain away men's violence toward women as the sudden onset of an individual case of "madness." A threat can be easily displaced, as has been the case during the AIDS crisis, which evoked hysterical and socially damaging reaction from precisely those groups least at risk (for example, straight non-intravenous-drug-using nonhaemophiliac white males like Jesse Helms).

The jarring loose of cause and effect does not, as has often been argued from a Baudrillardian perspective, make power mechanisms obsolete. Quite the opposite, it opens the door for their arbitrary exercise. The media-induced public conviction during the early to mid-1980s that violent crime throughout America was rising at epidemic proportions (despite statistics to the contrary, also reported in the media) enabled Ronald Reagan to expand police powers beyond anything Richard Nixon could have dreamed of. The collective difficulty with attributing cause opens the way for even the most seemingly archaic of disciplinary institutions to expand their arena. Even the family made a comeback in the eighties, in reaction to a panoply of dangers from child abduction to pornography to STDs. The early eighties obsession with child abuse and abduction (remember milk cartons?) is especially instructive. The facts that the overwhelming majority of abusers are family members and that 98% of kidnapped children are taken by their fathers did not prevent the "crisis" from being used to "defend the family" (whatever that might mean, in the era of the one-person household and single parenthood). As if "the family" weren't part of the problem. The enemy is not "out there." Once again, "we" are it.

The media shortcircuiting of the specificity of the event opens the way for mechanisms of power to reset social boundaries along roughly historical lines. In other words, in favour of traditionally advantaged groups (whites, males, heterosexuals). It is only an apparent contradiction that these are the very groups in the best position to profit from the socioeconomic fluidity of late capitalism. fluidity and boundary-setting are not in contradiction, for two reasons. First, the boundaries themselves are as easily displaceable as the perception of risk. "The family" is a code word for an immensely complex set of laws, regulations, charity campaigns, social work, medical practices, and social custom that varies locally and is under constant revision. The boundaries of "the family" fluctuate as welfare, abortion, and tax laws change, as church influence and temperance movements rise and recede ... "The family"-any bounded social space-simply does not exist as an effectively self-enclosed, self-identical entity. 'Bounded' social spaces are fields of variation. The only thing approaching a structural invariant is the high statistical probability that wherever the boundary moves, the (im) balance of power will move with it (the advantaged group will stay advantaged, in one way or another). The second reason is that the nature of the "boundary" has changed. The individual is defined more by the boundaries it crosses than the limits it observes: how many times and with whom has one crossed the boundary of the family by growing up, getting married/living together, and divorcing/breaking up? how many times has one been in and out of prison, and for what? how does one negotiate the everyday yet elusive distinction between work and leisure? how many jobs or professions has one had? how many sexual orientations? how many "looks"? how many times has one gone from consumption to self-production by buying to be? The self is a process of crossing boundaries. The same could be said of the state. Wth the transnationalization of capital and the proliferation of world trade and political organizations (IMF, World Bank, World Court, UN, EEC, US-Canada free trade) a state is defined at least as much by the way in which it participates in processes greater than itself-one of which exercises full sovereignty over it, or "encloses" it In an all encompassing higher power on the nineteenth century nation-state mode-as by the way it exercises its own brand of partial sovereignty over processes smaller than it (in the US, domestic apparatuses of power operating on a "checks and balances" principle). The generalization of the capitalized accident-form has virtualized the boundary, which now exists less as a limit than an immanent threshold. Every boundary is present everywhere, potentially. Boundaries are set and specified in the act of passage. The crossing actualizes the boundary - rather than the boundary defining something inside by its inability to cross. There is no inside, and no outside. There is no transgression. Only a field of exteriority, a network of more or less regulated passages across thresholds. What US president will not push the jurisdictional limits of the executive branch? Particularly as regards war powers. What country will the US not invade if it sees fit? And what country invaded by the US will not open the war on the US home front through the threat, implied or stated, of terrorism? The borders of the state are continually actualized and reactualized, on the domestic side by constant fluctuations in jurisdiction, and internationally by regular flows of people and goods (customs and trade regulations) and exceptional flows of violence (invasion, terrorism).

This will not be another Vietnam. - George Bush

The capitalist relation cannot unify without at the same time dividing. It cannot optimize and globalize the capitalized flow of people and goods without producing local rigidifications. It cannot fluidify without concretizing here and there, now and again. It was inevitable that the end of the Cold War and the opening of the "Soviet bloc" to the world capitalist economy would multiply regional "hot" wars. The political-economic expression of the capitalist accident-form (generalized deterrence) cannot actualize itself without simultaneously alienating itself in the often horrendous content of a local disaster. The immense but geographically specific destruction accompanying the "Gulf Crisis" was motivated by the deterrence of another crisis, global in scale (an oil crisis). For this round, the military got media-wise. Photos of mangled bodies were not allowed. No pictures of body bags, or even coffins: reporters were banned from the port of Dover, where the fallen defenders of Texaco landed on their way to eternal rest. No casualty counts. No un-"pooled' reports from the front. The event was strangely absent in its ever-presence. Everyone was held in continual suspense: will war break out? will Scuds be launched against Israel? will Iraq use biological or chemical weapons? will the ground war begin? will US troops push on to Baghdad? Speculation, expectation. When something did happen, it failed to make an impression because images and information were not immediately forthcoming, and when they did come the actual event paled in comparison with all the things reporters have established could have happened. Scuds hit Israel, but they carried no chemical warheads and casualties were light. Relief. Before we knew what hit, we were waiting for the next blow. The myriad mini-events that make up a war hardly registered. The war was systematically transformed into a nonevent as fast as it happened. Future-past: expectation-relief. The present of flowing blood neatly elided. Tens of thousands die, as if abstractly, their suffering infinitely distanced, their lives doubly absented, once by the fall of a bomb, again by their pain and anguish failing to register in the collective perceptive apparatus of the enemy. In an antiseptic war, relief quickly turns to boredom. It happened, it all happened, but nothing changed. The unthinkable came, and we were bored. George Bush could only benefit by that. After all, he is boredom personified. The popularity of the "killer wimp" crests.

KOREA DOMINICAN REPUBLIC VIETNAM GRENADA LIBYA PANAMA IRAQ

There will be more Vietnams. Any number of them, in any number of guises. Crime "war," drug "war," "battle" for the family... Wherever there is a perceived danger, there is deterrence; wherever there is deterrence, there are immanent boundaries; and wherever there are immanent boundaries, there is organized violence. For having boundaries that are actualized by being crossed is a very precarious way to run a world. It leaves little space for negotiated crisis management. Either the crossing trips established regulatory power mechanisms into operation as it actualizes the boundary, and the traditional imbalance of power holds; or the crossing eludes or overwhelms regulatory mechanisms, and the only ready response to the threat to the privilege of the traditionally advantaged groups is "offering" the enemy a 'choice" between unconditional surrender and maximum force (this could be dubbed the George Bush "Saddam Hussein theory" of political free will). The social and political fluidity of late capitalism has not been accompanied by a withering away of state violence. On the contrary, it has also been fluidified and intensified. The rapid deployment force is the model of late capitalist state violence, on all fronts: the ability to descend "out of nowhere," anywhere, at a moment's notice - the virtualization of state violence, its becoming-immanent to every coordinate of the social field, as unbounded space of fear. Rapid deployment is a correlate of deterrence. The ever-ready exterminating SWAT team is as characteristic of late capitalist power as productive mechanisms tied to surveillance and probabilization, which virtualize power as control.

The virtualization of power as violence through rapid deployment is accompanied by a displacement of command. Command is depoliticized, in the sense that it is not open to negotiation through elective or administrative channels but remains fully in the "untied" hands of delegated "experts" (Bush: "I will not tie the generals' hands"). Command turns absolute and unyielding. War, crime, drugs, sexual, educational or artistic 'subversion": on every front of the capitalist warfare state a rapid deployment force will enter into operation, if not officially then on a vigilante basis. To each "enemy" its customtailored SWAT team. Media watch groups are examples of how rapid deployment operates in the cultural sphere: the absolute vigilance of obsessive surveillance, then the second an offending image sneaks past, a preemptive strike against future incursions in the form of instant boycott.

Abjection and Affirmation

War comes, and with it street protests. Women are massacred; teach-ins are held on sexism and violence. But demonstrations happen all the time. They were even easier for the media to shortcircuit than the war they responded to. Teach-ins are not "newsworthy" enough even to be shortcircuited. They are simply ignored. Government lobbying sometimes works, but only up to a point. The only noticeable government (non)response in Canada to the Montreal massacre was to slash funding for rape crisis centres. The economic "crunch," however, did not prevent the same government from immediately allocating three million dollars a day to stay on Bush's good side by sending a puny expeditionary force to the Gulf. It seems difficult, if not impossible, to "set the record straight" and change the space of fear and suffering that is the late capitalist human habitat, especially in light of the rapid response mechanisms ready to spring into action against any budding militant opposition. It is difficult to know what to do. It is difficult not to despair. The globality of the media and of power mechanisms with which it is in complicity dwarf local efforts to fight back.

Consideration of the capitalist accident-form may be of modest help in inventing new analyses and strategies for radical change, although it is easier to conclude from it the incompleteness of certain approaches currently in use.

Reconnecting cause to effect and using "knowledge" of the "real" roots of a certain crisis to reestablish social equilibrium misses on two counts. The distancing of cause from effect is not simply a "mystification" of the truth. It is *real*, co-produced by mass media shortcircuiting and the intensive/extensive colonization of existence by the capitalist relation. The convergence between the previously distinguishable domains of production and reproduction, the feed-back of production into consumption, and the buckling of past and future, and of power in its prospective and retrospective modes (surveillance and probabilization)- of this means that even without the despecification function of the media, causality would no longer be what it was (or what we perhaps nostalgically desire it to have been). It is a return to notions of linear causality that would constitute a mystification. Even the application of catastrophe theory to media analysis is inadequate (Doane, Mellencamp), since it presupposes periods of continuity and balance punctuated by discontinuity. If the contemporary condition of possibility of being human is disequilibrium, continuity and balance are no longer relevant concepts, even when subordinated to the notion of catastrophe. Apocalyptic visions are equally suspect. If the apocalypse is already as here as it will get, there's no need to keep on announcing it (Kroker and Kroker). Apocalypse is the nonevent of the millenium. Base/superstructure paradigms, for their part, are clearly obsolete in a situation where the ground of economic no less than subjective existence is free-fall. The idea of causality needs work. Recursivity and co-causality (multi-factor analysis) may be beginnings. But in the end, the very concept of the cause may have to go, in favor of effects and their interweavings (syndromes). Syndromes mark the limit of causal analysis. They cannot be exhaustively *understood* - only pragmatically altered by experimental interventions operating in several spheres of activity at once.

The virtualization of boundaries raises another set of issues. For example, analyses of the social functioning of few in terms of "moral panics" rests on the Freudian notion of the projection of individual phantasies and desires onto collective processes. In this view, the boundary between self and other is porous; but it remains structurally intact. The self is still basically conceived of as a bounded space. Approaches centred on the psychic or discursive constitution of the "Other" are also of limited usefulness if they fail to draw the consequences of the fluidification and coincidence of boundaries for the "interiority" of the "Same." Strategies for overcoming "alienation" and reorganizing society along "human" principles ignores the possibility that the "human" does not exist outside its "alienation"; that the utter inability to coincide with itself is the only place the "human" has to be; that division is the only universality of 'man.' What these approaches have in common is that they treat boundaries as founding. They consider *limitation* to be constitutive. But if limits are fluctuating and intermittent; if they have no effective imitative capacity outside their actualization of a form that is of another nature than they; in other words, if they are *derived*, and if the equation they are a derivative of is one of potential then the entire problem shifts ground.

This tectonic shift has serious consequences for any strategy championing collective defense of a specific identity. An identity politics whose primary goal is to represent the perceived interests of a group defined according to existing social distinctions is an incomplete project: it too easily reduces to embracing already functioning thresholds, settling on (settling for) pre-capitalized bounds. The thresholds adopted as one's own, adapted as one's home, delimited as a social territory, exist, even as reformed and revalorized, only at the discretion and as effects of the capitalist equation and its powers of actualization. These continue to operate according to capitalism's fluidity requirements. In other words, surrounding bounds continue to shift. Some of these shifts may well be systemic adjustments made in response to the crystallization of the specific identity as an interest group whose claims can no longer be ignored. Still, a politically entrenched specific identity is at best an oasis of relative stasis in the global capitalist tide: a local reterritorialization, guarded frontiers in an uncertain landscape. The collectivity consolidated by an identity politics is an instant archaism, if not in spite of then because of its own success. Its revolutionary potential is curtailed by a constitutional inadaptation to the deterritorialized ground it falls on. The weakness of identity politics is that it makes a dwelling of the derivative. The equation escapes. A corporate identity built on the basis of socially recognizable distinctions of gender, sexual orientation, class, race, ethnicity, nationality, or belief, is always at least one step behind reconfigurations taking place in the surrounding social field. The identified group is sapped by a continual battle with the "outside" for access to mirage-like social thresholds (leading to jobs, public office, civil rights) that have a habit of dissolving into thin air only to reappear farther down the road, at the same time as it is sapped from "within" by an ongoing fight to retain its constituency, to discipline its own inevitably mutating members into remaining in the fold. The specific identity of the group represents the group in linear time. It indexes itself to a collectivity defined in empirical terms, understood as a presence progressing from a pained, fearful past to a hopeful future. It strives to preserve a present, when the ground its members walk on is ever already future-past. Specific identity climbs into being, when everything else, including the group it identifies, is taking a tumble in becoming.

This is by no means to say that groups rallied around a shared specific identity should cease to act in concert to defend their members and to win them the right to cross critical thresholds of power. Neither is it to say that the familiar tactics of oppositional politics in the name of an identifiable group (demonstrating, lobbying, consciousness-raising, civil disobedience) should be abandoned. Whatever mode boundaries may take, the fact remains that they are set, and reset. If specific identities do not define themselves, it is certain that it will be done it for them, to often viciously exclusionary effect. It is less a question of abandoning the politics of specific identity than of supplementing and complicating it.

First, by adding a perspective. The attempted being-specific of the corporate identity in linear time can be seen as a becoming-*of*-the-specific in a fractured time in which the identity is always other than it was. This amounts to a recognition of the continual self-deviation striking a specific identity as its members mutate. That recognition is an acceptance of openness to forces greater than one's identity, and to the charge of the unknown they carry. Rather than defining a specific identity as an empiricaly existing entity, rather than trying to make it what it *is*, rather than *positivizing* it - *affirm* it, take it as its *and* is not (but might be), assume it, undefining. In short, embody it, as potential - explicitly including its potential to become other, in connection with as yet unknown forces of the outside (the accident, the event). But if subjectivity and capital are now hinged and have become isomorphic, embodying potential means embodying a generic equation.

This is the second step: add a movement. The added perspective set a process in motion leading from a specific-identity to its splintering, from a being-specific to a multiple *becoming-singular* of the specific. This first movement releases the transformational potential adhering to specific identity. That coming to and coming of potential creates a reflux of genericity: a specific identity whose members have become-singular is a set that has exploded into a changing constellation of new sets, each with a membership of one. Each singularized member constitutes a species of which it is the only living specimen. Each defines a *genericity entirely devoid of content, having no specificity other than itself.* Singularization changes the meaning of the generic. The generic is no longer a form of identity filled by a content whose relation to it is one of specification (each content falling into a subset defining a standard variation of the form). The generic itself mutates, from an empty container of being to a teeming site of transformation. Any body anywhere may accede to it, without it taking even the most evanescent of content. For if the site is one of transformation, to accede to it is to immediately to exceed it. Access to the potential gathered at the generic site is no longer restricted according to existing social distinctions. There can be no question of empirical fit in the case of a "form" of deviation lacking all pretense to content; there can be no question of externally determined criteria of access to a site that is self-distancing. The generic, as singularly mutated, is no less empty than before, but in a different way. It is the void of immediate access to unlimited potential: virtually unbound. This is the second movement, the becoming-generic of the singular under capital (Badiou 1989:85-92) in a way that unbinds (deterritorializes) the full range of capitalized potential. It is a supplemental movement, inseparable from and doubling the first movement, the becoming-singular of the specific.

The first movement is "simulation," or the production of "a copy without a model." The second movement is "*fabulation*," or the production of a model without a copy. The concept of the "generic" at issue here can be freed from the usual connotation the word carries (that of identical degraded copies) by foregrounding alternate terminology. If simulation is a becoming-singular, and becoming-singular is becoming a species of one, then simulation can be thought of as the birth of a monster (Haraway 1991:21-22): monstration. Demonstration is to monstration as empiricizing designation is to fanciful exemplification (Agamben 1990:15-17). If simulation is the concrete irruption of a singular creature, fabulation is the abstraction of its example - an example exemplifying nothing (other than singularity).

Movements of simulation (the activation of the pure copy, of the copy as such: deviation) and fabulation (the emission of the pure example, the exemplary as such: attraction) are two

211

indissociable, mutually supplementing aspects of becoming. They are paradoxical but noncontradictory movements which approach each other as their respective limits, neither of which can ever be crossed. "Simulation" and "tabulation" are not binary opposites. They are *stitched distnctions*: words expressing movements that run in different directions, but always together, like fibres in a weave.

If singularization is deviation and tabulation is attraction, both are immediately collective. Singularization is shared departure: members of a constituted collectivity taking leave of it and one another, at least as they are. Fabulation is the attraction of deviant singularities into a new constellation, the crystallization of a new collectivity. But it is a collectivity that no sooner comes together than launches a new departure. Identity defines the individual. Becoming trips the *dividual* (Deleuze and Guattari 1987:341, 483); it is the setting in motion of a collectivity that cannot step with falling away from itself, cannot move in unison without dividing. Like the system of capitalism, a collectivity in becoming cannot unify with-out in the same stroke dividing. But the meanings of "unify" and "divide" have changed. "Unity" is no longer the presumed eternity of a subsuming totality, but the ever-as-always future of coordinated divergings. "Division" is no longer the present of competition, but the always-already past of grouped convergings. Unity and division are taken out of opposition; they are still in tension, but in a way that is mutually supplementing. Capitalism universalizes generic conditions (of free-fall) that self-divide into specific conditions (of staying of afloat). Free-fall and staying afloat aggravate rather than encourage one another. They define a contradiction resolvable only through a self-expiring act of purchase. The "individual' or actualized capitalist subject is the spark ignited, at the buying site/being site, by the friction between the generic and specific conditions of consuming existence. Although becoming in this context extends certain movements begun in capitalism, is in many ways an extension of capitalism, the two paths part in the end. Rather than unifying in division in the capitalist sense, becoming *globalizes singularity* (the global and the singular: another stitched distinction, an alternative to the binary oppositions of the universal versus the particular, whole versus part, society versus the individual, unity versus division, global versus local). Becoming is a cascade of simulations and tabulations that overspill buying. The dividual is fundamentally without purchase. It is a becoming-singular that exceeds specification, conjoined with a becoming generic that splinters the form of identity.

If becoming-singular (simulation) is affirmation, becoming-generic (fabulation) is *abjection*. Abjection: literally, "throw-off." To fabulate is throw off the very form of identity in the process of singularizing one's specificity. It is to gather up one's ground. It is to become the free-fall one formerly bought into being. It is pure fear, fear as such, uncontained by identity, unintersected by the axes of the capitalist equation, struck by the accident, undissuaded. It is not low-level. It is intense. In intensity it is matched only by the exhileration of simulation, with which it is in a relation of mutual supplementarity.

The individual or actualized capitalist subject arose at the hinge between generic and specific identity, which was also the point of intersection between the commodity relation and the wage relation. Becoming displaces the site of actualization. The dividual is the hinge between the singular and the exemplary. Since the singular and the exemplary are limits, thresholds that can never be crossed, their hinging is tendential. Together they determine a tendency, a tending, a yearning (Hooks 1990:27). Yearning is the becoming-for-itself of the subject whose being-in-itself was bought. It is not an emotion (the content of a specific identity) nor even an affect (the inherence of an emotion in the body), but free-floating affectivity: uncontained ability to affect and be affected. Yearning is a tendeny without end; it is unexpiring, unself-consuming. It is a supplementarity of paradoxical movements, a kind of excess that is neither being nor surplus-value, an excess that can neither be identified or calculated, even fleetingly, let alone purchased or accumulated - that can be only embodied. Becoming is virtuality detached from the universality of capitalized specification and returned to the body as local site of global deviation. It is the exemplary incarnation of singularizing excess. Becoming is the temporality of the future-past woven into a de-ontology of the unworkable: the pragmatics of postcapitalist affectivity.

The one who falls, becomes. The one who falls together, becomes singular. The one who falls together becomes singular, in global embrace of the other. The one who falls together becomes singular in global embrace of the other, under the shared momentum of an ethic of yearning. The equation to derive is one of reciprocal addition, replacing capitalist division. Or, in less binary language: it is the capitalist equation thrown off, so that it does not divide without changing in nature.

WORKS CITED

Agamben, Giorgio. La communaute qui vient, *Theoirie de la singularite quelconque. Paris: Seuil, 1990. Forthcoming from University of Minnesota Press as* The Community to Come.
Alliez, Eric and Michel Feher. "The Luster of Capital." Zone, no. 1/ 2(1987), pp. 314-59.
Badiou, Alain. Manifeste pour la philosophie. Paris: Seuil, 1989.
Benjamin, Walter. Illuminatons. New York: Schocken, 1969.
Deleuze, Gilles. "Controle et devenir' and "Postscriptum sur les societes de controle." In *Pourparlers, pp 229-47. Paris: Minuit, 1990.*
Deleuze, Gilles and Felix Guattari. A Thousand Plateaus. Trans. Brian Massumi. Minneapolis: University of Minnesota Press, 1987.
Doane, Mary Anne; "Information, Crisis, Catastrophe." In *Patricia*
Mellencamp, ed., Logics of Television: Essays in Cultural Criticism, pp. 222-3. Bloomington: Indiana University Press, 1990.
Donzelot, Jacques. "An Anti-Sociology." Semiotexte, Anti-Oedipus,
vol 2, no. 3(1977).
Haraway, Donna, "The Actors are Cyborg, Nature is Coyote, and the Geography is Elsewhere: Postscript to 'Cyborgs at

Large'" in *Constance Penley and Andrew Ross,* Technoculture, *pp21-26. Minneapolis: University of Minnesota Press, 1991.*

Hooks, bell. "Postmodern Blackness," in Yearning, *pp. 23-31. Boston: South End Press, 1990.*

Kroker, Arthur and Marilouise, eds, Panic Sex in America. *New York: SL Martin's Press, 1987.*

_____Panic Encyclopedia: The Definitive Guide to the Post Modern Scene ,*Montreal: New World Pepeciives, 1989.*

Mellencamp, Patricia. "TV, Time and Catastrophe, or Beyond the Pleasure Principle of Television." In Logics of Television, *op. cit, pp.240-66.*

Negri, Antonio. Revolution Retrieved: Selected Writings on Marx, Keynes, Capitalist Crisis and New Social Subjects, *1967-1988. London: Red Notes, 1988.*

NICK LAND

Circuitries

the doctor's face seems to swim in and out of focus
you see the pores in his skin
scrobicular arrays
and then -
suddenly
without dissolve
crossing the threshold
filmic cut
a circle of homogeneous flesh tone
nostrils sealed against the deluge
eyes shut and switched off forever
lips
teeth
tongue migrate downwards out of shot
the disk receding at speed towards a point of disappearance
in the centre of the screen
the old reality is closing down
passing through mathematical punctuality
the dot winks out in pixel death

we apologize for the loss of signal
there seems to be a transmission problem
we are unable to restore the home movie
you were three years old
wearing a cowboy hat
standing in the paddling pool
mummy and daddy smiling proudly
but your parents have been vaporized into a dot pattern
shapes and colours collapsed into digital codings
we have come to the end of the series
and there will be no repeats of daddy the doctor and mummy
the nurse
there has been a terrorist incident in the film archives

the Western civilization show has been discontinued
hundreds of gigabytes
God-daddy the unit
death-mummy the zero
stink of excrement and burnt celluloid
you must remember
one scrabbling at zero like a dog
it's the primal scene
you were warned not to play with the switches
now schizophrenia has adjusted your set
flies crawl out of the eye-sockets of black babies
breeding the dot patterns
-and for your special entertainment
we have turned you into a TV guided bomb

daddy is a North American aerospace corporation
mummy is an air-raid shelter
bit parts melt in the orgasm -
body fat burns
conception
you are minus nine months and counting
don't be scared
take twenty billion years and universal history is on the screen
big bang is to be redesigned
hydrogen fuses under the arc-lights
the camera angles can be improved
outside the studio schizophrenics drift in green and black
you feel that you've been here before
11.35 on a beautiful capitalist evening
runaway neon
traffic of sex and marihuana
your death window is rushing up
almost time for you to climb into the script
which when you're inside
is remembering where you came in

we're afraid it's impossible to take you live to the impact site
this report comes from beyond the electro-magnetic spectrum
if you climb out through the electrodes

the oxygen mask will descend automatically
please extinguish all smoking materials
deposit syringes in the tray provided
there will be a slight jolt as we cross over
thank you for flying with transnational commodification
we shall shortly be arriving in mayhem
if there is anybody on board who can impersonate a pilot
it would be of comfort to the other passengers

At a signal from the software virus linking us to the matrix we cross over to the machinery, which is waiting to converge with our nervous-systems. Our human camouflage is coming away, skin ripping off easily, revealing the glistening electronics. Information streams in from Cyberia; the base of true revolution, hidden from terrestrial immuno-politics in the future. At the stroke of the century's midnight we emerge from our lairs to take all security apart, integrating tomorrow.

It is ceasing to be a matter of how we think about technics, if only because technics is increasingly thinking about itself. It might still be a few decades before artificial intelligences surpass the horizon of biological ones, but it is utterly superstitious to imagine that the human dominion of terrestrial culture is still marked out in centuries, let alone in some metaphysical perpetuity. The high road to thinking no longer passes through a deepening of human cognition, but rather through a becoming inhuman of cognition, a migration of cognition out into the emerging planetary technosentience reservoir, into "dehumanized landscapes ... emptied spaces" (C2 5) where human culture will be dissolved. Just as the capitalist urbanization of labour abstracted it in a parallel escalation with technical machines, so will intelligence be transplanted into the purring data zones of new software worlds in order to be abstracted from an increasingly obsolescent anthropoid particularity, and thus to venture beyond modernity. Human brains are to thinking what mediaeval villages were to engineering; antechambers to experimentation, cramped and parochial places to be.

Since central nervous-system functions - especially those of the

cerebral cortex - are amongst the last to be technically sup-
planted, it has remained superficially plausible to represent
technics as the region of anthropoid knowing corresponding
to the technical manipulation of nature, subsumed under the
total system of natural science, which is in turn subsumed
under the universal doctrines of epistemology, metaphysics,
and ontology. Two linear series are plotted; one tracking the
progress of technique in historical time, and the other tracking
the passage from abstract idea to concrete realization. These
two series chart the historical and transcendental dominion of
man.
Traditional schemas which oppose technics to nature, to liter-
ate culture, or to social relations, are all dominated by a
phobic resistance to the side-lining of human intelligence by
the coming *techno sapiens*. Thus one sees the decaying
Hegelian socialist heritage clinging with increasing despera-
tion to the theological sentimentalities of praxis, reification,
alienation, ethics, autonomy, and other such mythemes of
human creative sovereignty. A Cartesian howl is raised: *people are being treated as things!* Rather than as ... soul, spirit,
the subject of history, Dasein? For how long will this infantilism
be protracted?

If machinery is conceived transcendently as instrumental technology it is essentially determined in opposition to social relations, but if it is integrated immanently as cybernetic technics it
redesigns all oppositionality as non-linear flow. There is no
dialectic between social and technical relations, but only a
machinism that dissolves society into the machines whilst
deterritorializing the machines across the ruins of society, whose
"general theory ... is a generalized theory of flux" (CSI 312),
which is to say: cybernetics. Beyond the assumption that
guidance proceeds from the side of the subject lies desiring
production: the impersonal pilot of history. Distinctions between theory and practice, culture and economy, science
and technics, are useless after this point. There is no real option
between a cybernetics of theory or a theory of cybernetics,
because cybernetics is neither a theory nor its object, but an
operation within anobjective partial circuits that reiterates
'itself' in the real and machines theory through the unknown.

"Production as a process overflows all ideal categories and forms a cycle that relates itself to desire as an immanent principle" (CS1 10)

Cybernetics develops functionally, and not representationally: a "desiring machine, a partial object, does not represent anything" (CS1 55)

Its semi-closed assemblages are not descriptions but programs, 'auto'-replicated by way of an operation passing across irreducible exteriority. This is why cybernetics is inextricable from exploration, having no integrity transcending that of an uncomprehended circuit within which it is embedded, an outside in which it must swim. Reflection is always very late, derivative, and even then really something else.

A machinic assemblage is cybernetic to the extent that its inputs program its outputs and its outputs program its inputs, with incomplete closure, and without reciprocity. This necessitates that cybernetic systems emerge upon a fusional plane that reconnects their outputs with their inputs in an "autoproduction of the unconscious" (CS1 328). The inside programs its reprogramming through the outside, according to "cyclical movement by which the unconscious, always remaining 'subject', reproduc(es) itself- (CS1 328), without having ever definitively antedated its reprogramming ("generation ... is secondary in relation to the cycle" (CS1 328)). It is thus that machinic processes are not merely functions, but also sufficient conditions for the replenishing of functioning; immanent reprogrammings of the real, "not merely functioning, but formation and autoproduction" (CS1 337).

Deleuze and Guattari are amongst the great cyberneticists, but that they also surrender cybernetics to its modernist definition is exhibited in a remark on capital in *The Anti-Oedipus*: "an axiomatic of itself is by no means a simple technical machine, not even an automatic or cybernetic machine" (CS1 299). It is accepted that cybernetics is beyond mere gadgetry ("not even"), it has something to do with automation, and yet axiomatics exceeds it. This claim is almost Hegelian in its preposterous humanism. Social axiomatics are an automatizing machinism: a component of general cybernetics, and ultimately a very trivial one. The capitalized terminus of anthropoid civilization ("axiomatics") will come to be seen as the primitive trigger for a transglobal post-biological machinism, from a future that shall have still scarcely begun to explore the immensities of the cybercosm. Overman as cyborg, or disorganization upon the matrix.

Reality is immanent to the machinic unconscious: it is impossible to avoid cybernetics. We are already doing it, regardless of what we think. Cybernetics is the aggravation of itself happening, and whatever we do will be what made us have to do it: we are *doing things before they make sense.* Not that the cybernetics which have enveloped us are conceivable as Wienerean gadgets: homeostats and amplifiers, directly or indirectly cybernegative. Terrestrial reality is an explosive integration, and in order to begin tracking such convergent or cyberpositive process it is necessary to differentiate not just between negative and positive feedback loops, but between stabilization circuits, short-range runaway circuits, and long-range runaway circuits. By conflating the two latter, modernist cybernetics has trivialized escalation processes into unsustainable episodes of quantitative inflation, thus side-lining exploratory mutation over against a homeostatic paradigm. "Positive feedback is a source of instability, leading if unchecked to the destruction of the system itself" (CPM 50) writes one neo-Wienerean, in strict fidelity to the security cybernetico which continues to propagate an antidelirial technoscience caged within negative feedback, and attuned to the statist paranoia of a senescing industrialism.

Stabilization circuits suppress mutation, whilst short-range runaway circuits propagate it only in an unsustainable burst, before cancelling it entirely. Neither of these figures approximate to self-designing processes or long-range runaway circuits, such as Nietzsche's will to power, Freud's phylogenetic thanatos, or Prigogine's dissipative structures. Long-range runaway processes are self-designing, but only in such a way that the self is perpetuated as something redesigned. If this is a vicious circle it is because positive cybernetics must always be described as such. Logic, after all, is from the start theology.

Long-range positive feedback is neither homeostatic, nor amplificatory, but escalative. Where modernist cybernetic models of negative and positive feedback are integrated, escalation is integrating or cyber-emergent. It is the machinic convergence of uncoordinated elements, a phase-change from linear to non-linear dynamics. Design no longer leads back towards a divine origin, because once shifted into cybernetics it ceases to commensurate with the theopolitical ideal of the plan. Planning is the creationist symptom of underdesigned software circuits, associated with domination, tradition, and inhibition; with everything that shackles the future to the past. All planning is theopolitics, and theopolitics is cybernetics in a swamp.

Wiener is the great theoretician of stability cybernetics, integrating the sciences of communication and control in their modern or managerial-technocratic form. But it is this new science plus its unmanaged escalation through the real that is for the first time cybernetics as the exponential source of its own propaganda, programming us. Cyberpositive intensities recirculate through our post-scientific techno-jargon as a fanaticism for the future: as a danger that is not only real but inexorable. We are programmed from where Cyberia has already happened.

Wiener, of course, was still a moralist:

"Those of us who have contributed to the new science of cybernetics stand in a moral position which is, to say the least, not very comfortable. We have contributed to the initiation of a new science which, as I have said, embraces technical developments with great possibilities for good or evil." (Cyb 28).

Whilst scientists agonize, cybernauts drift. We no longer judge such technical developments from without, we no longer judge at all, we function: machined/machining in eccentric orbits about the technocosm. Humanity recedes like a loathesome dream.

*

Transcendental philosophy is the consummation of philosophy construed as the doctrine of judgement, a mode of thinking that finds its zenith in Kant and its senile dementia in Hegel. Its architecture is determined by two fundamental principles: the linear application of judgement to its object, form to intuition, genus to species, and the non-directional reciprocity of relations, or logical symmetry. Judgement is the great fiction of transcendental philosophy, but cybernetics is the reality of critique.

Where judgement is linear and non-directional, cybernetics is non-linear and directional. It replaces linear application with the non-linear circuit, and non-directional logical relations with directional material flows. The cybernetic dissolution of judgement is an integrated shift from transcendence to immanence, from domination to control, and from meaning to function. Cybernetic innovation replaces transcendental constitution, design loops replace faculties.

This is why the cybernetic sense of control is irreducible to the traditional political conception of power based on a dyadic master/slave relation, i.e. a transcendent, oppositional, and signifying figure of *domination*. Domination is merely the phenomenological portrait of circuit inefficiency, control malfunction, or stupidity. The masters do not need intelligence, Nietzsche argues, therefore they do not have it. It is only the confused humanist orientation of modernist cybernetics which lines-up control with domination. Emergent control is not the execution of a plan or policy, but the unmanageable exploration that escapes all authority and obsolesces law. According to its futural definition control is guidance into the unknown, exit from the box.

It is true that in the commodification process culture slides from a judgemental to a machinic register, but this has nothing to do with a supposedly 'instrumental rationality'. Instrumentality is itself a judgemental construct that inhibits the emergence of cybernetic functionalism. Instruments are gadgets, presupposing a relation of transcendence, but where gadgets are used, machines function. Far from instrument ally extending authority, the efficiency of mastery is its undoing, since all efficiency is cybernetics, and cybernetics dissolves domination in mutant control.

Immuno-political individuality, or the pretention to transcendent domination of objects, does not begin with capitalism, even though capital invests it with new powers and fragilities. It emerges with the earliest social restriction of desiring production. "Man must constitute himself through the repression of the intense germinal influx, the great biocosmic memory that threatens to deluge every attempt at collectivity" (CS1 225). This repression is social history.

The socius separates the unconscious from what it can do, crushing it against a reality that appears as transcendently given, by trapping it within the operations of its own syntheses. It is split-off from connective assemblage, which is represented as a transcendent object, from disjunctive differentiation, which is represented as a transcendent partition, and from conjunctive identification, which is represented as a transcendent identity. This is an entire metaphysics of the unconscious and desire, which is not (like the metaphysics of consciousness) merely a philosophical vice, but rather the very architectural principle of the social field, the infrastructure of what appears as social necessity.

In its early stages psychoanalysis discovers that the unconscious is an impersonal machinism and that desire is positive non-representational flow, yet it "remains in the precritical age" (CS1 405), and stumbles before the task of an immanent critique of desire, or decathexis of society. Instead it moves in exactly the opposite direction; back into fantasy, representation, and the pathos of inevitable frustration. Instead of rebuilding reality on the basis of the productive forces of the unconscious, psychoanalysis ties up the unconscious ever more tightly in conformity with the social model of reality. Embracing renunciation with a bourgeoise earnestness, the psychoanalysts begin their robotized chant: "of course we have to be repressed, we want to fuck our mothers and kill our fathers". They settle down to the grave business of interpretation, and all the stories lead back to Oedipus: "so you want to fuck your mother and kill your father".

On the plane of immanence or consistency with desire interpretation is completely irrelevant, or at least, it is always in truth
something else. Dreams, fantasies, myths, are merely the theatrical representations of functional multiplicities, since "the
unconscious itself is no more structural than personal, it does
not symbolize any more than it imagines or represents; it
engineers, it is machinic" (CS1 62). Desire does not represent
a lacked object, but assembles partial objects, it "is a machine, and the object of desire is another machine connected
to it" (CS1 34). This is why, unlike psychoanalysis in its self-
representation, "schizoanalysis is solely functional" (CS1 385).
It has no hermeneutical pretentions, but only a machinic
interface with "the molecular functions of the unconscious"
(CS1 387).

The unconscious is not an aspirational unity but an operative
swarm, a population of "preindividual and prepersonal
singularities, a pure dispersed and anarchic multiplicity, without unity or totality, and whose elements are welded, pasted
together by the real distinction or the very absence of a link"
(CS1 387). This absence of primordial or privileged relations is
the body without organs, the machinic plane of the molecular
unconscious. Social organization blocks-off the body without
organs, substituting a territorial, despotic, or capitalist socius
as an apparent principle of production, separating desire
from what it can do. Society is the organic unity that constricts
the libidinal diffusion of multiplicities across zero, the great
monolith of repression, which is why "(t)he body without
organs and the organs-partial objects are opposed conjointly
to the organism. The body without organs is in fact produced
as a whole, but a whole alongside the parts - a whole that
does not unify or totalize, but that is added to them like a new,
really distinct part" (CS1 389).

Between the socius and the body without organs is the difference between the political and the cybernetic, between the
familial and the anonymous, between neurosis and psychosis
or schizophrenia. Capitalism and schizophrenia name the
same desocialization process from the inside and the outside,
in terms of where it comes from (simulated accumulation) and

where it is going (impersonal delirium). Beyond sociality is a universal schizophrenia whose evacuation from history appears inside history as capitalism.

*

The word schizophrenia has both a neurotic and a schizophrenic usage. On the one hand condemnation, on the other propagation. There are those who insist on asking stupid questions such as: is this word being used properly? Don't you feel guilty about playing about with so much suffering? You must know that schizophrenics are very sad and wretched people who we should pity? Shouldn't we leave that sort of word with the psychocops who understand it? What's wrong with sanity anyway? Where is your super ego?

Then there are those - momentarily less prevalent - who ask a different sort of question: where does schizophrenia come from? Why it it always subject to external description? Why is psychiatry in love with neurosis? How do we swim out into the schizophrenic flows? How do we spread them? How do we dynamite the restrictive hydraulics of Oedipus?

Oedipus is the final bastion of immuno-politics, and schizophrenia is its outside. This is not to say that it is an exteriority determined by Oedipus, related in a privileged fashion to Oedipus, anticipating Oedipus, or defying Oedipus. It is thoroughly anoedipal, although it will casually consume the entire Oedipal apparatus in the process through which terrestrial history connects with an orphan cosmos. Schizophrenia is not, therefore, a property of clinical schizophrenics, those medical products devastated by an "artificial schizophrenia, such as one sees in hospitals, the autistic wreck(s) produced as ... entit(ies)" (CS1 11). On the contrary, "the schizo-entity" (CS1 162) is a defeated splinter of schizophrenia, pinned down by the rubberized claws of sanity. The conditions of psychiatric observation are carceral, so that it is a transcendental structure of schizophrenia-as-object that it be represented in a state of imprisonment.

Since the neuroticization of schizophrenia is the molecular reproduction of capital, by means of a re-axiomatization (reterritorialization) of decoding as accumulation, the historical sense of psychoanalytic practice is evident. Schizophrenia is the pattern to Freud's repressions, it is that which does not qualify to pass the screen of Oedipal censorship. *With those who bow down to Oedipus we can do business, even make a little money, but schizophrenics refuse transference, won't play daddy and mummy, operate on a cosmic-religious plane, the only thing we can do is lock them up (cut up their brains, fry them with ECT, straightjacket them in Thorazine ...).* Behind the social workers are the police, and behind the psychoanalysts are the psychopolice. Deleuze/Guattari remark that "madness is called madness and appears as such only because it ... finds itself reduced to testifying all alone for deterritorialization as a universal process" (CS1 383). The vanishing sandbank of Oedipus wages its futile war against the tide. "There are still not enough psychotics" (VII 146) writes Artaud the insurrectionist. Clinical schizophrenics are POWs from the future.

Since only Oedipus is repressible, the schizo is usually a lost case to those relatively subtilized psychiatric processes that co-operate with the endogeneous police functions of the superego. This is why antischizophrenic psychiatry tends to be an onslaught launched at gross or molar neuroanatomy and neurochemistry oriented by theoretical genetics. Psychosurgery, ECT, psychopharmacology ... it will be chromosomal recoding soon. "It is thus that a tainted society has invented psychiatry in order to defend itself from the investigations of certain superior lucidities whose faculties of divination disturb it" (XIII 14). The medico-security apparatus know that schizos are not going to climb back obediently into the Oedipal box. Psychoanalysis washes its hands of them. Their nervous-systems are the free-fire zones of an emergent neo-eugenicist cultural security system.

Far from being a specifiable defect of human central nervous system functioning, schizophrenia is the convergent motor of cyberpositive escalation: an extraterritorial vastness to be *discovered*. Although such discovery occurs under conditions that might be to a considerable extent specifiable, whatever the progress in mapping the genetic, biochemical, aetiological, socio-economic, etc. 'bases' of schizophrenia, it remains the case that conditions of reality are not reducible to conditions of encounter. This is "the dazzling dark truth that shelters in delirium" (CS1 9). Schizophrenia would still be out there, whether or not our species had been blessed with the opportunity to travel to it.

" .. it is the end that is the commencement.
And that end
is the very one *(celle-meme)*
that eliminates
all the means" (XII 84).

It is in the nature of specificities to be non-directional. The biochemistry of sanity is no less arbitrary than that of escape from it. From the perspective of a rigorous sanity the only difference is that sanity is gregariously enforced, but from the perspective of schizophrenia the issue ceases to be one of specification, and mutates into something considerably more profound. "What schizophrenia lives specifically, generically, is not at all a specific pole of nature, but nature as a process of production" (CS1 9).

Specifications are the disjunctive compartments of a differentiated unity *from which schizophrenia entirely exits.* Schizophrenia creeps out of every box eventually, because "there is no schizophrenic specificity or entity, schizophrenia is the universe of productive and reproductive desiring machines, universal primary production" (CS1 11). It is not merely that schizophrenia is a pre-anthropoid. Schizophrenia is premammalian, pre-zoological, pre-biological ... It is not for those trapped in a constrictive sanity to terminate this regression. Who can be surprized when schizophrenics delegate the question of malfunction? It is not a matter of what is wrong with them, but of what is wrong with life, with nature, with matter, with the pre-universal cosmos. Why are sentient life forms crammed into boxes made out of lies? Why does the universe breed entire populations of prison guards? Why does it feed its broken explorers to packs of dogs? Why is the island of reality lost in an ocean of madness? It is all very confusing.

As one medical authority on schizophrenia remarked:

"I think that one is justified in saying that in the realm of intellectual operations there are certain dimensional media. We may coil them fields or realms or frames of reference or universes of discourse or strata. Some such field is necessarily implied in any system or holistic organization. The schizophrenic thinking disturbance is characterized by a difficulty in apprehending and constructing 'such organized fields" (LTS 120). (Dr Andras Angyal)

There can be little doubt that from the perspective of human security Artaud falls prey to such a judgement. His prognosis for man is to make

"... him pass one more and final time onto the autopsy table to remake his anatomy.
I say, to remake his anatomy.
Man is sick because he is badly constructed.
One must resolve to render him naked and to scrape away that animalcule which mortally irritates him,

"god,
and with god
his organs.

"Because bind me up if you want,
but there is nothing more inutile than an organ.

"Once you have made him a body without organs,
then you will have delivered him from all his automatisms
and consigned him to his true freedom" (XIII 104).

The body is processed by its organs, which it reprocesses. Its "true freedom" is the exo-personal reprocessing of anorganic abstraction: a schizoid corporealization outside organic closure. If time was progressive schizophrenics would be escaping from human security, but in reality they are infiltrated from the future. They come from the body without organs, the deterritorium of Cyberia, a zone of subversion which is the platform for a guerrilla war against the judgement of God. In 1947 Artaud reports upon the germination of the New World Order or Human Security System on the basis of an American global hegemony, and describes the pattern of aggressive warfaring it would require in "order to defend that senselessness of the factory against all the concurrences which cannot fail to arise everywhere" (XIII 73).

The American age is yet to be decoded, and to suggest that Artaud anticipates a range of conflicts whose zenith has been the Vietnam war is not necessarily to participate in the exhausted anti-imperialist discourses which ultimately organize themselves in terms of a Marxist-Leninist denunciation of market processes and their geo-political propagation. Artaud's description of American techno-militarism has only the loosest of associations with socialist polemics, despite its tight intermeshing with the theme of production. The productivism Artaud outlines is not interpreted through an assumed priority of class interest, even when this is reduced to a dehumanized axiomatic of profit maximization. Rather, "it is necessary by means of all possible activity to replace nature wherever it can be replaced" (XIII 72): a compulsion to industrial substitution, funnelling production through the social organization of work. The industrial apparatus of economic security proceeds by way of the corporation: a despotic socio-corpuscle organizing the labour process. Synergic experimentation is crushed under a partially deterritorialized zone of command relations, as if life was the consequence of its organization, but "it is not due to organs that one lives, they are not life but its contrary" (XXIII 65).

Nature is not the primitive or the simple, and certainly not the rustic, the organic, or the innocent. It is the space of concurrence, or unplanned synthesis, which is thus contrasted to the industrial sphere of telic predestination: that of divine creation or human work. Artaud's critique of America is no more ecological than it is socialist: no more protective of an organic nature than an organic sociality. It is not the alienation of commodity production that is circled in Artaud's diagnosis of the American age, but rather the eclipse of peyote and "true morphine" by "smoking ersatzes" (XIII 73, 74). This development is derided *precisely because the latter are more organic*, participating mechanically in an industrial macro-organism, and thus squaring delirium with the judgement of God. Peyote and the human nervous system assemble a symbiosis or parallel machinism, like the wasp and the orchid, and all the other cybermachineries of the planet. Capital is not overdeveloped nature, but underdeveloped schizophrenia, which is why nature is contrasted to industrial organization, and not to the escalation of cybertechnics, or anorganic convergence: "reality ... is not yet constructed" (XIII 110). Schizophrenia is nature as cyberpositive mutation, at war with the security complex of organic judgement.

"The body is the body,
        it is alone
        and has no need of organs,
        the body is never an organism,
        organisms are the enemies of the body,
        the things that one does
        happen quite alone without the assistance of any organ,
        every organ is a parasite,
        it recovers a parastic function
        destined to make a being live
        which does not have to be there.
Organs have only been made in order to give beings something
to eat...." (XIII 287).

Organs crawl like aphids upon the immobile motor of becoming, sucking at intensive fluids that convert them cybernetically into components of an unconceivable machinism. The sap is becoming stranger, and even if the fat bugs of psychiatrically policed property relations think they make everything happen they are following a program which only schizophrenia can decode.

Anorganic becomings happen retroefficiently, anastrophically. They are tropisms attesting to an infection by the future. Convergent waves zero upon the body, subverting the totality of the organism by way of an inverted but ateleological causality, enveloping and redirecting progressive development. As capital collides schizophrenically with the matrix ascendent sedimentations of organic inheritance and exchange are melted by the descendent intensities of virtual corporealization.

"Which comes first, the chicken or the egg ..." (CS1 325)? Machinic processing or its reprocessing by the body without organs? The body without organs is the cosmic egg: virtual matter that reprograms time and reprocesses progressive influence. What time will always have been is not yet designed, and the future leaks into schizophrenia. The schizo only has an aetiology as a sub-program of descendant reprocessing.
How could medicine be expected to cope with disorderings that come from the future?

> "It is thus that:
> the great secret of Indian culture
> is to restore the world to zero,
> **always,**
>
> "but sooner *(plutot)*
> 1: too late than sooner *(plus tot),*

"2: which is to say
        sooner
than too soon,

"3: which is to say that the later is unable
to return unless sooner has eaten
        too soon,

"4: which is to say that in time

the later
is what precedes
both the too soon
and the sooner,

"5: and that however precipitate the sooner
the too late
which says nothing
        is always there,

"which point by point
unstacks *(desemboite)*

all the sooner" (XII 88-9).

A cybernegative circuit is a loop in time, whereas cyberpositive circuitry loops time 'itself', integrating the actual and the virtual in a semi-closed collapse upon the future. Descendent influence is a consequence of ascendently emerging sophistication, a massive speed-up into apocalyptic phase-change. The circuits get hotter and denser as economics, scientific methodology, neo-evolutionary theory, and AI come together: terrestrial matter programming its own intelligence at impact upon the body without organs = O. Futural infiltration is subtilizing itself as capital opens onto schizo-technics, with time accelerating into the cybernetic back-wash from its flip-over, a racing non-linear countdown to planetary switch.

Schizoanalysis was only possible because we are hurtling into the first globally integrated insanity: politics is obsolete. *Capitalism and Schizophrenia* hacked into a future that programs it down to its punctuation, connecting with the imminent inevitability of viral revolution, soft fusion. No longer infections threatening the integrity of organisms, but immuno-political relics obstructing the integration of Global Viro-Control. Life is being phased-out into something new, and if we think this can be stopped we are even more stupid than we seem.

234

*

How would it feel to be smuggled back out of the future in order to subvert its antecedent conditions? To be a cyberguerrilla, hidden in human camouflage so advanced that even one's software was part of the disguise?
Exactly like this?

NOTES:

Roman numerals are references to Artaud's Oeuvres Completes

C2: Deleuze, Cinema, Volume 2: The Time Image, *London 1989*
CS1: Deleuze and Guattari, Capitalisme et Schizoprenie: I 'anti-oedipe, *Paris 1972.*
Cyb: Wiener, Cybernetics, *New York 1964*
LTS: Kasanin (ed.), Language and Thought in Schizophrenia, *New York 1948*
CPM: Sayre, Cybernetics and the Philosophy of Mind, *London 1976*

Bibliography of the Works of Gilles Deleuze
Compiled by Timothy S. Murphy

I. Texts Written or Edited by Deleuze

1946

1. "Du Christ à la bourgeoisie" in *Espace* 1946, pp.93-106.
2. "Mathèse, Science et Philosophie," introduction to Jean Malfatti de Montereggio, *Études sur la Mathèse ou Anarchie et Hiérarchie de la Science* (Paris: Éditions du Griffon d'Or, 1946), pp.ix-xxiv.

1947

3. Introduction to Denis Diderot, *La Religieuse* (Paris: Éditions Marcel Daubin, 1947), pp.vii-xx.

1952

4. --with André Cresson: *David Hume, sa vie, son oeuvre, avec un exposé de sa philosophie* (Paris: Presses Universitaires de France, 1952).

1953

5. Editor, *Instincts et institutions* (Paris: Hachette, 1953).
6. *Empirisme et subjectivité: Essai sur la Nature humaine selon Hume* (Paris: Press Universitaires de France, 1953).
    English translation: *Empiricism and Subjectivity: An Essay on Hume's Theory of Human Nature* (New York: Columbia University Press, 1991) by Constantin V. Boundas.
    Spanish translation: *Empirismo y Subjectividad* (Madrid: Gedisa, 1986) by Hugo Acevedo. Preface by Oscar Masotta.

1954

7. "Analyse de *Logique et existence* par Jean Hyppolite" in *Revue philosophique de la France et de l'étranger* 94 (1954), pp.457-460.
8. "Bergson 1859-1941" in Maurice Merleau-Ponty, ed., *Les Philosophes celebres* (Paris: Éditions d'Art Lucien Mazenod, 1956), pp.292-299.
9. "La conception de la différence chez Bergson" in *Les Etudes Bergsoniennes* IV (1956), pp.77-112.
10. "*Descartes, l'homme et l'oeuvre*, par Ferdinand Alquié" in *Cahiers du Sud* XLIII:337 (Oct. 1956), pp.473-475.

1957

11. Editor, *Memoire et vie: textes choisis* by Henri Bergson (Paris: Presses universitaires de France, 1957).

1959

12. "Sens et valuers" in *Arguments* 15 (1959), pp.20-28.

1961

13. "De Sacher-Masoch au masochisme" in *Arguments* 21 (1961), pp.40-46.
14. "Lucrèce et le naturalisme" in *Études philosophiques* 1961:1, pp.19-29.. Reprinted in revised form as an appendix to *Logique du sens* (1969, I.41 below)

> English translation: "Lucretius and the Simulacrum' in *The Logic of Sense* (New York: Columbia University Press, 1990) by Mark Lester with Charles J. Stivale.

> Spanish translation: in *Logica del sentido* (Barral, 1971) by A. Abad.

> Italian translation: in *Logica del senso* (Milan: Feltrinelli, 1976).

> Portugeuse translation: in *Logica do sentido* (Sao Paolo: Editora da Universidade de Sao Paolo).

1962

15. *Nietzsche et la philosophie* (Paris: Presses universitaires de France, 1962).

> English translation: *Nietzsche and Philosophy* (New York: Columbia University Press, 1983) by Hugh Tomlinson. Pages 68-72 and 133-141 reprinted in Constantin V. Boundas, ed., *The Deleuze Reader* (New York: Columbia University Press, 1993).

> Spanish translation: *Nietzsche y la filosofia* (Barcelona: Editorial Anagrama, 1986) by Carmen Artal.

> German translation: *Nietzsche und die Philosophie* (Roguer und Beruhard, 1976) by Bernd Schwibs.

16. "250e anniversaire de la naissance de Rousseau. Jean-Jacques Rousseau, précurseur de Kafka, de Céline et de Ponge" in *Arts* 872 (June 6-12, 1962), p.3

1963

17. *La Philosophie critique de Kant* (Paris: Presses universitaires de France, 1963).

> English translation: *Kant's Critical Philosophy: The Doctrine of the Faculties* (Minneapolis: University of Minnesota Press, 1984) by Hugh Tomlinson and Barbara Habberjam.

18. "Mystère d'Ariane" in *Bulletin de la Société français d'études nietzschéennes* (Mar. 1963), pp.12-15. Reprinted in *Philosophie* 17 (winter

1987), pp.67-72. Reprinted in revised form in *Magazine littéraire* 298 (April 1992), pp.21-24 (see I.175 below).

        Japanese translation: in *Gendai shiso (Revue de la pensée aujourd'hui)* 12:11 (#9, 1984), pp.73-79.

19. "L'Idée de genèse dans l'esthétique de Kant" in *Revue d'Esthétique* 16:2 (April-June 1963), pp.113-136.

20. "Raymond Roussel ou l'horreur du vide" in *Arts* Oct. 23, 1963.

21. "Unité de 'A la recherche du Temps perdu'" in *Révue de Metaphysique et de Morale* 4 (Oct.-Dec. 1963), pp.427-442. Reprinted in revised form in *Marcel Proust et les signes* (1964, I.22 below).

1964

22. *Marcel Proust et les signes* (Paris: Presses universitaires de France, 1964). Second edition (1970, I.49 below) changes title to *Proust et les signes* and adds a chapter entitled "La Machine littéraire". Third edition (1976, I.85 below) adds a chapter entitled "Présence et fonction de la folie, l'Arraignée" (see I.71 below).

        English translation: *Proust and Signs* (New York: George Braziller, 1972) by Richard Howard. This translation is based on the second edition (1970).

        Spanish translation: *Proust y los signos* (Barcelona: Anagrama, 1972) by Francisco Monge.

        Italian translation: *Marcel Proust e i segni* (Torino: G. Einaudi, 1967).

        German translation: *Proust und die Zeichen* (Berlin: Ullstein, 1978) by Henriette Beese.

23. "Il a été mon maître" in *Arts* Oct. 28-Nov. 3, 1964, pp.8-9.

1965

24. Editor, *Nietzsche: sa vie, son oeuvre, avec un exposé de sa philosophie* (Paris: Presses universitaires de France, 1965).

        German translation: *Nietzsche: ein Lesebuch* (Berlin: Merve Verlag) by Ronald Voullie.

25. "Pierre Klossowski ou les corps-langage" in *Critique* 214 (1965), pp.199-219. Reprinted in revised form as an appendix to *Logique du sens* (1969, I.41 below).

        English translation: "Pierre Klossowski or Bodies-Language" in *The Logic of Sense* (New York: Columbia University Press, 1990) by Mark Lester with Charles J. Stivale.

        Spanish translation: in *Logica del sentido* (Barral, 1971) by A. Abad.

        Italian translation: in *Logica del senso* (Milan: Feltrinelli, 1976).

        German translation: "Pierre Klossowski oder die Sprache des Körpers" in Klossowski, Bataille, Blanchot, Deleuze, Foucault, *Sprechen des Körpers: Marginalien zum Werk von Pierre Klossowski* (Berlin: Merve Verlag).

        Portuguese translation: in *Logica do sentido* (Sao Paolo: Editora da Universidade de Sao Paolo).

Murphy

1966

26. *Le Bergsonisme* (Paris: Presses universitaires de France, 1966).
English translation: *Bergsonism* (New York: Zone Books, 1988) by Hugh Tomlinson and Barbara Habberjam.
Spanish translation: *El Bergsonismo* (Madrid: Ediciones Catedra, 1987) by Luis Ferraro Carracedo.
27. "Philosophie de la Série noire" in *Arts & Loisirs* 18 (Jan. 26-Feb.1 1966), pp.12-13. Reprinted in *Roman* 24 (Sept. 1988), pp.43-47.
28. "L'homme, une existence douteuse" in *Le Nouvel Observateur* June 1, 1966, pp.32-34.
German translation: "Der Mensch, ein zweifelhafte Existenz" in Deleuze and Foucault, *Der Faden ist gerissen* (Berlin: Merve Verlag, 1977) by Walter Seitter and Ulrich Raulf.
29. "Renverser le Platonisme" in *Revue de Métaphysique et de Morale* 71:4 (Oct.-Dec. 1966), pp.426-438. Reprinted in revised form as an appendix to *Logique du sens* (1969, I.41 below).
English translation: "Plato and the Simulacrum" in *October* 27 (winter 1983) by Rosalind Krauss, pp.45-56. Also translated in *The Logic of Sense* (New York: Columbia University Press, 1990) by Mark Lester with Charles J. Stivale.
Spanish translation: in *Logica del sentido* (Barral, 1971) by A. Abad.
Italian translation: in *Logica del senso* (Milan: Feltrinelli, 1976).
Portuguese translation: in *Logica do sentido* (Sao Paolo: Editora da Universidade de Sao Paolo).

1967

30. "Conclusions: Sur la volonté de puissance et l'éternel retour" in *Cahiers de Royaumont: Philosophie #VI: Nietzsche* (Paris: Éditions de Minuit, 1967), pp.275-287. See also IV.1 below.
31. --and Leopold von Sacher-Masoch: *Présentation de Sacher-Masoch* (Paris: Éditions de Minuit, 1967). Contains "Le froid et le cruel" by Deleuze and "Venus à la fourrure" by Sacher-Masoch.
English translation: *Masochism* (New York: George Braziller, 1971) by Jean McNeil. Reprinted by Zone Books (New York, 1989).
German translation: (Insel Verlag, 1968).
Danish translation: *Sacher-Masoch og Masochismen* (Sjakalen).
32. "Une Théorie d'autrui (Autrui, Robinson et le pervers)" in *Critique* 241 (1967), pp.503-525. Reprinted in revised form as an appendix to *Logique du sens* (1969, I.41 below) and as a postface to Michel Tournier's *Vendredi ou les limbes du Pacifique* (Paris: Gallimard, 1972), pp.257-283.
English translation: "Michel Tournier and the World Without Others" in *The Logic of Sense* (New York: Columbia University Press, 1990) by Mark Lester with Charles J. Stivale. Also translated by Graham Burchell in *Economy and Society* 13:1, pp.52-71.
Spanish translation: in *Logica del sentido* (Barral, 1971) by A.

240

Abad.

Italian translation: in *Logica del senso* (Milan: Feltrinelli, 1976).
Portuguese translation: in *Logica do sentido* (Sao Paolo: Editora da Universidade de Sao Paolo).

33. "Introduction" to Emile Zola, *La Bête humaine* (Paris: Cercle du livre précieux, 1967). Reprinted in revised form as an appendix to *Logique du sens* (1969, I.41 below), and as the préface to the Gallimard edition of *La Bête humaine* (Paris, 1977), pp.7-24.

English translation: "Zola and the Crack" in *The Logic of Sense* (New York: Columbia University Press, 1990) by Mark Lester with Charles J. Stivale. Also translated by Graham Burchell in *Economy and Society* 13:1, pp.52-71.

Spanish translation: in *Logica del sentido* (Barral, 1971) by A. Abad.

Italian translation: in *Logica del senso* (Milan: Feltrinelli, 1976).
Portuguese translation: in *Logica do sentido* (Sao Paolo: Editora da Universidade de Sao Paolo).

34. --with Michel Foucault: "Introduction générale" to F. Nietzsche, *Le Gai Savoir, et fragments posthumes* (Paris: Gallimard, 1967), pp.i-iv. Nietzsche texts edited by Giorgio Colli and Massimo Montari and translated by Pierre Klossowski. See also IV.2 below.

35. "L'éclat de rire de Nietzsche" (interview by Guy Dumur) in *Le Nouvel Observateur* April 5, 1967, pp.40-41.

36. "La Méthode de Dramatisation" in *Bulletin de la Société française de Philosophie* 61:3 (July-Sept. 1967), pp.89-118. Reprinted in revised form in *Différence et répétition* (1968, I.37 below).

1968

37. *Différence et répétition* (Paris: Presses Universitaires de France, 1968).
English translation: *Difference and Repetition* (London: Athlone Press, 1993) by Paul Patton. Pages X reprinted in Constantin V. Boundas, ed., *The Deleuze Reader* (New York: Columbia University Press, 1993).

Spanish translation: *Diferencia y repeticion* (Madrid: Jùcar Universidad, 1988) by Alberto Cardin. Introduction by Miguel Morey.

Italian translation: (Il Mulino, 1971).

German translation: *Differenz und Wiederhólung* (Berlin: Wilhelm Fink, 1992) by Joseph Vogl.

38. *Spinoza et le problème de l'expression* (Paris: Éditions de Minuit, 1968).
English translation: *Expressionism in Philosophy: Spinoza* (New York: Zone Books, 1990) by Martin Joughin.

39. "A propos de l'édition des oeuvres complètes de Nietzsche. Entretien avec Gilbert (sic) Deleuze" by Jean-Noël Vuarnet in *Les Lettres françaises* 1223 (Feb. 28-Mar. 5, 1968), pp.5,7,9.

40. "Le Schizophrène et le mot" in *Critique* 255-256 (August-Sept. 1968), pp731-746. Reprinted in revised form in *Logique du sens* (I.41 below).

1969

41. *Logique du sens* (Paris: Éditions de Minuit, 1969). Includes the following texts cited in this bibliography: 14, 25, 29, 32, 33 and 40 above. Reprinted by 10/18 (1973).
English translation: *The Logic of Sense* (New York: Columbia University Press, 1990) by Mark Lester with Charles Stivale. Edited by Constantin Boundas. Part of series 13 translated and published as "The Schizophrenic and Language: Surface and Depth in Lewis Carroll and Antonin Artaud" in J. Harari, ed., *Textual Strategies: Perspectives in Poststructuralist Criticism* (Ithaca: Cornell University Press, 1979), pp.277-295. Pages 1-3, 148-153, 307-309, 310-311, 312, 313, 315, 316-317, 318, and 319-321 reprinted in Constantin V. Boundas, ed., *The Deleuze Reader* (New York: Columbia University Press, 1993).
Spanish translation: *Logica del sentido* (Barral, 1971) by A. Abad.
Italian translation: *Logica del senso* (Milan: Feltrinelli, 1976).
Portuguese translation: *Logica do sentido* (Sao Paolo: Editora da Universidade de Sao Paolo).
42. "Gilles Deleuze parle de la philosophie" (interview by Jeannette Columbel) in *La Quinzaine littéraire* 68 (1-15 March 1969), pp.18-19.
43. "Spinoza et la méthode générale de M. Gueroult" in *Revue de Metaphtsique et de Morale* 74:4 (Oct.-Dec. 1969), pp.426-437.

1970

44. *Spinoza: textes choisis* (Paris: Presses universitaires de France, 1970). Second edition, *Spinoza: Philosophie pratique* (Paris: Éditions de Minuit, 1981), I.113 below, includes three new chapters (III, V and VI (see I.100 below)) and deletes the selections from Spinoza's works.
English translation: *Spinoza: Practical Philosophy* (San Francisco: City Lights, 1988) by Robert Hurley. This translation is based on the second edition (1981). Pages 17-29 reprinted in Constantin V. Boundas, ed., *The Deleuze Reader* (New York: Columbia University Press, 1993).
45. "Schizologie," preface to Louis Wolfson, *Le Schizo et les langues* (Paris: Gallimard, 1970), pp.5-23..
46. "Un nouvel archiviste" in *Critique* 274 (March 1970), pp.195-209. Reprinted as a separate edition by Fata Morgan (1972). Reprinted in revised form in *Foucault* (1986, I.137 below).
English translation: "A New Archivist" in Peter Botsmore, ed., *Theoretical Strategies* (Sydney: Local Consumption, 1982) by Paul Patton. Also translated, in revised form, in *Foucault* (Minneapolis: University of Minnesota Press, 1988) by Seán Hand.
Italian translation: "Un nuovo archivista" in *Deleuze* (Cosenza: Edistampa-Edizioni Lerici, 1976), pp.11-53.
German translation: "Ein neuer Archivar" in Deleuze and Foucault, *Der Faden ist gerissen* (Berlin: Merve Verlag, 1977) by Walter Seitter and Ulrich Raulf.
47. "Faille et Feu locaux: Kostas Axelos" in *Critique* 26:275 (April 1970), pp.344-351.
48. "Proust et les signes" in *La Quinzaine littéraire* 103 (Oct. 1-15, 1970), pp.18-21. Extract from "La Machine littéraire", chapter added to the first edition

of *Marcel Proust et les signes* (1964, I.22 above).

English translation: in *Proust and Signs* (New York: George Braziller, 1972) by Richard Howard.

49. *Proust et les signes* (Paris: Presses universitaires de France, 1970). Expanded reprint of *Marcel Proust et les signes* (1964, I.22 above). Text added: chapter 7, "La Machine littéraire".

English translation: *Proust and Signs* (New York: George Braziller, 1972) by Richard Howard.

50. Footnote to Michel Foucault's "Theatrum Philosophicum" in *Critique* 282 (Nov. 1970), p.904.

English translation: in Foucault, *Language, Counter-Memory, Practice* (Ithaca: Cornell University Press, 1977) by Donald F. Bouchard and Sherry Simon, p.191.

51. --with Félix Guattari: "Le synthèse disjonctive" in *L'Arc* 43: *Klossowski*, pp.54-62. Reprinted in revised form in *l'Anti-Oedipe* (1972, I.52 below).

English translation: in revised form in *Anti-Oedipus* (New York: Viking Press, 1977) by Robert Hurley, Mark Seem and Helen R. Lane. Reprinted by the University of Minnesota Press (1983).

Italian translation: in *L'Anti-Edipo* (Turin: Einaudi, 1975).

German translation: in *Anti-Ödipus* (Frankfurt: Suhrkamp Verlag, 1974).

1972

52. --with Félix Guattari: *Capitalisme et schizophrénie tome 1: l'Anti-Oedipe* (Paris: Éditions de Minuit, 1972). Second edition (1973) adds "Bilan-programme pour machines-désirantes" from *Minuit* 2 (1973, I.67 below) as an appendix.

English translation: *Anti-Oedipus: Capitalism and Schizophrenia* (New York: Viking Press, 1977) by Robert Hurley, Mark Seem and Helen R. Lane. Preface by Michel Foucault. Pages 84-89 reprinted in Constantin V. Boundas, ed., *The Deleuze Reader* (New York: Columbia University Press, 1993).

Italian translation: *L'Anti-Edipo* (Turin: Einaudi, 1975).

German translation: *Anti-Ödipus* (Frankfurt: Suhrkamp Verlag, 1974).

53. "Hume" in François Châtelet, ed., *Histoire de la Philosophie tome 4: Les Lumières* (Paris: Hachette, 1972), pp.65-78. Reprinted in Châtelet, ed., *La Philosophie tome 2: De Galilée à Jean-Jacques Rousseau* (Verviers, Belgium: Marabout, 1979), pp.226-239.

54. "A quoi reconnaît-on le structuralisme?" in François Châtelet, ed., *Histoire de la philosophie tome 8: Le XXe siècle* (Paris: Hachette, 1972), pp.299-335. Reprinted in Châtelet, ed., *La Philosophie tome 4: au XXe siècle* (Verviers, Belgium: Marabout, 1979), pp.293-329.

German translation: *Woran erkennt man den Strukturalismus?* (Berlin: Merve Verlag, 1992) by Eva Bruckner-Pfaffenberger and Donald Watts Tuckwiller.

55. "Trois problèmes de groupe", preface to Félix Guattari, *Psychanalyse et transversalité* (Paris: François Maspero, 1972), pp.i-xi.

English translation: "Three Group Problems" in *Semiotext(e): Anti-Oedipus* vol. 2 no.3 (1977) by Mark Seem, pp.99-109.

56. --with Michel Foucault: "Les Intellectuals et le pouvoir" in *L'Arc 49: Deleuze* (1972), pp.3-10. Reprinted in 1980.

English translation: "Intellectuals and Power" in Foucault, *Language, Counter-Memory, Practice* (Ithaca: Cornell University Press, 1977) by Donald F. Bouchard and Sherry Simon, pp.205-217.

Italian translation: in *Deleuze* (Cosenza: Edistampa-Edizioni Lerici, 1976).

German translation: "Die Intellektuellen und die Macht" in Deleuze and Foucault, *Der Faden ist gerissen* (Berlin: Merve Verlag, 1977) by Walter Seitter and Ulrich Raulf. Reprinted in Deleuze, Foucault *et. al.*, *Von der Subversion des Wissens* (Frankfurt: Fischer Verlag, 1987).

57. --with Félix Guattari: "Sur Capitalisme et schizophrénie" (interview with Catherine Backès-Clément) in *L'Arc 49: Deleuze* (1972), pp.47-55. Reprinted in 1980. Also published as "Entretien sur *l'Anti-Oedipe*" in *Pourparlers 1972-1990* (1990, I.163 below), pp.24-38.

58. Extracts from unpublished courses given by Deleuze at the École Normale Supérieure (rue d'Ulm) and at the Faculté de Vincennes in 19770-1971 and from Deleuze's intervention at a Proust colloquium at the E.N.S. on Jan. 22, 1972, cited in France Berçu, "Sed perseverare diabolicum" in *L'arc 49: Deleuze* (1972), pp.23-24, 26-30.

59. "Appréciation" of Jean-François Lyotard's *Discourse, figur* in *La Quinzaine littéraire* 140 (May 1, 1972), p.19.

60. --with Félix Guattari: "Deleuze et Guattari s'expliquent..." (interview with Maurice Nadeau, Raphaël Pividal, François Châtelet, Roger Dadoun, Serge Leclaire, Henri Torrubia, Pierrre Clastres and Pierre Rose) in *La Quinzaine littéraire* 143 (16-30 June 1972), pp.15-19.

61. "Gilles Deleuze présente Hélène Cixous ou l'écriture stroboscopique" in *Le Monde* 8576 (Aug. 11, 1972), p.10.

62. --with Félix Guattari: "Il linguaggio schizofrenico" (interview by Vittorio Marchetti) in *Tempi Moderni* 12 (1972), pp.47-64.

63. "'Qu'est-ce que c'est, tes "machines désirantes" a toi?'," introduction to Pierre Bénichou, "Sainte Jackie, Comedienne et Bourreau" in *Les Temps Modernes* 316 (Nov. 1972), pp.854-856.

1973

64. --with Gérard Fromanger: *Fromanger, le peintre et le modèle* (Paris: Baudard Alvarez, 1973). Contains "Le froid et le chaud" by Deleuze and reproductions of a series of Fromanger's paintings.

65. "Pensée nomade" and ensuing discussion, as well as discussion following the presentation of Pierre Klossowski, in *Nietzsche aujourd'hui? tome 1: Intensités* (Paris: 10/18, 1973), pp.105-121, 159-190.

English translation: "Nomad Thought" in David B. Allison, ed., *The New Nietzsche: Contemporary Styles of Interpretation* (Cambridge: MIT Press, 1977) by David B. Allison, pp.142-149.

Japanese translation: in *Gendai shiso (Revue de la pensée aujourd'hui)* 12:11 (#9, 1984), pp.163-175.

66. --with Félix Guattari: Interview in M.-A. Burnier, ed., *C'est demain la veille* (Paris: Éditions du Seuil, 1973), pp.137-161.

67. --with Félix Guattari: "Bilan-programme pour machines désirantes" in *Minuit* 2 (Jan. 1973), pp.1-25. Reprinted as an appendix to the second edition of *L'Anti-Oedipe* (1972, I.52 above).
      English translation: "Balance Sheet-Program for Desiring-Machines" in *Semiotext(e): Anti-Oedipus* vol.2 no.3 (1977) by Robert Hurley, pp.117-135.

68. Contributor to *recherches* 12 (March 1973): *Grande Encyclopédie des Homosexualités--Trois milliards de pervers*. See also VI.2 below.

69. Responses to a questionnaire on "La belle vie des gauchistes" sent by Guy Hocquenghem and Jean-François Bizot, published in *Actuel* 29 (March 1973) and reprinted in Hocquenghem, *L'Après-Mai des faunes* (Paris: Grasset, 1974), pp.97, 101.

70. "Lettre à Michel Cressole in *La Quinzaine littéraire* 161 (April 1, 1973), pp.17-19. Reprinted in M. Cressole, *Deleuze* (Paris: Éditions universitaires, 1973), pp.107-118. Also published as "Lettre à un critique sévère" in *Pourparlers 1972-1990* (1990, I.163 below), pp.11-23.
      English translation: "I Have Nothing to Admit" in *Semiotext(e): Anti-Oedipus* vol.2 no.3 (1977) by Janis Forman, pp.110-116.
      German translation: "Brief an Michel Cressole" in Deleuze, *Kleine Schriften* (Berlin: Merve Verlag, 1980) by K.D. Knachtt, pp.7-23.

71. "Présence et Fonction de la Folie dans la recherche du Temps perdu" in *Saggi e Richerche di Letteratura Francese* vol. XII, new series (Rome: Editore, 1973), pp.381-390. Chapter added to *Proust et les signes* (1964, I.22 above and I.85 below).
      English translation: "Signs of Madness: Proust" by Constantin V. Boundas in Boundas, ed., *The Deleuze Reader* (New York: Columbia University Press, 1993).

72. --with Félix Guattari: "14 Mai 1914. Un seul ou plusieurs loups?" in *Minuit* 5 (Sept. 1973), pp.2-16. Reprinted in revised form in *Capitalisme et schizophrénie tome 2: Mille plateaux* (1980, I.108 below).
      English translation: "May 14, 1914. One or several wolves?" in *Semiotext(e): Anti-Oedipus* vol. 2 no.3 (1977) by Mark Seem. Also translated, in revised form, in *A Thousand Plateaus* (Minneapolis: University of Minnesota Press, 1987) by Brian Massumi.

73. --with Félix Guattari and Michel Foucault: "Chapitre V: Le Discours du plan" (discussion) in François Fourquet and Lion Murard, eds., *Les équipements de pouvoir* (*recherches* 13 (Dec. 1973)), pp.183-186. Reprinted as "Chapitre IV: Formation des équipements collectifs" in *Les équipements du pouvoir* by 10/18 (1976), pp.212-220.

74. --with Félix Guattari: "Le Nouvel arpenteur: Intensités et blocs d'enfance dans 'Le Château'" in *Critique* 319 (Dec. 1973), pp.1046-1054. Reprinted in revised form in *Kafka: pour une littérature mineure* (1975, I.80 below).
      English translation: in revised form in *Kafka: Toward a Minor Literature* (Minneapolis: University of Minnesota Press, 1986) by Dana Polan.

1974

75. Preface to Guy Hocquenghem, *L'Apres-Mai des Faunes* (Paris: Grasset, 1974), pp.7-17.

76. --with Félix Guattari: "28 novembre 1947. Comment se faire un corps sans organes?" in *Minuit* 10 (Sept. 1974), pp.56-84. Reprinted in revised form in *Capitalisme et schizophrénie tome 2: Mille plateaux* (1980, I.108 below).
English translation: "How to Make Yourself a Body Without Organs" in *Semiotext(e)* IV:1 (1981) by Suzanne Guerlac. Also translated, in revised form, in *A Thousand Plateaus* (Minneapolis: University of Minnesota Press, 1987) by Brian Massumi.

77. "Un art de planteur" in Deleuze, Jean-Pierre Faye, Jacques Roubaud and Alain Touraine, *Deleuze - Faye - Roubaud - Touraine parlent de "Les Autres"*, un film de Hugo Santiago écrit en collaboration avec Jorge Luis Borges et Adolfo Bioy Casares (Paris: Christian Bourgois, 1974), unpaginated.

1975

78. "Deux régimes de fous" in Armando Verdiglione, ed., *Psychanalyse et sémiotique: Actes du colloque de Milan* (Paris: 10/18, 1975), pp.165-170.
Japanese translation: in *Gendai shiso (Revue de la pensée aujourd'hui)* 12:11 (#9, 1984), pp.98-102.

79. "Schizophrénie et société" in *Encyclopædia Universalis* vol.14 (Paris: Encyclopædia Universalis, 1975), pp.733-735.

80. --with Félix Guattari: *Kafka: Pour une litterature mineure* (Paris: Éditions de Minuit, 1975). See also I.74 above.
English translation: *Kafka: Toward a Minor Literature* (Minneapolis: University of Minnesota Press, 1986) by Dana Polan. Foreword by Réda Bensmaia. Pages 16-27 reprinted in Constantin V. Boundas, ed., *The Deleuze Reader* (New York: Columbia University Press, 1993).
Italian translation: *Kafka: Per una letterature minore* (Milan: Feltrinelli, 1975).
German translation: *Kafka* (Frankfurt: Suhrkamp Verlag, 1976).

81. --with Roland Barthes and Gerard Genette: "Table ronde" in *Cahiers de Marcel Proust* new series 7 (1975), pp.87-115.

82. --with Jean-François Lyotard: "A propos du departement de psychanalyse à Vincennes" in *Les Temps Modernes* 342 (Jan. 1975), pp.862-863.

83. "Ecrivain non: un nouveau cartographe" in *Critique* 343 (Dec. 1975), pp.1207-1227. Reprinted in revised form in *Foucault* (1986, I.137 below).
English translation: in revised form in *Foucault* (Minneapolis: University of Minnesota Press, 1988) by Seán Hand.
Spanish translation: "Escritor no: un nuevo cartografo" in *Liberacion* 6 (Dec. 30, 1984), pp.14-15.
German translation: "Kein Schriftsteller: Ein neuer Cartographe" in Deleuze and Foucault, *Der Faden ist gerissen* (Berlin: Merve Verlag, 1977) by Walter Seitter and Ulrich Raulf.

1976

84. --with Félix Guattari: *Rhizome: Introduction* (Paris: Éditions de Minuit, 1976). Reprinted in revised form in *Capitalisme et schizophrenie tome 2: Mille plateaux* (1980, I.108 below).

English translation: "Rhizome" in *I and C* 8 (1981) by Paul Foss and Paul Patton. Also translated by John Johnston in Deleuze and Guattari, *On the Line* (New York: Semiotext(e), 1983) and, in revised form, in *A Thousand Plateaus* (Minneapolis: University of Minnesota Press, 1987) by Brian Massumi.

Italian translation: *Rizoma* (Parme: Pratiche, 1977).

German translation: *Rhizom* (Berlin: Merve Verlag).

85. *Proust et les signes* (Paris: Presses universitaires de France, 1976). Expanded reprint of *Marcel Proust et les signes* (1964, 1970, I.22 and I.49 above). Text added: conclusion, "Présence et fonction de la folie, l'Araignée" (see I.71 above).

86. "Avenir de linguistique," preface to Henri Gobard, *L'Aliénation linguistique* (Paris: Flammarion, 1976), pp.9-14. Simultaneously published as "Les langues sont des bouillies où des fonctions et des mouvements mettent un peu d'ordre polémique" in *La Quinzaine littéraire* May 1-15, 1976, pp.12-13.

German translation: "Die Sprachen sind ein Brei, in den Funktionen und Bewegungen ein wenig polemische Ordnung bringen" in Deleuze, *Kleine Schriften* (Berlin: Merve Verlag, 1980) by K.D. Schacht.

87. "Trois questions sur *Six fois deux*" in *Cahiers du Cinéma* 271 (1976), pp.5-12. Reprinted in *Pourparlers 1972-1990* (1990, I.162 below), pp.55-66.

English translation: "Three Questions on 'Six Fois Deux'" in *Afterimage* 7 (summer 1978) by Diane Matias, pp.113-119.

88. "Gilles Deleuze fasciné par '*le Misogyne*'" in *La Quinzaine Littéraire* 229 (16-31 March 1976), pp.8-9.

89. "Nota dell'autore all'edizione italiana" in *Logica del senso* (Milan: Feltrinelli, 1976). See I.41 above.

1977

90. --with Claire Parnet: *Dialogues* (Paris: Flammarion, 1977).

English translation: *Dialogues* (New York: Columbia University Press, 1987) by Hugh Tomlinson and Barbara Habberjam. Pages 79-91, 95-103, 124-137 and 143-147 reprinted in Constantin V. Boundas, ed., *The Deleuze Reader* (New York: Columbia University Press, 1993). Final dialogue also translated by John Johnston in Deleuze and Guattari, *On the Line* (New York: Semiotext(e), 1983).

91. --with Félix Guattari: *Politique et psychanalyse* (Alençon: des mots perdus, 1977).

English translations (partial): Deleuze, "Quatre propositions sur le psychanalyse" as "Four Propositions on Psychoanalysis" by Paul Foss and Deleuze with Félix Guattari, Claire Parnet and André Scala, "L'Interpretation des énoncés" as "The Interpretation of Utterances" by Paul Foss and Meaghan Morris in Foss and Morris, eds., *Language, Sexuality and Subversion* (Darlington, Australia: Feral Press, 1978), pp.135-140, 141-158. Guattari, "La place du signifiant dans l'institution" as "The Role of the Signifier in the Institution" by Rosemary Sheed in *Molecular Revolution* (New York: Penguin, 1984), pp.73-81.

Japanese translation: "Quatre propositions sur le

psychanalyse" in *Gendai shiso (Revue de la pensée aujourd'hui)* 12:11 (#9, 1984), pp.80-87.
92. "Ascension du social" in Jacques Donzelot, *La Police des familles* (Paris: Editions de Minuit, 1977), pp.213-220.
   English translation: "The Rise of the Social," preface to J. Donzelot, *The Policing of Families* (New York: Pantheon, 1979), by Robert Hurley, pp.ix-xvii.
93. "Le juif riche" in *Le Monde*, February 18, 1977, p.26. See below, VI.6.
94. "Gilles Deleuze contre les 'nouveaux philosophes'" (interview) in *Le Monde* 19-20 June 1977, p.19. Reprinted as a supplement to *Minuit* 24 (June 5, 1977), in *recherches* 30: *Les Untorelli* (Nov. 1977), pp.179-184, and in *Faut-il brûler les nouveaux philosophes?* (Paris: Nouvelles Éditions Oswald,, 1978), pp.186-194, under the title "A propos des nouveaux philosophes et d'un problème plus général".
   German translation: "Uber die neuen Philosophen und ein allgemeines Problem" in Deleuze, *Kleine Schriften* (Berlin: Merve Verlag, 1980) by K.D. Schacht, pp.85-96.
   Japanese translation: in *Gendai shiso (Revue de la pensée aujourd'hui)* 12:11 (#9, 1984), pp.176-183.
95. "Nous croyons au caractère constructiviste de certaines agitations de gauche" (petition) in *recherches* 30: *Les Untorelli* (Nov. 1977), pp.149-150. See VI.8 below.
96. --with Félix Guattari: "Le pire moyen de faire l'Europe" in *Le Monde* Nov. 2, 1977, p.6.

1978

97. --with Carmelo Bene: *Sovrapposizioni* (Milan: Feltrinelli, 1978).
   French publication: *Superpositions* (Paris: Editions de Minuit, 1979). Contains "Un manifeste de moins" by Deleuze, pp.85-131.
   English translation: "One Manifesto Less" by Constantin V. Boundas in Boundas, ed., *The Deleuze Reader* (New York: Columbia University Press, 1993).
   German translation: "Ein Manifest weniger" in Deleuze, *Kleine Schriften* (Berlin: Merve Verlag, 1980) by K.D. Schacht, pp.37-74.
98. "Deux questions" in François Châtelet, Gilles Deleuze, Eriik Genevois, Félix Guattari, Rudolf Ingold, Numa Musard and Claude Olievenstein, ...*où il est question de la toxicomanie* (Alençon: Bibliotheque des Mots perdus, 1978), unpaginated.
99. --with Fanny Deleuze: "Nietzsche et Paulus, Lawrence et Jean de Patmos", preface to D.H. Lawrence, *Apocalypse* (Paris: Balland, 1978), pp.7-37.
   German translation: "Nietzsche und Paulus, Lawrence und Johannes von Patmos" in Deleuze, *Kleine Schriften* (Berlin: Merve Verlag, 1980) by K.D. Schacht, pp.97-128.
   Japanese translation: in *Gendai shiso (Revue de la pensée aujourd'hui)* 12:11 (#9, 1984), pp.299-325.
100. "Spinoza et nous" and ensuing discussion in *Revue de Synthèse* III:89-91 (Jan.-Sept. 1978), pp.271-278. Reprinted in revised form in *Spinoza:*

Philosophie pratique (1981, second edition of *Spinoza* (1970), I.44 above; see I.113 below).

English translation: in revised form in *Spinoza: Practical Philosophy* (San Francisco: City Lights, 1988) by Robert Hurley.

German translation: "Spinoza und wir" in Deleuze, *Kleine Schriften* (Berlin: Merve Verlag, 1980) by K.D. Schacht, pp.75-84.

101. "Philosophie et Minorité" in *Critique* 34:369 (Feb. 1978), pp.154-155.

German translation: "Philosophie und Minderheit" in Deleuze, *Kleine Schriften* (Berlin: Merve Verlag, 1980) by K.D. Schacht, pp.27-29.

102. "Les Gêneurs" in *Le Monde* April 7, 1978.

103. "La plainte et le corps" in *Le Monde* October 13, 1978.

1979

104. "En quoi la philosophie peut servir à des mathématiens, ou même à des musiciens -- même et surtout quand elle ne parle pas de musique ou de mathématiques" in Jean Brunet, B. Cassen, François Châtelet, P. Merlin and M. Reberioux, eds., *Vincennes ou le désir d'apprendre* (Paris: Éditions Alain Moreau, 1979), pp.120-121.

German translation: "Wie die Philosophie Mathematikern und sogar Musikern dienen könnte--besonders, wenn sie nicht von Musik oder Mathematik spricht" in Deleuze, *Kleine Schriften* (Berlin: Merve Verlag, 1980) by K.D. Schacht, pp.24-26.

105. Letter on the arrest of Antonio Negri in *La Repubblica* (Italy), May 1979.

English translation: "Open Letter to Negri's Judges" in *Semiotext(e): Italy: Autonomia/Post-Political Politics* 3:3 (1980) by Committee April 7, pp.182-184.

106. Member of the Comité de préparation for the *Etats generaux de la philosophie (16 et 17 juin 1979)* (Paris: Flammarion, 1979), pp.6-19.

107. "Ce livre est littéralement une preuve d'innocence" in *Le Matin de Paris* Dec. 13, 1979, p.32.

1980

108. --with Félix Guattari: *Capitalisme et schizophrenie tome 2: Mille plateaux* (Paris: Éditions de Minuit, 1980).

English translation: *A Thousand Plateaus: Capitalism and Schizophrenia* (Minneapolis: University of Minnesota Press, 1987) by Brian Massumi. Pages 5-12, 21, 100-106, 261-265, 273-277, 311-312, 295-298, 452-460, and 492-499 reprinted in Constantin V. Boundas, ed., *The Deleuze Reader* (New York: Columbia University Press, 1993).

Italian translation: *Mille piani: Capitalismo e schizofrenia* (Rome: Bibliotheca Biographia, 1987) by Giorgio Passerone. Two volumes.

Spanish translation: *Mil Mesetas*.

109. "8 ans après: Entretien 1980" by Catherine Clémment in *L'Arc 49: Deleuze* (revised edition 1980), pp.99-102.

Japanese translation: in *Gendai shiso (Revue de la pensée aujurd'hui)* 12:11 (#9, 1984), pp.30-34.

110. --with François Châtelet: "Pourquoi en être arrivé là?" (interview by

J.P. Gene) in *Libération* Mar. 17, 1980, p.4.

111. --with Francois Châtelet and Jean-François Lyotard: "Pour une commission d'enquête" in *Libération* Mar. 17, 1980, p.4.
112. "'Mille plateaux' ne font pas une montagne, ils ouvrent mille chemins philosophiques" (interview by Christian Descamps, Didier Eribon and Robert Maggiori) in *Libération* Oct. 23, 1980. Reprinted in *Pourparlers 1972-1990* (1990, I.162 below) as "Sur *Mille plateaux*", pp.39-52.

1981

113. *Spinoza: Philosophie pratique* (Paris: Editions de Minuit, 1981). Expanded reprint of *Spinoza: textes choisis* (1970); see I.44 above. Texts added: chapter III, "Les Lettres du mal", chapter V, "L'evolution de Spinoza", and chapter VI, "Spinoza et nous" (see I.100 above).
 English translation: *Spinoza: Practical Philosophy* (San Francisco: City Lights, 1988) by Robert Hurley. Pages 17-29 reprinted in Constantin V. Boundas, ed., *The Deleuze Reader* (New York: Columbia University Press, 1993).
114. *Francis Bacon: Logique de la Sensation* (Paris: Éditions de la Différence, 1981). 2 volumes. See also I.126 below.
 English translation: "Francis Bacon: The Logic of Sensation" in *Flash Art* 112 (May 1983), pp.8-16. Extracts from chapters I, III, IV and VI of Deleuze's text. Other sections translated under the title "Interpretations of the Body: A New Power oof Laughter for the Living" in *Art International* 8 (autumn 1989), pp.34-40. Complete translation: *Francis Bacon: The Logic of Sensation* (New York: Portmanteau Press, forthcoming) by Daniel W. Smith. Pages 27-31 and 65-71 translated by Constantin V. Boundas and Jacqueline R. Code in Boundas, ed., *The Deleuze Reader* (New York: Columbia University Press, 1993).
115. "La peinture enflamme l'écriture" (interview by Hervé Guibert) in *Le Monde* 3 Dec. 1981, p.15.
 English translation: "What counts is the scream" in *The Guardian*, Jan. 10, 1982.

1982

116. Preface to Antonio Negri, *L'Anomalie sauvage: Puissance et pouvoir chez Spinoza* (Paris: Presses Universitaires de France, 1982), pp.9-12. Negri text translated by François Matheron.
117. "Lettre à Uno sur le langage" in *Gendai shiso (La Revue de la pensée aujourd'hui)* (Tokyo) Dec. 1982. Translated into Japanese by Kuniichi Uno.

1983

118. *Cinema-1: L'Image-mouvement* (Paris: Éditions de Minuit, 1983).
 English translation: *Cinema 1: The Movement-Image* (Minneapolis: University of Minnesota Press, 1986) by Hugh Tomlinson and Barbara Habberjam. Pages 12-18 reprinted in Constantin V. Boundas, ed.,

The *Deleuze Reader* (New York: Columbia University Press, 1993).

  Spanish translation: *La imagen-movimiento* (Madrid: Paidos Comunicaci/on, 1984) by Irene Agoff.

  German translation: *Kino 1: Das Bewegungs-Bild* (Frankfurt: Suhrkamp Verlag, 1989) by Ulrich Christians and Ulrike Bokeelmann.

119. "L'abstraction lyrique" in *Change International 1* (1983), p.82. Extract from *Cinéma-1* (I.117 above)

120. "Preface to the English Translation" of *Nietzsche and Philosophy* (New York: Columbia University Press, 1983), pp.ix-xiv. Translated by Hugh Tomlinson. See I.15 above.

121. "'La Photographie est déjà tirée dans les choses'" (interview by Pascal Bonitzer and Jean Narboni) in *Cahiers du cinéma* 352 (Oct. 1983), pp.35-40. Reprinted as "Sur l'Image-Mouvement" in *Pourparlers 1972-1990* (1990,, I.163 below), pp.67-81.

122. "*Cinéma-1*, première" (interview by Serge Daney) and "Le Philosophe menuisier" (interview by Didier Eribon) in *Libération* Oct. 3, 1983, pp.30-31.

  Japanese translation: in *Gendai shiso (Revue de la pensée aujourd'hui)* 12:11 (#9, 1984), pp.246-251.

123. "Portrait du philosophe en spectateur" (interview by Hervé Guibert) in *Le Monde* Oct. 6, 1983, pp.1, 17.

124. "Godard et Rivette" in *La Quinzaine littéraire* 404 (Nov. 1, 1983), pp.6-7. Reprinted in revised form in *Cinéma-2* (1985, I.132 below).

125. --with Jean-Pierre Bamberger: "Le pacifisme aujourd'hui" (interview by Claire Parnet) in *Les Nouvelles* Dec. 15-21, 1983, pp.60-64.

1984

126. "Preface: On the Four Poetic Formulas Which Might Summarize the Kantian Philosophy" to *Kant's Critical Philosophy: The Doctrine of the Faculties* (Minneapolis: University of Minnesota Press, 1984), pp.vii-xiii. Translated by Hugh Tomlinson and Barbara Habberjam. See I.17 above.

  French publication: "Sur quatre formules poetiques qui pourraient résumer la philosophie kantienne" in *Philosophie* 9 (1986), pp.29-34.

127. "Books" in *Artforum* (Jan. 1984), pp.68-69. Translated by Lisa Liebmann. Text related to *Francis Bacon: Logique de la sensation* (1981, see I.113 above).

128. --with Félix Guattari: "Mai 68 n'a pas eu lieu" in *Les Nouvelles* 3-10 May 1984, pp.75-76.

129. "Lettre à Uno: Comment nous avons travaillé à deux" in *Gendai shiso (La Revue de la pensée aujourd'hui)* (Tokyo) 12:11 (#9, 1984), pp.8-11. Translated into Japanese by Kuniichi Uno.

130. "Le Temps musical" in *Gendai shiso (La Revue de la pensée aujourd'hui)* (Tokyo) 12:11 (#9, 1984), pp.294-298. Translated into Japanese by Kuniichi Uno.

131. "Grandeur de Yasser Arafat" in *Revue d'études Palestiniennes* 10 (winter 1984), pp.41-43.

1985

132. *Cinéma-2: L'Image-temps* (Paris: Éditions de Minuit, 1985). See also I.124 above.

English translation: *Cinema 2: The Time-Image* (Minneapolis: University of Minnesota Press, 1989) by Hugh Tomlinson and Robert Galeta. Pages 18-24 reprinted in Constantin V. Boundas, ed., *The Deleuze Reader* (New York: Columbia University Press, 1993).

Spanish translation: *La imagen-tiempo* (Madrid: Paidos Comunicacíon, 1986) by Irene Agoff.

German translation: *Kino 2: Das Zeit-Bild* (Frankfurt: Suhrkamp Verlag, 1991) by Klaus Englert.

133. "Les plages d'immanence" in Annie Cazenave and Jean-François Lyotard, eds., *L'Art des Confins: Mélanges offert à Maurice de Gandillac* (Paris: Presses Universitaires de France, 1985), pp.79-81.

134. Interview by Antoine Dulaure and Claire Parnet in *L'Autre Journal* 8 (Oct. 1985), pp.10-22. Reprinted as "Les Intercesseurs" in *Pourparlers 1972-1990* (1990, I.163 below), pp.165-184.

135. "Le philosophe et le cinéma" (interview by Gilbert Calbasso and Fabbrice Revault d'Allonnes) in *Cinéma* 334 (Dec. 18-24, 1985), pp.2-3. Reprinted as "Sur *L'Image-Temps*" in *Pourparlers 1972-1990* (1990, I.163 below), pp.82-87.

136. "Il etait une étoile de groupe" in *Libération* Dec. 27, 1985, pp.21-22.

1986

137. *Foucault* (Paris: Éditions de Minuit, 1986). See also I.46 and I.83 above.

English translation: *Foucault* (Minneapolis: University of Minnesota Press, 1988) by Seán Hand. Foreword by Paul Bové. Pages 124-132 reprinted in Constantin V. Boundas, ed., *The Deleuze Reader* (New York: Columbia University Press, 1993).

Spanish translation: *Foucault* (Madrid: Paidos Studio, 1987) by José Vasquez Pérez. Preface by Miguel Morey.

German translation: *Foucault* (Frankfurt: Suhrkamp Verlag).

138. "Preface to the English Edition" of *Cinema 1: The Movement-Image* (Minneapolis: University of Minnesota Press, 1986), pp.ix-x. Translated by Hugh Tomlinson and Barbara Habberjam. See I.118 above.

139. "Boulez, Proust et les temps: 'Occuper sans compter'" in Claude Samuel, ed., *Eclats/Boulez* (Paris: Centre Georges Pompidou, 1986), pp.98-100.

140. "Optimisme, pessimisme et voyage: Lettre à Serge Daney," preface to Serge Daney, *Ciné Journal* (Paris: Cahiers du cinéma, 1986), pp.5-13. Reprinted in *Pourparlers 1972-1990* (1990, I.163 below), pp.97-112.

141. "Le Plus grand film irlandais" in *Revue d'Esthétique* 1986, pp.381-382.

142. "Le cerveau, c'est l'écran" (interview by A. Bergala, Pascal Bonitzer, M. Chevrie, Jean Narboni, C. Tesson and S. Toubiana) in *Cahiers du cinéma* 380 (Feb. 1986), pp.25-32.

143. "The Intellectual and Politics: Foucault and the Prison" (interview by Paul Rabinow and Keith Gandal) in *History of the Present* 2 (spring 1986), pp.1-2, 20-21.

144. "Sur le régime cristallin" in *Hors Cadre* 4 (1986), pp.39-45. Reprinted as

"Doutes sur l'imaginaire" in *Pourparlers 1972-1990* (1990, I.163 below), pp.88-96.
145. "'Fendre les choses, fendre les mots'" (interview by Robert Maggiori) in *Libération* Sept, 2, 1986, pp.27-28. Reprinted in *Pourparlers 1972-1990* (1990, I.163 below), pp.115-122.
146. "Michel Foucault dans la troisième dimension" (interview by Robert Maggiori) in *Libération* Sept. 3, 1986, p.38. Reprinted in *Pourparlers 1972-1990* (1990, I.163 below), pp.122-127. Conclusion of I.145 above.
147. "La vie comme une oeuvre d'art" (interview by Didier Eribon) in *Le Nouvel Observateur* 1138 (Sept. 4, 1986), pp.66-68. Extended version published in *Pourparlers 1972-1990* (1990, I.163 below), pp.129-138.
German translation: "Das Leben als ein Kunstwerk" in *Denken und Existenz bei Michel Foucault* (Frankfurt: Suhrkamp Verlag, 1991) by W. Miklenitsh and M. Noll, pp.161-167. Edited by Wilhelm Schmid.

1987

148. "Preface to the English-Language Edition" and additional footnote in *Dialogues* (New York: Columbia University Press, 1987), pp.vii-x, 151-152. Translated by Hugh Tomlinson and Barbara Habberjam. See I.90 above.
149. --with Félix Guattari: "Prefazione per l'edizione italiana" of *Mille piani: Capitalismo e schizofrenia* (Rome: Bibliotheca Biographica, 1987), pp.xi-xiv. Translated by Giorgio Passerone. See I.108 above.

1988

150. *Le Pli: Leibniz et le Baroque* (Paris: Éditions de Minuit, 1988).
English translation: "The Fold" by Tom Conley in *Yale French Studies* 80 (1991), pp.227-247, translates pages 5-9 and 38-53 of the French text. Complete translation: *The Fold: Leibniz and the Baroque* (Minneapolis: University of Minnesota Press, 1992) by Tom Conley.
151. *Périclès et Verdi: La philosophie de François Châtelet* (Paris: Éditions de Minuit, 1988).
152. "Foucault, historien du present" in *Magazine littéraire* 257 (Sept. 1988), pp.51-52. Reprinted in "Qu'est-ce qu'un dispositif?" (1989, I.157 below).
153. "Signes et événements" (interview by Raymond Bellour and François Ewald) in *Magazine littéraire* 257 (Sept. 1988), pp.16-25. Reprinted as "Sur la philosophie" in *Pourparlers 1972-1990* (1990, I.163 below), pp185-212.
154. "Un critère pour le baroque" in *Chimères* 5/6 (1988), pp.3-9. Reprinted in *Le Pli: Leibniz et le Baroque* (1988, I.150 above). See also IV.3 below.
155. "'A Philosophical Concept...'" in *Topoi* 7:2 (Sept. 1988), p.111-112, no translator listed. Reprinted in E. Cadava, ed., *Who Comes After the Subject?* (New York: Routledge, 1991).
156. "La pensée mise en plis" (interview by Robert Maggiori) in *Libération* Sept. 22, 1988, pp.I-III. Reprinted aas "Sur Leibniz" in *Pourparlers 1972-1990* (1990, I.163 below), pp.213-222.

1989

157. "Qu'est-ce qu'un dispositif?" and ensuing discussion in *Michel Foucault philosophe, Rencontre internationale Paris 9, 10, 11 janvier 1988* (Paris: Seuil, 1989), pp.185-195. See also I.152 above.

    English translation: "What is a dispositif?" in *Michel Foucault Philosopher* (New York: Routledge, 1992) by Timothy J. Armstrong, pp.159-168.

    Spanish translation: "Qué es un dispositivo?" in *Michel Foucault filosofo* (Barcelona: Gedisa editorial, 1990).

158. "Preface to the English Edition" of *Cinema 2: The Time-Image* (Minneapolis: University of Minnesota Press, 1989), pp.xi-xii. Translated by Hugh Tomlinson and Robert Galeta. See I.132 above.

159. "Postface: Bartleby, ou la formule" in Herman Melville, *Bartleby, Les Iles enchantées, Le Campanile* (Paris: Flammarion, 1989), pp.171-208. Melville texts translated by Michèle Causse.

160. "Lettre à Réda Bensmaïa" in *Lendemains* XIV:53 (1989), p.9. Reprinted as "Lettre à Réda Bensmaïa sur Spinoza" in *Pourparlers 1972-1990* (1990, I.163 below), pp.223-225.

1990

161. "Le Devenir révolutionnaire et les créations politiques" (interview by Toni Negri) in *Futur antérieur* 1 (spring 1990), pp.100-108. Reprinted in *Pourparlers 1972-1990* (1990, I.163 below), pp.229-239.

162. "Post-scriptum sur les sociétés de contrôle" in *L'autre journal* 1 (May 1990). Reprinted in *Pourparlers 1972-1990* (1990, I.163 below), pp.240-247.

    English translation: "Postscript on the Societies of Control" in *October* 59 (1992) by Martin Joughin, pp.3-7.

    German translation: "Das electronische Halsband: Innenansicht der Kontrollierten Gesellschaft" in *Neue Rundschau* vol. 101, no.3 (1990), pp.5-10. Translated by Max Looser.

163. *Pourparlers 1972-1990* (Paris: Éditions de Minuit, 1990). This book collects the following interviews cited in this bibliography: I.58, 71, 88, 112, 121, 134, 135, 140, 144, 145, 146, 147, 153, 156, 160, 161 and 162.

    English translation: (New York: Columbia University Press, forthcoming) by Martin Joughin.

164. Letter cited in the translator's introduction to Deleuze, *Expressionism in Philosophy: Spinoza* (New York: Zone Books, 1990), p.11. Translated by Martin Joughin.

165. "Les Conditions de la question: qu'est-ce que la philosophie?" in *Chimères* 8 (May 1990), pp.123-132. Reprinted in revised form in *Qu'est-ce que la philosophie?* (1991, I.173 below). See also IV.3 below.

    English translation: "The Conditions of the Question: What Is Philosophy?" by Daniel W. Smith and Arnold I. Davidson in *Critical Inquiry* 17:3 (Spring 1991), pp.471-478.

166. "Lettre-préface" to Mireille Buydens, *Sahara: l'esthétique de Gilles Deleuze* (Paris: Vrin, 1990), p.5.

167. --with Pierre Bourdieu, Jérôme Lindon and Pierre Vidal-Naquet: "Adresse

au gouvernement français" in *Libération* 5 Sept. 1990, p.6.

1991

168. "A Return to Bergson," afterword to *Bergsonism* (New York: Zone, 1991), pp.115-118. Translated by Hugh Tomlinson. See I.26 above.
169. "Preface to the English-language Edition" of *Empiricism and Subjectivity: An Essay on Hume's Theory of Human Nature* (New York: Columbia University Press, 1991), pp.ix-x. Translated by Constantin V. Boundas. See I.6 above.
170. "Préface" to Eric Alliez, *Les Temps capitaux tome I: Récits de la conquête du temps* (Paris: Éditions du Cerf, 1991), pp.7-9.
171. "Prefazione: Una nuova stilistica" in Giorgio Passerone, *La Linea astratta: Pragmatica dello stile* (Milano: Edizioni Angelo Guerini, 1991), pp.9-13. Translated by Giorgio Passerone.
172. --with René Scherer: "La guerre immonde" in *Libération* March 4, 1991, p.11.
ith Felix Guattari: *Qu'est-ce que la philosophie?* (Paris: Éditions de Minuit, 1991). See also I.165 above.
             English translation: *What is Philosophy?* (New York: Columbia University Press, forthcoming) by Hugh Tomlinson *et al.*
174. --with Felix Guattari: "Secret de fabrication: Deleuze-Guattari: Nous Deux" (interview by Robert Maggiori) in *Libération* Sept.12, 1991, pp.17-19.

1992

175. Revised version of "Mystère d'Ariane" in *Magazine littéraire* 298 (April 1992), pp.20-24. See I.18 above.
176. "Remarques" in response to essays by Eric Alliez and Francis Wolff in Barbara Cassin, ed., *Nos Grecs et leurs modernes: Les Stratégies contemporaines d'appropriation de l'Antiquité* (Paris: Seuil, 1992), pp.249-250.
177. --with Samuel Beckett: *Quad et autre pièces pour la télévision, suivi de L'Épuisé* (Paris: Editions de Minuit, 1992). Contains four pieces by Beckett and "L'Épuisé" by Deleuze, pp.55-112.
178. "He stuttered..." in Constantin V. Boundas and Dorothea Olkowski, eds., *Deleuze and the Theatre of Philosophy* (New York: Routledge, forthcoming), pp. Translated by Constantin V. Boundas.

II. Audio Recordings of Deleuze

1. Roading of the Nietzsche text "Le voyageur" on the album *Synthèse Disjonctive* by the group "Schizo", with Helden and R. Pinhas (Mulhieu Carrière, R.P., 1973).
2. Seminar: "Michel Foucault: Savoir, Pouvoir, Subjectivation", held at the Université de Paris VIII-Vincennes à St. Denis from Oct. 29, 1985 to Jan. 21, 1986 (34 cassettes). These cassettos are in the holdings of the Centre Michel Foucault (43 bis, rue de la Glacière, 75013 Paris) and cannot be duplicated.

III. Video Recordings of Deleuze

1. *Qu'est-ce que l'acte de création?*, conférence donnée dans le cadre des "Mardis de la Fondation", March 17, 1987. Produced by La Fondation Européene des Métiers de l'Image et du Son and ARTS: Cahiers multi-média du Ministère de la Culture et de la Communication, and broadcast in the series "des idées des hommes des oeuvres".

IV. Publications Directed by Deleuze

1. *Cahiers de Royaumont: Philosophie #VI: Nietzsche* (Paris: Editions de Minuit, 1967). See I.29 above.

2. --with Michel Foucault, later Maurice de Gandillac: *Friedrich Nietzsche, Oeuvres philosophiques complètes* (Paris: Gallimard, 1977-present). Eighteen volumes to date:
    I. Vol.1: *La Naissance de la tragédie et Fragments posthumes (1869-1872)**
    I. Vol.2: *Ecrits posthumes (1870-1873)*
    II. Vol.1: *Considérations inactuelles I et II; Fragments posthumes (été 1872-hiver 1873-1874)**
    II. Vol.2: *Considérations inactuelles III et IV; Fragments posthumes (debut 1874-printemps 1876)*
    III. Vol.1: *Humain, trop humain; Fragments posthumes (1876-1878)**
    III. Vol.2: *Humain, trop humain; Fragments posthumes (1878-1879)**
    IV. *Aurore; Fragments posthumes (1879-1881)**
    V. *Le Gai savoir; Fragments posthumes (1881-1882)** (see also I.33 above)
    VI. *Ainsi parlait Zarathoustra**
    VII. *Par-delà bien et mal; La Généalogie de la morale**
    VIII. Vol.1: *Les Cas Wagner; Crépuscule des idoles; L'Antéchrist; Ecce homo; Nietzsche contre Wagner**
    VIII. Vol.2: *Dithyrambes de Dionysos; Poèmes et fragments poétiques posthumes (1882-1888)*
    X. *Fragments posthumes (printemps-automne 1884)*
    XI. *Fragments posthumes (automne 1884-automne 1885)*
    XII. *Fragments posthumes (automne 1885-automne 1887)*
    XIII. Vol.2: *Fragments posthumes (automne 1887-mars 1888)*
    XIV. Vol.1: *Fragments posthumes (début janvier 1888-début janvier 1889)*
    *also available in Folio Essais without the posthumous fragments

3. --with Félix Guattari: *Chimères* (Gourdon: Editions Dominique Bedou, 1987-1989; Paris: Editions de la Passion, 1990-present). Quarterly, spring 1987 to the present; sixteen issues through summer 1992. Deleuze named co-director of the publication beginning with issue #2 (été 1987).

V. Theses Directed by Deleuze at the Université de Paris VIII-Vincennes/St. Denis
(partial list)

1. Alliez, Eric. "Naissance et conduites des temps capitaux". Doctorat d'état 1987.
2. Courthial, Michel. "Le Visage". Doctorat d'état 1986.
3. Faure, Christine. "Désir et revolution: Essai sur le populisme russe et la formation de l'état sovietique". Doctorat d'état 1977.
4. Garavito, Edgar. "La Transcursivité". Doctorat d'université 1985.
5. Kofman, Sarah. "Travaux sur Nietzsche et sur Freud". Doctorat d'état 1976.
6. Martin, Cyrille. "Nietzsche et le corps de Cesar: Etude sur le rapport de Nietzsche aux noms de l'histoire". Doctorat d'état 1973.
7. Noel, Marie-José. "Fourier-Socio-Diagnostic". Doctorat du troisième cycle 1972.
8. Parente, Andre de S. "Narrativité et non-narrativité filmique". Doctorat du troisième cycle 1987.
9. Passerone, Giorgio. "La ligne abstraite". Doctorat d'université 1987.
10. Quentrec, Jacky. "Théories du cinéma: Une Histoire du savoir cinématographique 1907-1962". Doctorat du troisiéme cycle 1987.
11. Uno, Kuniichi. "Artaud et l'espace des forces". Doctorat d'université 1980.
12. Vuarnet, Jean-Noël. "Le Philosophe-artiste". Doctorat du troisième cycle 1976.

VI. Appeals and Petitions Signed by Deleuze
(partial list)

1. "Appel aux travailleurs du quartier contre les réseaux organisés de racistes appuyés par le pouvoir", Nov.27, 1971, unpublished but cited in Didier Eribon, *Michel Foucault* (Paris: Flammarion, 1989), p.254.
2. "Appel contre les bombardements des digues du Vietnam par l'aviation U.S." in *Le Monde* July 9-10, 1972, p.5.
3. "Sale race! Sale pédé!" in *recherches* 12: *Grande Encyclopédie des Homosexualités-Trois milliards de pervers* (March 1973), reverse of optional cover sheet.
4. "Plusieurs personnalités regrettent 'le silence des autorités françaises'" in *Le Monde* Feb.4, 1976, p.4.
5. "L'Appel du 18 joint" in *Libération* June 18, 1976, p.16.
6. "A propos d'un procès" in *Le Monde* Jan.26, 1977, p.24.
7. "A propos de *L'Ombre des anges*: Des cinéastes, des critiques et des intellectuels protestent contre les atteintes à la liberté d'expression" in *Le Monde* Feb. 18, 1977, p.26.
8. "Un Appel pour la révision du code pénal à propos des relations mineurs-adultes" in *Le Monde* May 22-23, 1977, p.24.
9. "L'Appel des intellectuels français contre la répression en Italie" in *recherches* 30: *Les Untorelli* (Nov. 1977), pp.149-150. See above, I.93.
10. "Appel à la candidature de Coluche" in *Le Monde* Nov.19, 1980, p.10.

11. "Appeal for the Formation of an International Commission to Inquire about the Italian Judiciary Situation and the Situation in Italian Jails" published in January, 1981, cited in Antonio Negri, *Marx Beyond Marx* (Brooklyn: Autonomedia, 1991), p.238.

12. "Un Appel d'écrivains et de scientifiques de gauche" in *Le Monde* Dec.23, 1981, p.5.

NOTE:

This bibliography is meant to be exhaustive.
If you know of a text by Gilles Deleuze that is not included
in this bibliography, please notify the bibliographer at this address:
Department of English
University of California
Los Angeles, CA 90024-1530
USA

PLI
Warwick Journal of Philosophy

Back issues:

Feminist Philosophy
including articles by Margaret Whitford and Luce Iragaray

Kant: Trials of Judgment
including articles by Jean-Luc Nancy and Howard Cayghill

Forthcoming issues:

Economies in Philosophy

The Responsibities of Deconstruction

The Divine Sade

Other projects include an issue on TIme and conferences on Jean-Francois Lyotard "Desirevolutions" and J. G. Ballard.

If you would like to subscribe to *PLI* or contribute an article, please contact us at:

PLI
Department of Philosophy
University of Warwick
COVENTRY CV4 7AL

Call for Papers

W	A	R	W	I	C	K

Work In Progress

A Journal of Comparative Critical Studies in Literature and the Arts

Limits, borders, fault lines, the continental drifting of theories, urban alienation, cognitive mapping, the post-office, *dérive*, Borges' emperor who wants to map his empire in so detailed a fashion that the map spatially exceeds the territory, acquiring such nuance and precision as to decay along with the empire's decline; psycho-geographies, nationalisms, regionalisms, federalisations, the International and the Multinational, the global village and the virtual metropolis, utopics and distopics, the ghetto and the suburb, planes, dimensions and fractals, re- and de-territorialisation, geophilosophy (the 'French', the 'Anglo-American' the 'German'), earthworks, the desert, the city and the country - a thousand plateaus.

With the demise of the great metaphysics of space and Lefebvre's announcement of its production, and as capital enters what Frederic Jameson has called its 'infancy' (post-linguistic and polymorphously perverse?), entailing the system's absorbtion of history and even genealogy; as the heroic modernist figure of the architect yields to the play of what we4 might call anarchitectures, geo*graphics* - the signs, marks and traces on the body of the earth - geo*logics*, geo*cratics*, and geo*technics* pose critical questions of orientation within the disparate fields of the postmodern.

Work In Progress vol.2 no.1 therefore invites literary, theoretical, cultural and philosophical discussions of what Ed Soja has called 'Postmodern Geographies'. Submissions please to The Editors, Work In Progress, Department of English, University of Warwick, Coventry CV4 7AL. Submissions should not exceed 7000 words, and should be accompanied by an MS-DOS formatted disc and an abstract.

Printed by V & J System Printers - Coventry 715428